THE COMPLETE BOOK OF
VEGETABLES & HERBS

ROY GENDERS

KU-610-239

WARD LOCK LIMITED/LONDON

© Roy Genders 1972

Reprinted 1972

ISBN 0 7063 1513 8

First published in Great Britain 1972 by Ward Lock
Limited, 116 Baker Street, London, W1M 2BB

All Rights Reserved. No part of this publication
may be reproduced, stored in a retrieval system, or
transmitted, in any form or by any means, elec-
tronic, mechanical, photocopying, recording, or
otherwise, without the prior permission of the
Copyright owners.

Text filmset in 10 point Monophoto Bembo
by Yendall & Company Ltd.

Printed and bound by
Editorial Fher SA Bilbao.

THE COMPLETE BOOK OF VEGETABLES & HERBS

CONTENTS

INTRODUCTION

The seed houses report that more vegetable seeds are now sold each year than flower seeds. With the high cost of vegetables and lack of variety in the shops, gardeners are once again growing their own and receiving so much assistance in the production of good crops that it would not have been thought possible only a few years ago. Plants of hybrid vigour and disease resistant strains have revolutionised vegetable growing and where once five or six pounds per plant was considered a satisfactory yield with indoor tomatoes, varieties of hybrid vigour have doubled the yields expected from an average crop.

Many new varieties showing increased hardiness and earlier maturity, raised for those who garden under adverse conditions, have made it possible to grow many of the more interesting vegetables such as sweet corn and melons when once it was necessary to rely on the more favourably situated commercial growers to produce a reliable crop. Aubergines and hybrid cucumbers, which ripen within 60 days, and which show high resistance to mosaic and downy mildew; peas with edible pods; green-budded broccoli; and golden beetroot are new vegetables to add interest to the diet and make vegetable growing a really worth while occupation. And to make vegetable culture as easy as possible, pelleted seed for precision drilling and correct spacing, thereby eliminating much time and labour on thinning and transplanting, is a welcome innovation.

Seedsmen now supply treated seed to safeguard the crop from all manner of diseases. Virus tested tomato seed ensures that it is free from seed-borne virus infection, whilst celery seed soaked in Thiram ensures its freedom from seed-borne fungal diseases. Leek and onion seed which has been fumigated with mythol bromide against eelworm infection has eliminated the most troublesome pests of these crops whilst peas and broad beans for autumn sowing will have been treated by Fernasan orthocide to prevent seed decay and pre-emergence damping off. Automatic spades and modern mechanical equipment, the use of plastic materials for protecting early crops; soil-testing outfits; and plant-raising materials which ensure that the seedlings are free from root disturbance has contributed to the successful production of modern vegetables. Their culture is now an interesting and rewarding occupation and a small plot of ground may be expected to feed the family throughout the year with delicious and unusual crops.

Part 1

THE VEGETABLE GARDEN

1
Planning and Designing

Not every would-be vegetable grower is fortunate enough to possess a walled garden to give protection from winds and act as a sun trap. Instead, it will be necessary to utilise whatever land is available to the best advantage. Almost all vegetables require an open sunny situation and will not produce good crops if the ground is surrounded by mature trees which will deprive the soil of moisture and nourishment, whilst for the crops to reach maturity in reasonable time, they must have sunlight and so the first consideration is an open, sunny situation. This is especially important where early crops are wanted. If the ground has a slope towards the south or west, so much the better for this will ensure earlier ripening of fruits and vegetables and full advantage may be taken of the early spring sunshine.

Wind protection   To divide the ground from that of one's neighbour and to give some protection from cold winds, a hedge should be planted or a fence erected on the side of the prevailing wind. In Britain this is usually from the north-east or south-west, the former bringing the cold winds of early spring which may cause considerable damage by 'burning' or browning the foliage of plants. It is therefore on the north and east side that the land must be given protection and the best method is to erect a fence 5–6 feet tall of wattle hurdles or interwoven fencing. The latter is slightly more expensive but has greater durability. Osier hurdles may be obtained from Farmans of North Walsham, Norfolk and from others in the area. Light to handle, they may be erected around those plants requiring wind protection such as sweet corn or the taller growing outdoor tomatoes. This is done by driving stout stakes into the ground and tying the hurdles to them. Used in this way, a permanent fence is not essential. Interwoven or overlap fencing panels, made to any height and usually in 6 feet or 2 metre lengths, are obtainable from Larch Lap Limited of Stourport-on-Severn; E.C. Cases of Taffs Well, Glamorgan; and Coates of Bridgwater; whilst most country gardeners will be able to purchase the panels made by local craftsmen, possibly to one's exact requirements.

Permanent fencing should be made secure, so that strong winds cannot cause movement which would distort the panels, often resulting in breakage. Fix the panels to 3 inch by 4 inch stakes, driven well into the ground and if the soil is of a sandy nature, it will be advisable to cement the stakes in. A well constructed fence will give years of valuable wind protection but a fence carelessly erected will cause only trouble, requiring constant attention. Against the fence, facing south or west, cordon gooseberries may be planted or runner beans grown up laths which may rest on top of the fence. Tomatoes may also be grown close to the fence and other tall growing plants and those crops requiring concentrated sunlight for their ripening. The value of fencing in comparison to a hedge of privet or beech is that the ground may be utilised right up to the fence and every inch used, whereas with a hedge, planting cannot be done nearer than about 3 feet. A fence will also require no further attention when once it has been erected, neither will it take up moisture and nourishment from the soil which is better employed by the vegetables.

A fence may be erected on three sides of the vegetable plot, which is usually the case where the plot is sited at the end of the garden, divided from the rest of the garden by a trellis or rustic screen covered with roses or clematis. It will be advantageous to place a row of frames sloping gently towards the south and 4 to 5 feet from the end of the plot so that the frames may receive the maximum amount of sunlight whilst the lights when not in use, may be reared over those crops growing against the fence and requiring protection from late frosts. Sufficient room must be allowed for the removal of the frame lights which will rest against the back frame boards when open. And a path must be made along the front of the frames to enable them to be reached for watering and ventilation. A path made of brick or paving stones will be both permanent and clean to use.

Making the paths   Paths are important for, if well made, this will enable a barrow to be easily moved about the plot, in addition to mechanical cultivators, whilst the lady of the house will be able to pull a few radishes or spring onions or cut a cabbage or lettuce without the need to change her shoes in wet weather on every occasion. Permanent paths will be an asset but they should not be constructed until the vegetable garden has been laid out. Following the accepted 4-course rotation of crops, the ground is divided into four main rectangular sections and so that the paths may be made with the minimum of difficulty.

The paths should be made 2 feet wide, this being the minimum width necessary for moving the various implements about with ease. First mark out the various sections and the paths required, then begin making them by removing about 4 inches of soil, the depth of a brick placed on its side. On either edge of the path, bricks are laid with their side uppermost which will give the path a neat appearance. The space between the two rows of bricks is filled with clinker, rubble, or crushed brick to a depth of about 3 inches which is made firm and compact. On top of the base, a layer of cement is spread to a depth of 1 inch so that the finished surface is level with the sides of the bricks. As an alternative make the base 2 inches deep and spread over it a thin layer of cement. On to this lay paving stones or concrete flagstones. If the flagstones are 2 feet wide (which is usual), allow for the necessary width when the bricks are laid, marking out the ground accurately with lines.

Apart from a spade, the only tool needed will be a builder's spirit level which will not only enable a more professional job to be done but will ensure that the surface is made level. Obtain a builder's level long enough to span the sides of the bricks and in this way the surface may be made level throughout. To make good paths will require effort and money but they will repay for their making a hundredfold in ease in moving about the garden and in cleanliness. The work should be done in stages when gardening work permits but do not use cement when there is frost about during the winter months.

On one side of the plot will be placed the greenhouse. This should be erected in a north to south direction so that it will receive the maximum amount of sunlight throughout the day. The various types of greenhouse and their erection are described in the following chapter. On the north side of the greenhouse and so that it does not cause shade, will be the potting shed where cuttings may be prepared for rooting, composts and fertilisers stored, and tools and equipment housed and maintained. If fruits and rootcrops are to be stored there during winter, it will be advisable to line the shed with hardboard when the space between the inner and outer walls should be filled with an insulating material such as fibreglass which is both mould and insect-proof. This will go some way towards making the shed frost proof and will provide extra warmth for those who work in the shed in winter. A window light in the roof will assist ventilation in summer and provide additional light for implement cleaning and the preparation of cuttings, etc. during winter. Electricity in the greenhouse and shed will enable earlier crops to be grown and will permit work to be done during hours of darkness so that more daylight hours may be spent in the garden. Much can be done in greenhouse and shed during winter when adverse weather may prevent any outdoor work.

Planning the garden When planning the garden, those crops of a permanent nature must first be considered and the most suitable position chosen for them. Rhubarb will be happy in semi-shade and may be planted where few other crops will flourish. Mint, too, enjoys cool conditions and a moist soil, likewise the dandelion, land cress and horse radish, each of which should be given a corner of the garden to themselves as once established plants are difficult to eradicate if this is thought necessary. Those vegetables such as endive and spinach which quickly run to seed in hot, dry weather, may also be grown in partial shade but most vegetables require an open, sunny situation. Herbs, too, with but one or two exceptions, require full sun and should be planted at the centre point of the garden. The herb garden may take the form of a large circle with the taller herbs at the centre or of a 'wheel' radiating from a central hub. In the spaces between the imaginary spokes (an old cart wheel may be pressed into the surface of the soil and dwarf herbs planted in the spaces between the spokes) herbs such as the thymes, majoram, balm and winter savory are planted, whilst the taller growing herbs such as fennel and dill should be grown against the fencing, in full sun and where they are allowed to seed themselves undisturbed. Or make a herb border in front of the fence facing south with the taller plants at the back, the most dwarf to the front.

To make a vegetable garden as attractive as possible, dwarf hedges or aromatic plants, kept tidy by regular clipping, may be planted around the outer sides of the various plots and they will also give protection from cold winds. Here, lavender and rosemary, hyssop and sage, all of them perennial plants and of woody habit, should be grown. They will add a touch of old world charm to that part of the garden which is usually less aesthetically pleasing than the rest of the garden, besides providing valuable material to use in pot pourris and scent bags and for stuffings. Rows of

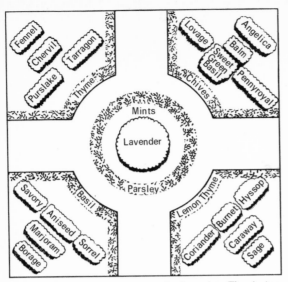

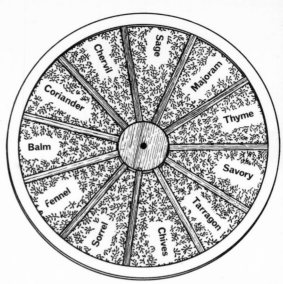

A layout for a permanent square herb garden. The design could just as easily be adapted to a rectangular plot, and would look just as attractive edged with box edging. The paths should be gravel.

A layout for a permanent herb bed made between the spokes of an old cartwheel. Alternatively the design can be carried out with the spokes represented by gravel paths and a sun-dial in the centre.

parsley and chives may be grown by the inner path edges so that they are, at all times, readily available to the housewife without dirtying her shoes.

The asparagus bed will be permanent and should be given an open, sunny position where it may be left undisturbed for years. There should also be a section for a seed bed which should be brought to a fine tilth, and here radishes and spring onions may be sown in shallow drills and seed of lettuce, Brussels sprouts, cabbage and cauliflower, the young plants being transplanted when large enough to handle.

If given a specially prepared bed, the seedlings may be more readily controlled for pest and disease and can be covered with cloches if necessary during adverse weather, whilst their watering is the easier if growing together. The seed bed may be prepared on ground which is close to the greenhouse and cold frames while nearby should be a supply of mains water which will be readily available for those plants growing in the seed bed or under glass and which will need constant supplies of moisture to keep them growing. If mains water is not available, rain water should be collected from the roof of the greenhouse and shed and stored in a tank or barrel for use when required.

Rotational cropping　The cropping of all available ground is of the utmost importance for only a limited area of the garden will be available for vegetable growing and the best possible use must be made of it. A 4-course rotation of crops should be followed where possible for there are many advantages to be gained by it. The crops will make use of the different plant foods stored up in the soil in varying degree so that one may use up larger quantities of nitrogen whilst another will use up more potash and phosphates. It is therefore important to divide the ground in such a way that one crop may follow another each year in systematic rotation.

Again, to keep the soil in good 'heart', it is necessary to ensure that it does not lack lime but whereas certain crops require ample supplies, others e.g. the potato require an acid condition of the soil. Yet if lime is not present, the inert plant foods stored up in the soil will not be made available to the growing crops and however well the ground has been manured, the plants will obtain little benefit. Not only does rotational cropping maintain a balance between the various plant foods but the different methods of cultivation required by each group of plants will ensure that the ground is thoroughly tilled and to a considerable depth rather than merely at the surface. This will open up and aerate the soil and enable bacteria to obtain supplies of oxygen so necessary to convert the manures and fertilisers into food which can be readily absorbed by the crops.

The correct rotation of cropping will also make for the most economical use of the ground for

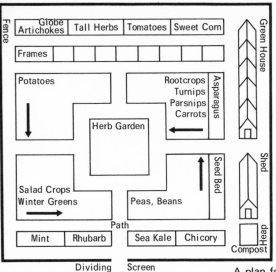

A plan for a vegetable garden showing the positions of the greenhouses, the shed and compost heap, as well as those of the permanent plants, the herb garden and the sequence for the rotation of crops.

less fertilisers will be needed. For example, cabbages and cauliflowers take large amounts of nitrates from the soil whilst the legumes (peas and beans) actually leave the soil richer in nitrogen, due to the ability of the root nodules to fix the nitrogen in the soil. The 'green' crops should therefore follow beans and peas and with the 'greens' may be grown the salad crops or the salads may be grown as 'catch' crops in each section. Moving the crops around will also prevent the accumulation of those pests and diseases in the soil which may be endemic to one group of plants, whilst to grow the crops in rotation will prevent the ground from building up an adverse reaction to any specific plant. This is known as 'soil sickness' and makes for continually decreased crops. When moved to fresh ground, the plants will show a much improved vigour.

On even the smallest vegetable garden, rotational cropping should be practised. First manure one part for the potatoes, planting early, second early and main crop varieties. They will clean the ground as no other crop will do and by moving them around the vegetable garden, this will ensure that the soil is kept free from weeds. A heavy application of manure for potatoes will mean that only limited supplies will be needed for other crops during the next three years and until the ground is made ready for potatoes again.

Root crops should follow potatoes and they require a soil which is not deficient in lime, whilst they always do better in one which has been manured for a previous crop. Fresh manure causes the roots to grow forked whilst it is also detrimental to their keeping qualities.

Follow root crops with legumes of all kinds and which will increase the nitrogen content of the soil and make it available for the 'greens' which will follow the peas and beans. For the small garden, the rotation will be as follows:

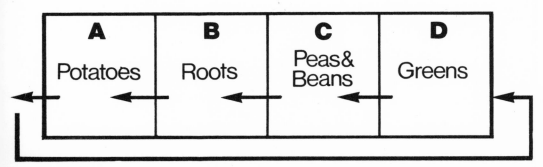

Root crops to give an all-year supply:

	Variety	When to sow	To mature
Beet	Boltardy	April	July–August
	Little Ball	April–May	September–November
	Show Bench	May	August–November
Carrot	★Amstel	February–March	May–June
	Concord	April	October onwards
	Early Nantes	March–June	July–October
	Scarlet Perfection	April	September onwards
	★Sweetheart	January–March	April–June
Parsnip	Hollow Crown	April	September onwards
	Tender & True	April–May	October onwards
	The Student	March	August–October
Swede	Purple Top	April	October onwards
Turnip	★Early Snowball	March	June–July
	Golden Ball	April–May	October onwards
	Tokyo Cross	March	June–July
	Utility	April–May	October onwards

★ *Sow under glass*

The larger garden will be able to grow a larger number of varieties in each section which will give a greater spread of vegetables throughout the year but the cropping rotation should be the same. This is, however, a general rule and it must not be thought that between rows of peas and beans and other crops, lettuce salad crops be grown. As they will occupy the ground for only a short time, and it is necessary to crop the land as intensively as possible, salads are ideal for planting between most other crops for they will have been removed from the ground before the other plants reach maturity.

An all year supply of salads:

	Variety	When to sow	To mature
Cucumber	★Burpee's Hybrid	April	July–September
Endive	Batavian Broad Leaf	April–July	July–October
Lettuce	Arctic King	September	April–May
	★Cheshunt Early Giant	September–October	January–March
	Constant Heart	March–April	June–August
	Sugar Cos	April–May	July–September
	★Suzan	September–October	April–May
	Webb's Wonderful	April–May	July–September
	Winter Density	May–June	September–November
Mustard and Cress	Super Salad	All year	All year
Onion, Spring	Evergreen bunching	August	April–May
	or White Lisbon	March–April	June–August
Radish	★Cherry Belle	February–March	April–May
	Chinese Rose	July	October–December
	Sparkler	March–June	April–August

★ *Sow and grow on under glass*

There are also those plants which follow no definite rotation (celery is one) because the ground must be trenched each year. The plants, however, will benefit from being planted in fresh ground as frequently as possible.

Intensive cropping Climate will also play a part in determining the cropping programme. Those gardening in the favourable areas of the south west, from a line drawn from Bristol to Southampton will be able to take several more crops during a season than those gardening in the north. In the south west, where winter temperatures rarely cause damage to crops of lettuce and broccoli,

	Variety	When to sow	To mature
Broccoli (Large heading)	Leamington	August	March–April
	Markanta	June	April–June
	Sutton's Progress	June	May–June
	Sutton's Thanet	June	April–May
	Veitch's Self Protecting	April–May	October–December
Broccoli (Sprouting)	Purple Sprouting	April–May	February–April
	White Sprouting	April–May	March–May
Brussels Sprouts	Cambridge No. 5	April	October–December
	Continuity	April	August–December
	Irish Elegance	April	October–February
	King of the Lates	April	November–March
	Peer Gynt	April	September–November
	Sanda	April	October–January
Cabbage	Babyhead	March–April	August–October
	Flowers of Spring	July	April–May
	Golden Acre	April–May	September–December
	Greyhound	March–April	August–November
	January King	April–May	November–March
	*May Star	February–March	May–June
	Sutton's Earliest	March	June–July
	Wheeler's Imperial	July–August	March–May
Calabrese (Large heading)	Green Comet	April–May	August–October
Calabrese (Sprouting)	Green Sprouting (Autumn Spear)	April–May	September–November
Cauliflower	All the Year Round	April	August–October
	Beacon	May–June	September–November
	Canberra	April–May	October–December
	Harrison's Novo	May	September–November
	*Sutton's Classic	February–March	June–July
	Unwin's Snowflake	April–May	August–October
Kale (Borecole)	Asparagus	March–April	October onwards
	Dwarf Green Curled	March–April	October onwards
Savoy	Irish Giant	April	October–March
	Omega	April	November–February
	Savoy King	April	September–January

*Sow under glass

these are grown for harvesting in the early spring, to be followed by a crop of French beans sown early in April as the ground is cleared. The beans are followed by quick-maturing cabbage or cauliflower, broccoli to cut in spring, taking their place. Thus four crops of quick-maturing varieties may be obtained from the same piece of ground in a single season whereas, those gardening in the north will be fortunate if they can harvest two crops.

In the less favourable areas, inter-cropping assumes a greater importance and here it will also be advisable to bring on the plants under glass, making use of cloches to start them off whilst spring frosts are still troublesome. In this way, at least a month's start will be gained over plants raised outdoors. In northern districts, quick-maturing varieties are now making it possible to obtain additional crops in a season. At the same time, sowings should be made in frames and under cloches so that as soon as one crop has been harvested, further plantings will be ready to take its place. Every day saved in bringing the crop to maturity will make for greater productivity and this is especially important if the garden is small. Spring cabbage may be followed by French beans with carrots sown along-side and followed by hardy winter broccoli which will give all the year round cropping.

Again, early potatoes or peas can be followed by lettuce, autumn cauliflowers or winter cabbage. It is not necessary to allow the ground to remain idle after harvesting the early crops. Well cultivated land may be kept continuously productive, following rotational cropping as widely as possible though quick-maturing 'catch' crops may be grown in all parts of the garden wherever the opportunity presents itself. This is made possible by the introduction of new vegetables of quick maturity and of compact habit which are ideal for the small garden.

Vegetables for small gardens for successional cropping:

	Variety	When to Sow	To mature
Beet	Little Ball	April–May	September–November
Broad Bean	The Midget (or The Sultan)	October	May–June
Broccoli	Leamington	August	March–April
(Large heading)	Matchless	June	May–June
Broccoli (Sprouting)	Dwarf Green Curled	April	November–March
Brussels sprouts	Dobies Early Dwarf	March	November–February
	Early Button	Early March	September–November
Cabbage	Babyhead	April	August–October
	Primata	March	August–September
	Wheeler's Imperial	July	March–May
Cauliflower	Dwarf Monarch	April	October–November
	*Early Snowball	February	June–July
	Snowflake	April	August–September
French bean	Earligreen	Mid-April	July
Kale	Dwarf Curled	April	November–March
Lettuce	Little Gem	April	June–July
	Tom Thumb	March	June–July
Pea	Lincoln	March	July–August
	Meteor	October	June
	Peter Pan	April	July
Runner Bean	Hammond's Dwarf	Late April	August–September
Savoy	Asmer Shortie	March	October–December
Turnip	Golden Ball	March	October–November
Vegetable Marrow	Gold Nugget	April	July–September

*Sow under glass

All these vegetables are quick to mature for they do not take as long a time as the more robust varieties to complete their growth:

Keeping records   When sowing seeds under glass or in the open ground, make a note of the date of sowing and place a small wooden label in the ground at the end of each row. By keeping a record of sowing times and of varieties, it will be possible to find out the time taken for germination and it will be additionally helpful if day-to-day records of the weather are also kept. The correct sowing time for each crop may then be determined. In this way the plants will not occupy the boxes or frames for too long a time, nor the open ground rows thereby causing them to become 'drawn' and starved of plant food before they can be moved to the open ground where they are to grow on to maturity. This will usually be dictated by weather conditions. Again, delayed sowing may mean the loss of valuable time in harvesting the crop with the result that there may not be time for the growing of other crops that season.

Records should also be made of the size and quality of each crop. Mushrooms and tomatoes can be weighed and the varieties compared as to which gives the higher yield, together with the cultural methods employed and the fertilisers used, how often and at what strength. A note should also be made of the culture of all outdoor crops, the time taken for them to reach maturity, their size and quality so that those varieties giving best results in certain soils and in a particular district may be noted for future planting and unsatisfactory varieties discarded.

2
Greenhouses and Frames

Whilst a frame will be almost as much a part of the vegetable garden as a spade, being used for hardening off and for the production of early crops, a greenhouse though not essential will enable a wider variety of crops to be grown, especially where gardening in the cooler parts of Britain. Here, crops of tomatoes and cucumbers can be produced much earlier than if relying on open air planting or on a frame and if some form of heating is available, then out of season crops may be enjoyed. Things like this make vegetable growing all the more attractive.

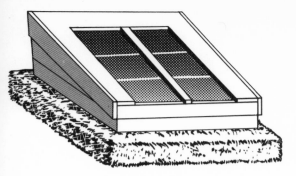

Hot-beds are still the finest way of raising early crops of tomatoes, cucumbers and other tender vegetables without a heated greenhouse. The diagram shows how the frame should be seated on top of the hot-bed.

Tomatoes and cucumbers may be raised early in the year and grown on in gentle heat to begin cropping in May. Aubergines and peppers may be given the extended cropping season they require, whilst a winter mushroom crop may be grown in semi-darkness beneath the greenhouse bench where space should also be kept for forcing rhubarb, a crop that is always appreciated in the early weeks of the New Year when fruits and vegetables are scarce and uninteresting. If those plants requiring the maximum amount of light are grown close to the roof, then pots of French beans can be grown at the front of the bench and with them, extra early crops of tomatoes and peppers, the plants being grown in pots and stopped after setting the first trusses so that the fruit will ripen more quickly. Lettuce, such as 'Cheshunt Early Giant', which produces a good solid heart during the time of year when daylight hours are short, may be grown in boxes at the front of the bench or between rows of tomatoes growing in ground beds where the Dutch-light house is in use.

Greenhouse construction Of numerous greenhouse types, the Dutch-light house is popular for growing tomatoes and all those crops such as winter lettuce which require the maximum amount of light. This type of house is used mostly without heat, though soil warming equipment will enable earlier crops to be grown. The house is usually constructed on a brick base of 3–4 courses and each light, composed of a single sheet of glass, is clipped into position, the sides having a gentle slope to allow for maximum light penetration. Made of aluminium or cedar wood, the house is quickly erected and is equally quickly dismantled to move elsewhere as required. If two bases can be prepared, it will be possible to alternate their planting with tomatoes each year so as to allow the ground beds a period of recuperation from their exposure to the elements. The lights may also be used as frame lights if so desired. With the Crittall-Hope house and others, a sliding door with finger-tip control gives easy access and additional ventilation, whilst wind damage is reduced to a minimum. No glazing is required, the lights being sent out complete and ready for erecting sectionally.

Several makes of the Dutch-light houses are supplied with a portable concrete base which may be laid directly on to the ground and the house erected over the base, there being no need for tedious brick laying. Or the house may be erected on old railway sleepers which, like the concrete blocks, may be moved about the garden if the house is being used to cover various crops growing in the open.

The more conventional greenhouse with a brick or wooden base extending to a height of 2 feet and with glass sides extending for a further 3 feet before meeting the roof, will require less heat to maintain a temperature similar to that of a Dutch-light house and will enable a wider range of horticultural activities to be performed. Tomatoes and cucumbers may be grown at the back, planting them in deep boxes or pots and first training them in an upright direction, then to the top of the roof whilst other crops may be grown at the front of the bench, or seedlings raised and cuttings rooted. Along the front of the bench may be tacked sacking or canvas, to exclude light and here, in boxes or directly on the ground, mushrooms may be grown and rhubarb and seakale forced.

A lean-to greenhouse, which may also be used as a garden room, will enable out of season crops to be grown which may be readily attended directly from the home if a suitable wall can be found against which it may be erected. The greenhouse may then be entered through a door-way made in the back wall. With electric lighting and heating, the greenhouse plants may be attended in the evening or on winter days when the garden may be under snow and ice.

A sunny position should be selected for a lean-to house, preferably a wall facing south or west, where tomatoes and cucumbers may be grown at the front and seedlings raised on benches or shelves fixed against the back wall and built up in tiers to take full advantage of available space. If the lean-to house is of Dutch-light design, all the horticultural activities that normally take place in the greenhouse can be carried out here.

Where garden space is at a premium, the circular greenhouse manufactured by Messrs. Humex Ltd. is to be recommended. It is 7 feet high and 8 feet in diameter and is topped by a dome 3 feet in diameter which lifts to provide top ventilation in addition to the all round intake of air at ground level. Instant shading is by means of spring roller blinds in green p.v.c. material which take only seconds to move up or down. Heating costs are minimised by the elimination of unnecessary headroom whilst staging provides support for plants at all levels. Heating consists of a close coiled mineral-insulated copper-sheathed cable operating at a low surface temperature and providing an all-round even distribution of heat which will raise the temperature at least 25°F. above outside temperatures.

Methods of heating Efficient heating is all-important when growing out-of-season crops. Violent fluctuations of temperature must be avoided whilst in case of a sharp fall in outside temperatures there should be sufficient reserve in the heating system to raise the temperature of the house to that demanded by the plants. Where raising seedlings, economies may be made by the use of a propagator which will raise the temperature to 60°–70°F. to ensure rapid germination, with the minimum of expense.

To calculate the amount of heat required to raise the temperature of a conventional greenhouse to 25°F. above that of the outside temperature, the total area of base and glass must be obtained. For a house 12 feet long and 8 feet wide, with a 2-foot base of brick or wood, and a door 7 feet high, the area will be approximately 284 square feet made up as follows:

2 sides with glass 12 feet × 3 feet	72 square feet
2 roof sections with glass 12 feet × 4 feet 6 inches	108 square feet
2 ends, average height of glass 8 feet × 4 feet	64 square feet
2 sides, brick 12 feet × 2 feet ÷ 2	24 square feet
2 ends, brick 8 feet × 2 feet ÷ 2	16 square feet
Total area	284 square feet

This is multiplied by 10 to give the number of watts required, which to be on the safe side should be 3000.

Of a number of efficient heaters on the market, the Autoheat 3000 will provide sufficient warmth for out of season crops for a house of these dimensions. It is a fan heater with a built-in thermometer and has a temperature control knob to enable the heater to be set to the degree required. Accurate thermostatic control means no wasted heat and low running costs. The sensitive element is placed behind the dial where it is unaffected by the radiant heat of the sun and where it can measure with accuracy, the intake air temperature. The heater can be instantly connected to the mains and may be allowed to stand on a wooden block or on bricks where used for heating a Dutch-light house.

An efficient heater is the Parwin P70, made of rust-proof steel. It has three elements which are doubly insulated to prevent shorting through the case, thus eliminating dangers from condensation, whilst the thermostat, 2-way switch and mains cable entry are enclosed in a drip-proof, dirt-resistant chamber.

The 3kW model will give frostproof protection for a greenhouse 20 feet × 12 feet and temperature control is selective from 35°F. upwards. The 2-way switch allows for the stopping and starting of the circulation fan as the thermostat cuts the heating elements to off and on. This is desirable for in winter a continuously running fan would circulate air around the cold glass and quickly cool the air again. The heater has three elements so arranged that should one fail, two are left for frost protection.

It should be said that circulating air (warm in winter, cool in summer) is vital for healthy plant growth and helps to prevent botrytis, mildew and other moulds which are encouraged by a stagnant atmosphere.

Tubular heaters are also effective and may be fitted to the walls where the greenhouse has a base of wood or brick. Where wall mounting is not practical, the tubes may be held in place by spikes of galvanised iron, inserted into the ground. The loading is 60 watts per foot of tube and additional lengths can be added should higher temperatures be required. The tubes may be tucked away beneath the staging and provide effective heat for the minimum of care and expense. With thermostatic control, the heaters may be left for weeks unattended.

Where no electric supply is available or where the house is too far from the home, the Module 7500 paraffin-oil-fired heater, thermostatically controlled will prove invaluable to greenhouse owners. With it, there is no wick-trimming and as it is supplied with a 5-gallon oil storage tank, frequent filling is not necessary. Fuel is metered into the vaporising burner by two orifices (the longer being marked with a dot). When the supply is turned on, sufficient oil flows continuously through the small orifice to maintain the flame in the burner at a low level. The thermostatic valve controls the fuel through the longer orifice, so that when the valve opens, fuel flows through both orifices and the flame burns at a higher level.

The unit is installed on bricks at the end of the greenhouse, with the oil storage tank on the bench for it must be no more than 3 feet nor less than 2 feet 6 inches away from the orifices as its height determines the fuel rate. The fuel line is clipped to the staging and to connect it to the burner, push the nipple into the fuel inlet. Then turn on the tap and when the wick is moist, apply a light. In about 30 minutes, adjust the thermostatic valve and the levelling screws so that the flame is even.

The 5-gallon tank will need filling once a month and to heat a greenhouse 120 feet long and 8 feet wide to a temperature of about 50°F. during the winter, 200 therms will be needed and will cost about £15.

A greenhouse may require shading during summer, if in an exposed position open to the sun which is where a greenhouse usually is sited. Hessian canvas, or tinted polythene sheeting may be extended down the outside of the roof. A less expensive method is to spray the outside of the greenhouse with Sun-brella, a waterproof preparation, pale green in colour which eliminates sun glare and provides the right conditions for peak production during summer. The paste is gradually diluted with water and is applied with a sprayer when the glass is quite dry. At the end of summer it is readily removed with a brush and warm soapy water.

To reduce the inside temperature of a greenhouse, at either end, above the door, the Vent-Axia air extraction system is efficient, one ventilator introducing fresh air, whilst the other removes the stale air, thus maintaining the house in a fresh, buoyant condition during the warmest of days.

Soil warming Where an electric supply is available, soil warmth for seed germination, the propagation of cuttings and for early salad crops may be inexpensively obtained by the use of warming wires and cables. A low voltage transformer unit which reduces the mains supply to a low safe voltage, is used to heat a plastic covered galvanised wire laid under a bed of soil or sand. These wires will also heat the soil in a frame used for early crops or for seed raising and where there is danger of cultivations disturbing them, warming wires should be used instead of cables. For rotational cropping, a warming wire is laid 10 inches deep in several frames and the transformer moved to each in turn, as required.

Where making an electric hot bed, a minimum of 6 watts per square foot of bed is allowed and current is switched on, generally at night, for a long enough period to burn 70 watts per square foot in every 24 hours. In addition, air warming cables can be fitted around the inside of frame, using stainless steel clips to fix the cables to the sides. For a frame 6 feet × 4 feet, one 150 watt soil warming cable and one 300 watt air heating cable will be required. Soil retains its temperature for a considerable time when heated and even after turning off the heater, there will be no rapid fall in temperature as there is with air heating. The use of soil warming wires in a heated greenhouse will enable the air temperature to be reduced to a minimum whilst keeping the plants growing by gentle bottom heat. Where a hotbed cannot be made from manure, electric soil warming is a reliable substitute.

For raising seedlings and striking cuttings, a sand propagating frame may be made in a cold greenhouse by using either low voltage or mains warming cables. A wooden box is made with 9 inch boards, the base being covered with felt. Over this is placed a 2 inch layer of washed sand before laying down the warming wires which are covered with a further 3 inch layer of sand on which the seed boxes or pots are stood; or cuttings (to be rooted) may be inserted directly into the sand. 8 watts per square foot of bed should be allowed, whilst a soil thermostat is necessary to control the temperature of the bed.

Greenhouse hygiene   When growing vegetable crops under glass, cleanliness is of the utmost importance. Each year, when the tomato crop is cleared in autumn, inspect the house for broken glass so that it may be replaced before the winter. It will not be possible to adequately heat a greenhouse where the warm air is continually escaping through damaged glass or where the ventilators will not close properly. Nor is it possible to fumigate efficiently for the control of pest and disease. It is usual at this time to wash the glass with warm soapy water, both inside and outside for dirty glass will prevent the sun's rays from penetrating and this is also the case with frame lights.

As a precaution against pest and disease, fumigation must also be carried out. A simple and effective method is to burn sulphur cones or candles inside the house, either before or after the crop has been removed but sulphur should not be used where there are growing plants.

To fumigate, close up all ventilators and if the greenhouse is of some size, begin by lighting the cones or candles at the far end, and working towards the door. Sulphur fumes are irritating and must not be inhaled. Sulphur should be used at the rate of 1 pound for every 1000 cubic feet of air space or use one cone or candle for a house 8 feet × 6 feet.

As an alternative, wash down the inside and soak the soil, if ground beds are used, with formalin solution used at a strength of 1 part formalin in 50 parts of water. It is a clear liquid and should be applied with a power sprayer which will enable the liquid to penetrate all cracks of the woodwork and into the glass overlaps where pests usually congregate. The discovery that formaldehyde gas, released from formalin solution, would cure mushroom house sickness and make a greenhouse 'sweet' and clean after tomato and cucumbers, revolutionised the growing of these crops for commercial growers.

After formalin has been used 4 to 5 weeks should be allowed before new planting is done in the soil beds. The fumes given off are poisonous to plants, humans and animals and after fumigating the house, allow the gas 24 hours to achieve its maximum penetration before opening up the door and ventilators. The house should then be aired for 48 hours to allow time for the fumes to clear, before being worked in again.

When the house has been fumigated, an additional precaution may be taken by passing the flame of a blow lamp over the woodwork, whilst all seed boxes and pots should be sterilised by immersing them in a tank of formalin solution, diluted to 1 part in 50 of water. Or use Ster-Izal which may also be used for disinfecting the greenhouse and soil.

Should eelworm have been troublesome as it may be with tomatoes, the pest is eradicated by injecting the soil with the liquid fumigant D.D. It will be necessary to allow the soil a month for the fumes to escape before further planting is done. The greenhouse may be kept free from pests by the use of an aerosol which is a suspension of minute solids or liquid particles in gaseous form, thereby creating a mist which envelopes each plant. The aerosol will consist of a metal container with a thermostatically controlled heating element to vaporise the liquid pesticide. The Mistosol 99 is suitable for the larger house. It is worked by a high speed motor of one-eighth h.p. which develops 16,000 r.p.m., the spinning disc system enabling an excellent mist to be produced from the water based insecticides or disinfectants.

A more simple method is to fit a disc impregnated with pesticide (or fungicide) over an electric light bulb which when switched on, will release the fumigant with the heat of the bulb.

One of the earliest preparations to be used in aerosol form was Azobenzene, discovered by

Prof. Blauvelt of Carnell University: it will eliminate red spider from glasshouses.

Where raising one's own plants, it will be advisable to have a supply of sterilized soil always available. One method is to obtain loam of a fibrous nature and to water it with formalin solution or with Sterilite soil disinfecting fluid, used at a strength of 1 pint to 10 gallons of water. As the soil is made damp, make it into a heap 2–3 feet high and cover with a tarpaulin or plastic sheeting to retain the fumes. Leave for a week, then remove the cover to allow the soil to be turned for the fumes to escape. It should be turned several more times until quite free of any fumes. This will take about a month when it may be used.

The Autosoil electric soil steriliser is most effective. It will sterilise a bushel of soil at one time and is automatically controlled, switching off after sterilisation is complete. Steam sterilisation may be done with the Sterilatum, a machine whereby steam is driven through soil contained in a chamber, a useful method where larger quantities of soil are to be sterilised. It should be stated that soil will be sterilised in a temperature of 160°F. (71°C.) held for 4 hours. It is inadvisable for the temperature to exceed 176°F. (80°C.) and should it exceed 212°F. (100°C.), the soil will be completely sterile and unable to support any form of plant life.

After the soil has been sterilised, the various John Innes composts may be made up according to the proven formula. The composts should not be made up before the soil has been sterilised.

3 Tools and Equipment

Good tools are essential to growing good crops of vegetables, they make the work easier and enable cultivations to be done more efficiently. Of first importance is a spade, for it will be used for turning over the soil and for trenching, also for earthing up and lifting the crops. It will be in constant use and although a spade of any reliable make will be an efficient tool, for best results select one with a blade of stainless steel. It will not only be almost indestructible but it will be lighter and easier to use for soil will not stick to its mirror polished surface. Especially should a stainless steel spade be used if working a clay soil into which it will cut with the greatest ease. A Spear and Jackson spade with a blade of Sheffield stainless steel and fitted with a D-type handle moulded from polypropylene will be light and easy to handle and will last the average gardener a lifetime. For working rough clay soil, the Claymaster spade, fitted with four pointed cutting teeth and with a handle of tubular steel will allow the most stubborn soil to be brought into condition. Select a spade in the same way that a professional cricketer selects his bat. Try several, to get the 'feel' or balance and it is surprising how each will differ, however slightly. But when one is using it most days of the year, a spade must need to feel comfortable in the hands of he (or she) who will most use it.

As a complement to the spade, a garden fork of stainless steel will be the ideal tool for forking over the surface and for mulching; in addition it will be needed for lifting potatoes and other crops and conveying garden refuse to the barrow or compost heap. Here again, a stainless steel fork will remain clean and polished where working wet soil, especially of a heavy nature. A small 'border' fork 9 inches wide instead of the usual 12½ inches, will prove easier for a lady to manage, whilst it has additional value in that it may be used between rows made only 12 inches apart. A spade and fork will be the vegetable grower's most important tools and after use they should be wiped clean with an oily rag before putting away in the garden shed. Treat them with the respect they deserve.

Those who find digging difficult will obtain some relief if using the Terrex digger manufactured by Wolf Tools, This implement entirely eliminates the strain caused by lifting and turning the soil. The tool is pushed into the soil until the rear lever is resting on the ground. Then, with a slight movement of the handles backwards and downwards, the soil is made loose and turned over. There is no laborious lifting and the tool may be used by a person with only one arm. Both spades and forks may be obtained in this semi-automatic form, and when it is realised that a spadeful of soil will weigh about 14 pounds, it is obvious that the semi-automatic spade will take most of the hard work out of digging.

After the ground has been given its basic preparations, an implement such as the Jalo Single-wheel Cultivator will prove valuable. After fitting it with a small plough or with a set of discs for breaking up lumpy soil, it is pushed through the soil which should be clean and friable. Rakes may also be attached to prepare a fine seed bed and cultivators for hoeing between the rows and for loosening hard top soil after winter.

For the larger garden, there are a number of efficient power-driven machines which will do the work of several men and with greater efficiency, in much less time. The Howard 'Bantam' manufactured by Rotary Hoes and fitted with a two-stroke engine, is capable of doing eight hours work on a gallon of petrol. For market garden work, Dashwood Engineering's 'Hornet' is only 12 inches wide and weighs 90 pounds. It will do a day's work on a half a gallon of petrol and will cultivate between rows 12 inches wide.

The compact Farmer's Boy made by the Raven Engineering Co. is an inexpensive machine to use. Besides doing all the usual garden cultivations, it will cut down bracken and drive a saw bench, thus utilising timber about the garden for fuel.

Of other tools, an efficient rake to pulverise the soil to make a seed bed and to make drills for seed sowing will be a necessity. It should have at least 12 teeth, preferably 14 or 16, to enable the work to be done more quickly. A series of hoes, including the Dutch type, a draw hoe and a scuffle hoe will also be an essential part of the equipment. Important, too, is a good trowel for planting and here, too, this should be of stainless steel to make for easier handling. Where working in damp soil, it will not be necessary to repeatedly clean the trowel if the blade is made of shining stainless steel. After use, wipe it clean with an oily cloth.

To use amongst plants which are growing closely together, a hand hoe will be useful. Generally known as an onion hoe, the head is 3–4 inches wide and the handle about 9 inches in length. It may also be used to thin out turnips, beetroot and other plants which may be growing close together in the rows. Wilkinson's swoe is a long-handled tool which functions in the same way. being a combination of a scuffler and a hoe.

A good tool rack is an integral part of one's kit. It should be fastened to the wall of a shed or outhouse, about 6 feet above the ground and here, the tools should always be placed at the end of the day after being cleaned and maintained in working order. There will then be no need to waste valuable time in looking for a certain tool, whilst all the tools will be kept in a clean and efficient condition.

An inexpensive tool for planting potatoes (and bulbs) is the B-B planter which is hand operated by two arms between which is a metal container to hold a potato or large bulb. The container has a sharp under-edge which allows it to be pressed into the ground, the potato or bulb being released by closing the arms together and withdrawing the implement.

No vegetable garden will be complete without a good barrow or truck which will be in constant use to move composts and fertilisers, harvested crops, pot plants and canes. It will save much hard work for otherwise everything must be moved by hand. An all-steel barrow is more durable though lighter to use than a wooden barrow. Fitted with a single rubber-tyred wheel and constructed of a strong tubular frame with a riveted and welded body of heavy gauge steel sheeting, the barrow has a 3 cubic feet capacity and is easily moved about the garden.

The water supply   If the mains water supply is not available (and with many allotments this is not so) a water barrow will be a necessity. It may also be used where mains water is available, to prepare liquid manures and is readily moved about the garden. Fitted with a strong galvanised tank of a capacity of 18 gallons or more, and mounted on solid rubber-tyred wheels, it may be filled from a pond or placed beneath a drain pipe to collect rain water from a shed or greenhouse. This natural water, containing many valuable trace elements which it obtains from the atmosphere on its way down, is better for growing plants than the hard chlorinated water from the mains supply as used in many gardens.

An efficient water supply is vital for vegetables and in a dry season, the water barrow or hose will be constantly in use. Labour saving and useful for those away from home for any length of time during the day, are the oscillating sprinklers, the Hozelock models providing adjustable watering over square or rectangular areas whilst a fingertip control dial enables one of four separate water patterns to be selected. Several models made of cast metal will water an area of 2000 or more square feet, whilst the gentle swaying action gives accurate irrigation. Smaller models rotate or spin and cover an area 40–60 feet in diameter, the nozzles being adjustable for spray intensity and direction.

To bring water to the sprinklers, an efficient hose is necessary, one made of plastic material being less expensive to purchase and lighter to handle than a hose made of rubber. The Hasel Throughfeed hose reel which unwinds and waters as one walks is fitted with hose guides which enable the hose to be drawn off at right angles to the reel and is most efficient. It may be fixed to a wall or post in the garden.

Where watering by hand, an automatic leverspray hose nozzle will enable the jet to reach greater distances or a jet spray may be obtained with a metal spike attached which will fit into the ground so that one part of the garden may be watered whilst the gardener is performing tasks elsewhere.

An efficient watering can is an essential part of vegetable garden equipment for watering in the open, in frames and beneath cloches where a gentle flow of water is required. Haws galvanised cans with their long spouts and fine rose sprinklers are the Rolls-Royce of cans and have a capacity of 4, 6 or 8 quarts. The cans are beautifully balanced to make for easier handling and even when filled with water, they never feel unduly heavy nor are they tiring to use.

Where the water supply is to be obtained from a well, spring or pond and has often to be brought a distance to the land, a petrol-driven pump will be a worthwhile investment. It will pump and convey 100 or more gallons an hour over a distance of 100 yards or so, the cost of the machine depending upon the capacity of water pumped per minute. The water may be pumped directly through lengths of perforated plastic or galvanised tubes, extended to any length and irrigate large areas of growing crops during periods of drought.

It is rarely possible to find a garden where the soil is in exactly the right condition to grow good crops of vegetables. Usually it will be too heavy and badly drained so that excess moisture remains about the roots of the plants in winter, causing them to decay and autumn sown peas and broad beans will be unable to survive such conditions. Or the soil may be dry and sandy and lacking in moisture so that the crops make little headway during the drier summer months when growth should be most vigorous. Some soils lack lime whilst others contain an excess, a condition that must be corrected to ensure heavy crops.

4 Soil Preparation and Drainage

Soil testing   The soil of every garden differs from the next but as a general rule soils may be divided into four main groups: (1) those of a clay nature, containing about $33\frac{1}{3}$rd per cent clay particles; (2) those which may be classed as rich loam, containing no more than about 20 per cent clay; (3) those classed as light and containing about 75 per cent sand; and (4) calcareous soils which have a high chalk or lime content and which are generally 'hot' shallow soils. All soils differ however slightly, in that some are too acid (lacking in lime) whilst others are too alkaline (containing too much lime) so that the first necessity is to discover the pH value. pH stands for the hydrogen ion concentration of moisture in the soil and the acidity or alkalinity varies accordingly. The scale extends from 0 to 14, with neutrality at 7.0. The change of a single unit represents a hydrogen ion value of 10 which is considerable so that for example, where soil shows a pH value of 6.0, a soil will be ten times more acid than one which is neutral and few vegetables (the potato being an exception) will grow well in a soil of such high acidity. The colour charts provided with soil testing kits show the pH values.   The range passes from deep purple which denotes the highest degree of acidity to deep green which denotes the highest degree of alkalinity.

The B.D.H. indicator kit consists of a bottle of indicator solution; a quantity of barium sulphate; glass test tubes; some distilled water; and a colour chart all housed in a compact wooden box in which the tubes stand upright.

The soil to be tested should be in a friable condition and be placed in the tube (half-full) with a spoon or spatula. To the soil add a small amount of barium sulphate, then fill almost to the top with distilled water and add a few drops of indicator. Place a rubber stopper into the end of the tube, shake up the contents and allow to settle, then compare the colour to that of the chart. Where the soil shows a lime deficiency, give 7 pounds of lime (hydrated) per 100 square feet of ground area for each hydrogen ion value. To make a soil acid, should this be considered necessary, dress with peat and give 1 pound per 100 square feet of sulphate of ammonia. Brassica crops require a soil of a high lime content, so do peas and beans and for most crops, the land should be well limed in winter.

Apart from its ability to correct the acidity of soil, lime has the power of being able to release the various plant foods pent up in the soil so that well manured land will not be beneficial to the growing crops unless lime is present to unlock the food content. Again, lime is able to improve the physical condition of the soil by breaking up the clay particles. For a heavy soil an application of caustic lime (unhydrated) will by its vigorous action break up the clay particles more quickly than will hydrated lime. Caustic lime is obtainable from a builder's merchant and must be kept dry. It is applied to the soil when the soil is in a reasonably dry condition, being dug well in when the moisture in the ground will cause an explosive action to take place, the clay soil disintegrating with the lime. Without lime, a heavy soil will consolidate with the winter rains and so deprive the roots of the plants of the necessary oxygen. The oxygen will also be cut off from bacteria in the soil and they will not be able to fulfill their function of converting humus into plant food.

Lime has a tendency to be washed down by rain and where used in hydrated form, it should be applied to the surface in mid-winter after the ground has been dug and the surface left in a rough condition, to be broken down by wind and frost.

The soil of town gardens which may contain heavy deposits of soot and sulphur which will contribute to its acid condition will benefit from a dressing of hydrated lime before any planting takes place for no matter how heavily the ground is manured, it will not grow good crops unless corrected for its acid condition.

A soil may also be tested for nitrogen, phosphorus and potash deficiency so that the correct requirements of each crop may be supplied and in the correct amounts, thus eliminating wastage and saving expense. A kit marketed by Sudbury Technical Products Ltd. contains 8 two ounce bottles of various soil testing solutions; filtration funnels and filter papers; a rack of 8 test tubes; a rod of pure tin for testing for phosphorous deficiency; and colour comparison charts.

To correct nitrogen deficiency, give a 4 ounce per square foot dressing with sulphate of ammonia for every 1 per cent deficiency shown on the chart.

To ensure the correct phosphatic content, use the solution marked 'phosphorus' and after shaking it up with the soil in the tube, allow to settle, then take the tin rod, scrape it and with it stir the solution for 30 seconds. The solution will then turn blue. If pale blue, this will denote an 10 per cent phosphorus deficiency and the ground should be given a dressing of superphosphate of lime at a rate of 2 pounds per 100 square feet.

To check the potash content, use the necessary indicators when a pale yellow solution will denote a 2 per cent deficiency. To correct this, rake into the surface of the soil in spring, at planting time, 2 ounces of sulphate of potash per 100 square feet of ground. A deep yellow solution will denote a 4 per cent deficiency and double the amount of potash will be required.

If the soil shows a deficiency of each of these plant foods, a compound fertiliser may be made up to the exact requirements and applied in spring, prior to planting. Soil testing can be done quickly on the spot but as soils may differ from one part of the garden to another, it is advisable to make several tests and to make an average of soil requirements before the necessary fertilisers are obtained.

A soil testing outfit may be used over and over again, as well as to test the correct alkalinity of mushroom compost, but where it is not thought necessary to obtain the outfit, the District Horticultural Officer will usually provide a soil test and give advice on soil treatment.

The value of humus Both light and heavy soils require humus. A clay soil so that it will open up and aerate the soil, to allow oxygen to penetrate to the plant roots and to assist drainage. A sandy soil needs humus to bind it and to provide a moisture-holding medium during the dry summer months when plants should be making most growth but will not be able to do so where the soil is lacking in moisture.

Humus may not contain much plant food. It may take the form of decayed leaves or straw that has been broken down (composted) by an activator. Peat is also useful but being slightly acid, the soil should be given liberal dressings of lime. Peat may be used for all types of soil and so greatly improves the soil texture as to allow plant roots to range far and wide without restriction. Whilst it opens up a heavy soil, the spongy texture of moss peat can also be used to enable a sandy soil to hold moisture. Sphagnum moss peats, produced in Ireland and in Somerset are of a light brown colour and are only partially decomposed, thus being able to retain the maximum amount of moisture. They can hold up to 20 times their own weight in water. A bale of peat moss (14 bushels) will cover the surface of the ground to an area of 200 square feet and to a depth of 1 inch. It should be lightly forked in and is best applied in spring. To bring the soil into a condition suitable for sowing or transplanting, take up a handful and squeeze it. It will be in the correct condition if it binds together. It the soil is dry and sandy, it is advisable to moisten the peat before using it. Being almost sterile, peat is to be recommended rather than leaf mould for with peat there is little chance of introducing either pest or disease to the soil. Poplar bark fibre may be used as an alternative but as peat and bark are almost sterile, they should be used with artificial fertilisers made to a balanced formula or with other humus forming materials which contain suitable plant foods. For those living near the coast, chopped seaweed, containing traces of nitrogen and potash and for those gardening in the industrial north, wool shoddy, rich in nitrogen will be both inexpensive and easy to use. Those living in country districts may be able to obtain some well decayed farmyard manure or used hops from a brewery, each supplying humus in addition to traces of the various plant foods. Old mushroom bed compost is also excellent. Where humus forming materials are in short supply, straw composted with an activator, such as Adco or Garotta will provide both humus and nutriment and will be easy and clean to handle.

To compost straw, obtain a bale and shake it well out in a corner of the garden, preferably where it can be surrounded with boards of corrugated iron sheeting. This will not only keep the heap tidy but will protect it from drying winds so that the straw may be more quickly composted. As the straw is spread out, soak it with water then spread a layer 12 inches deep and sprinkle over it some of the activator. Again, add more straw and more activator, building up the heap in this fashion to a height of about 5 feet. It will soon begin to heat up and in 10 days will be ready to turn, shaking out the straw and activator, giving more water if necessary and remaking the heap. Allow it to heat up for another 10 days before repeating the process and in three weeks the straw will have become dark brown, with a wholesome 'earthy' smell, whilst the bits of straw will have become quite short so that they may more easily be dug into the ground.

An excellent supply of humus can be obtained from the garden compost heap which may be formed alongside the straw compost heap, or made back to back, thus making the most economic use of the boards or currugated sheeting. Or use a 'bin' of strong wire netting. If correctly made, there will be no unpleasant smell from compost.

Compost making   The compost heap is built up in layers, using any unwanted 'greens' such as pea and bean haulm, tops of carrots and beetroot, endive which in dry weather may have run to seed, anything except potato haulm and diseased plants which should be burnt, and the stems of sprouts and cabbage which will be difficult to compost. Over each layer of garden refuse, cover with soil and give a dusting of lime. If a small quantity of farmyard or poultry manure can be obtained, add this also and to bring about rapid and thorough decomposition, use an organic liquid activator. This may be liquid manure or give a sprinkling of Adco or Garotta whilst a liquid feed made to a herbal formula and known as Q.R. will prove effective. Lawn mowings may be added, and clearings from ditches and ponds, peat and leaf mould, seaweed and used hops, in fact anything of an organic nature. At the end of six months, the heap will have been entirely composted and be ready to use on the land, being rich in plant foods whilst supplying valuable humus. It will be dark greenish-brown with the consistency of farmyard manure. Vegetables require ample supplies of both humus and plant food to be successful, hence the achievements of the old cottage gardeners who continuously worked into their land quantities of night-soil and rank manure so that the soil was kept well nourished and productive. This is even more important today when it is necessary to obtain full value for one's time and outlay. The ultimate aim with all soils is to bring to a fine tilth, deeply enriched with moisture holding humus, active in bacteria and which is spongy and friable when pressed in the hands. Such a soil will be well drained yet will be moisture retentive and will be ready to work at all times, except when covered with snow and ice. It will also warm up with the first spring sunshine so that the plants will get away to an early start.

A soil of a calcareous nature will usually have only a limited amount of top soil and whilst humus in the form of peat or garden compost will increase the depth, this may also be done by 'green' manuring. Calcareous soils are to be found in the region of the Chiltern Hills, in the Cotswolds, and along the South Coast, whilst limestone formations cover much of north eastern England, from Flamborough Head to the Border. Though the high alkalinity of the soil in these parts will not be detrimental to vegetable growing, calcareous soils are usually 'hot' soils owing to their lacking depth, and in dry weather the plants dry out rapidly and make only stunted growth.

'Green' manuring is best done in August. After clearing the ground of perennial weeds, it is thickly sown with rape seed. This will germinate quickly and be ready to dig into the soil during October. By then, a thick mat of fibrous roots and green top growth will have formed and should the rape have grown tall, it is cut down with shears or a scythe before digging it in to as great a depth as possible. Heavy land will also be improved by 'green' manuring and the soil should be left rough to enable the weather to improve further its structure.

There are several chemical compounds which are able to improve the condition of a heavy soil. One is Colimnus which is fortified by plant food and a 28 pound bag will treat about 400 square feet of ground. Another is Krillium. They are applied to the soil when in a reasonably dry condition, being sprinkled over the surface and dug in. Immediately, the compounds begin to break up the colloid matter in the soil which causes the clay particles to bind together. Thus a more friable condition is produced which is made more so by incorporating peat or composted straw or some other humus forming material.

Into a heavy soil, drainage materials may be incorporated at the same time, using crushed brick or mortar (with its valuable lime content), shingle or coarse sand. If the ground is low lying, an area of top soil should be removed to a depth of 3 feet and a base of crushed brick provided. Over this, drainage pipes should be laid of sufficient 'fall' to enable the water to be carried away to a ditch or to some other part of the garden where it will do less harm. The soil is then replaced, at the same time incorporating additional drainage and humus forming materials.

Aerosil, a product of British Gypsum Ltd. will also help to bring a heavy soil into a more workable condition. It will help to flocculate the colloid matter of a clay soil and will bind a sandy soil to enable it to retain moisture. It also provides valuable mineral foods such as calcium, magnesium and sulphur whilst it is inexpensive to use.

Organic and inorganic manures It is not possible to grow good vegetables without the use of organic manures for these are able to supply the plants with humus in addition to nutrients, whilst valuable trace elements are also present. Those vegetables requiring a long period to mature, possibly a year or more, will need a manure which releases its plant food slowly. Farm-yard manure and composted straw, material from the garden compost heap, seaweed and shoddy are all slow acting and are mostly nitrogenous manures. Bone meal is also slow acting and has a high phosphatic value. Nitrogen is needed to make sufficient vegetation to assist in the correct functions of the plant so that it will reach its maximum size and mature correctly. Lack of nitrogen will cause the plants to be stunted and sickly, though certain crops e.g. the potato, can have an excess of nitrogen and the quality deteriorates, while with others, leaf is made at the expense of 'heart'. Too much nitrogen and lack of phosphates will cause the cauliflower to form leaf at the expense of a large solid head. Thus, phosphates are required to bring the plants to full maturity whilst they also stimulate root activity. Where nitrogenous manures are being used, bone meal should accompany them especially in a lime deficient soil or phosphates should be provided by the quick acting fish meal or guano, both rich in nitrogen and in phosphatic content; or use the inorganic superphosphate of lime which contains only phosphatic compounds, though it is a fertiliser of acid reaction which should be used only in a well limed soil. Basic slag which has a similar phosphatic value has a high lime content and should be used in soils of acid reaction.

Nitrogen is necessary to start a plant into growth after a period of inactivity, possibly after occupying the ground over winter, or where cold winds have retarded growth. Nitrogen is given in the form of nitrate of soda which will also release pent-up potash in the soil whilst when compared to sulphate of ammonia, it does not prove so destructive to lime in the soil. Slower to release their nitrogen but less destructive to the soil are the inorganic fertilisers, soot and dried blood, both so valuable in the vegetable garden.

Potash is essential to all crops for it makes a plant grow 'hard', able to withstand adverse weather and disease. Soil deficient in potash will grow lush, soft plants which will succumb to the first frost or cold winds, or at the first sign of disease. Potash also accentuates flavour and colour. Vegetables lacking potash will have little flavour. Potash may be given in the form of wood ash, which should be stored dry as both it and it's potash content are readily washed away by rain. For this reason, light soils are usually devoid of potash and require replenishing with plant foods more often than heavy soils. A light soil is a hungry soil.

Fish meal, guano and poultry manure are also rich in potash but where the land is in good heart, the inorganic sulphate of potash, which has a high potash content, may be used instead, being given at planting time for it is quickly washed down to the plant's roots. Kainit also has a high potash content but contains $33\frac{1}{3}$ per cent salt and is mostly used on asparagus, beetroot and other maritime crops.

Another valuable fertiliser is liquid manure which contains a balanced diet for growing plants and is readily assimilated. It is applied through the growing season at regular intervals and may be used as a proprietary make (Liquinure) or as a concentrate such as Welgro; or it may be made up to one's own requirements. This is done by half filling a sack with farmyard or poultry manure and suspending it from a stout pole placed across a galvanised tank or bin. The tank should be filled with water and the sack completely immersed. After about a fortnight, the sack is removed and the tank topped up with water. The manure water will then be ready to use, diluting it further if considered necessary. After applying to the plants, it should be watered well down to the roots for best results.

Fertilisers and their food value

(Details of their use are given under each vegetable).

Fertiliser	Action	Nitrogen Content	Phosphatic Content	Potash Content
Basic Slag	Slow	15%		
Bone Meal	Slow	5%	20%	
Dried Blood	Medium	10%		
Farmyard manure	Slow	.5%	.25%	.5%
Fish meal	Quick	10%	8%	7%
Guano	Quick	15%	10%	7%
Kainit	Slow			13%
Nitrate of Soda	Quick	16%		
Nitro-Chalk	Quick	16%		
Potassium Nitrate	Quick	14%		40%
Poultry manure	Medium	3%	2%	6%
Rape meal	Slow	5%	2%	1%
Seaweed	Slow	5%		1.5%
Shoddy (Wool)	Slow	12%		
Sulphate of Ammonia	Quick	20%		
Sulphate of Potash	Medium			50%
Superphosphate	Medium		15%	
Used Hops	Slow	4%	2%	

Preparing the ground   No amount of care in the selection and use of fertilisers and manures will be of much value unless the soil is deeply worked and cleared of all perennial weeds which would compete with the vegetables for their food and moisture.

When first bringing the ground into condition, a start should be made in autumn whilst the soil is still friable and is easily worked. The ground must be cleared, the soil drained and aerated, the lime content increased if need be and be brought into a friable condition by the time the first sowings are made in spring. At this stage, double digging or trenching is essential for only by working the soil two spits (spades) deep will it be possible to incorporate the necessary humus and drainage materials and to remove the deep-rooting weeds. When once the land has been deeply worked, trenching or double digging will not be necessary again though, for a number of crops, trenching will be done each year to achieve best results. In this way, it is possible to concentrate the food requirements of the plants into a limited area so that they are more readily available whilst there will be less wastage.

Ground which has not been worked for some years is usually bastard trenched. This means removing the top 9 inches or so and placing it to one side of the ground which is being prepared whilst the lower spit is treated separately for this will be soil which has not been subjected to the aerating and sweetening influences of the weather, neither will it contain plant foods in readily assimilated form. During this operation, plant foods and drainage materials should be incorporated into the lower spit so that it will be in the best possible condition for the plant roots to penetrate, whilst a well drained soil will never become sour.

Before beginning the operation, several garden lines of strong twine should be available for the work will be easier if the ground is marked out to a plan. Whatever the area to be worked, divide it into two sections.

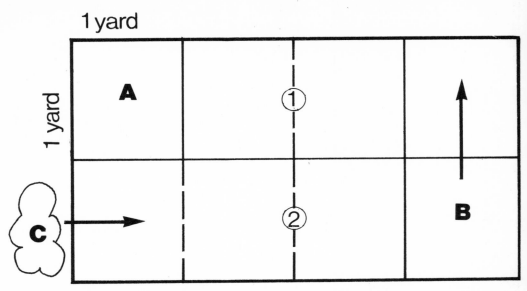

At (A), the top spit is removed and placed where shown (C) on the diagram. When the top spit of an area of 1 square yard has been removed, break up the lower spit, incorporating drainage and humus materials also, then cover it with the top soil, taken from the next yard of ground, at the same time removing all perennial weeds. Work across section (1) and replace the top soil at the end, with that from the end of the section (2) marked (B). The top soil at (C) will be used to complete operations. The ground should be limed at this stage, depending upon clay content and pH value whilst the ground should be treated for wireworm and millepedes by incorporating, as the work proceeds, Gamma–BHC powder but this should not be used if planting the ground with potatoes within 12 months.

Where there is a good depth of top soil and the ground is in a friable, well drained condition, ordinary double digging may be done. Again, the area should be marked out into sections of 1 square yard and soil two spits deep should be taken from (a) and placed at the side of the plot (E). Soil from the next yard of ground (B) two spits deep is then moved to (A) and so on until soil at (E) is used to complete the operation by replacing that moved from section (D). Throughout the operation, the soil is treated with wireworm fumigant whilst humus and fertilisers are incorporated as the work proceeds. The ground should be left in a rough condition for the winter weather to break down to a fine tilth.

Where couch grass and other weeds, difficult to eradicate, have taken a hold, it is advisable to plant potatoes (though not where Gamma–BHC has been used) in spring for they are an excellent means of cleaning the ground.

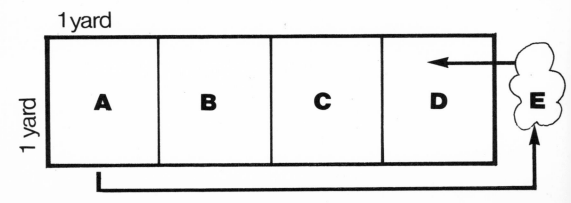

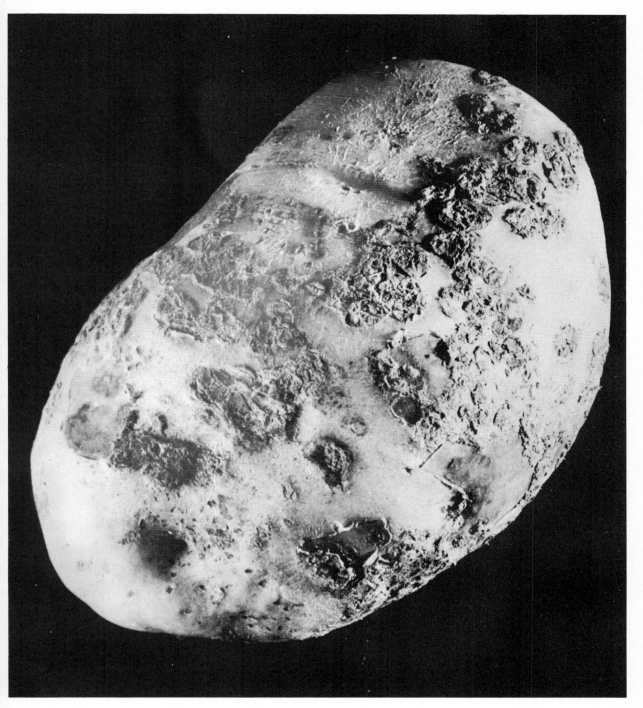

A severe attack of Scab, a fungus disease of potatoes
particularly prevalent on calcareous soils or soils that have
been heavily limed for a previous crop. Digging in green
manure will do much to prevent an outbreak.

Top Removing pollen from tomatoes with the 'Electric Bee'. This is a sophisticated technique for cross-pollinating tomatoes. Pollen of one variety is collected and transferred to emasculated fruit-bearing tomatoes growing in a separate house.

On the spot soil testing. The acid reaction of soil can vary from one part of a garden to another. Though vegetables need an alkaline soil, over-correction of acidity can be harmful. Accurate soil testing assists calculating the amount of lime required.

The work entailed in trenching and double digging is arduous but of vital importance where good vegetable crops are to be grown. Land which has been worked to a considerable depth and contains an abundance of humus will be greatly improved in its structure. It will resemble a sponge, being divided into a multitude of soil particles each surrounded by an air space into which moisture is able to penetrate and which is held in suspension around each particle of soil. The air spaces, though reduced in volume, remain to provide the plant roots with oxygen whilst sufficient moisture will be available to support healthy plant growth, even in periods of drought. Even so, after a winter of heavy rains, the surface of the soil may have formed a crust whereby the soil particles will have 'panned' together. In order to permit air and moisture to enter, the hoe must be used to break up the surface and to suppress annual weeds. Mulching is also important, especially between rows of broad beans and other crops which will occupy the ground during winter. A mulch will not only give some protection to the plants from frost but will suppress weeds and prevent the surface of the soil from 'panning'. It will also improve soil texture by the activities of worms which will carry the particles of humus down into the ground, whilst a summer mulch will prevent the too rapid evaporation of surface moisture. If composted straw or farmyard manure is used, additional plant food will be made available which will be washed into the soil by the rains.

There are those gardeners who make so great a use of mulches that all forms of digging and other cultivations are entirely eliminated. Peat and old mushroom bed compost may be spread over the surface of the soil to a depth of 3-4 inches and this may be augmented by well decayed farmyard manure or used hops. A large worm population and bacterial activity will maintain the soil in good heart and seed is sown and plantings made without the need for any additional soil preparations. This form of cultivation is excellent on light soils, but heavy clay soils still need to be double-trenched every six to eight years.

Upon the successful raising of the plants, the crop will depend. Vegetables are raised by several methods:

    (i) By sowing under glass in a propagator or in a warm greenhouse.
    (ii) By sowing over a hot bed in a frame, in an unheated frame or greenhouse, or under
        cloches.
    (iii) By sowing directly into the open ground.

Those plants requiring a long growing season to mature or where an early crop is to be raised such as tomatoes or cucumbers under glass, sowing in a heated greenhouse will be necessary, but where only small numbers of plants are needed, a simple propagating unit will be more economical to use. It may be placed in a garden room or greenhouse and run from the electricity supply. In a propagator, plants may be raised from seed which may prove difficult to germinate without heat.

Using a propagator Efficient is the Autogrow P40 thermostatic propagator. It is made with a galvanised frame and a polythene cover. It measures 30 inches × 16 inches, is 3 inches deep with a cover 12 inches high, and will accommodate four specially fitted seed trays. A reliable heating element, rated at 15 watts per square foot and an accurate 18 inch rod thermostat built into the base, gives reliable and economical heat.

After sowing, connect to the mains and turn the knob to the required temperature and await the germination of the seeds, all that is required being to keep the compost moist. Almost any temperature can be maintained, one light indicating that the supply is 'on', whilst the other comes 'on' and 'off' with the heating element to enable one to observe that the propagator is working correctly. After the plants leave the propagator, they may be grown on in lower temperatures than needed for the germination of the seeds. In a temperature of 65°F., tomato seed will germinate in about 7 days from an early January sowing. Cucumbers require a slightly higher temperature in which they will germinate in 3-4 days. Rapid germination ensures that 'damping off' is reduced to a minimum. After germination, the air temperature is reduced 5° so that the seedlings will grow sturdy.

The Humex Automatic propagator is equally efficient. Measuring 36 inches × 20 inches and

5
Propagation
and
Planting

12 inches deep, it is constructed of fibre glass and is completely automatic, the temperature being regulated by a rod–type thermostat which is adjusted to give any temperature from freezing point to 180°F. Complete safety is assured in that the low-voltage warming wire is enclosed in layers of sand on which the seed boxes are placed. The propagator is white on the inside to give the maximum amount of light for the seedlings. On a 40 watts consumption regulated by the thermostat, its running costs are only 5 pence a week which will ensure a considerable saving as compared with raising the plants in a greenhouse heated to similar temperatures.

Sowing seed indoors   Seeds are sown in boxes or pans but for those plants which do not transplant readily, seeds should be sown in half inch Solo-Grow cubes made of specially prepared plant food and Vermiculite. After germination, the cubes are planted (just as they are) in peat pots and the plants grown on in a reduced temperature.

Where sowing in boxes or pans, sow thinly or space out the seeds to an inch apart to allow the seedlings room to develop. Overcrowding at this stage will result in a drawn, 'leggy' plant which will never recover. Obtain the best seed from growers with a reputation to maintain. It will cost rather more but will amply repay its cost in reliable germination.

Sowing composts may vary slightly but as a general rule, the John Innes compost is to be recommended. It may be purchased from most garden stores but should be in a fresh condition. If made up for any length of time it may have become contaminated with disease spores while the superphosphate used in its formula and so valuable in promoting vigorous root action, will have lost its strength. The John Innes compost is composed of:

2 parts loam (sterilised)
1 part peat
1 part sand   } per bushel
1½ oz. superphosphate
¾ oz. ground limestone

Introduce the sowing compost to the greenhouse several days before sowing, to enable it to absorb some of the warmth of the house. Line the boxes or pans with moist moss or damp peat before covering with compost to a depth of 2 inches. The compost should be in a moist, friable condition and after sowing, the seeds are lightly covered with additional compost and watered in before placing in the propagator.

After germination, transplant the seedlings into boxes or pots containing the John Innes potting compost:

7 parts loam (sterilised)
3 parts peat
2 parts sand   } per bushel
¾ oz. ground limestone
½ lb. J.I. Base

The John Innes Base is made up of

2 parts Hoof or Horn meal
2 parts superphosphate
1 part sulphate of potash

In place of the limestone, crushed chalk, limestone flour as used for poultry, or whitening scraped from outhouse walls are forms of the same ingredient. Upon analysis, the J.I. base will provide approximately 10 per cent potash, 5 per cent nitrogen; 7.5 per cent phosphates, each of which is so important for healthy plant growth. If making up one's own composts, do not exceed the amounts stated for it has been established that seedlings grow better in a slightly acid compost than in one of an alkaline nature.

Soil-less composts such as Fison's Levington and Eff, composed mainly of peat and sand with added nutrients are less heavy to handle but require considerably more care with their watering for they dry out rapidly. Experience is needed in their use for best results.

It is important that where raising seedlings in a propagator or in a heated greenhouse, there is no undue delay in their transplanting, otherwise they will have used up the nutrients in their sowing compost and will grow hard and woody. The roots will be brown instead of white, the foliage yellow instead of green.

If the seed has been sown early in the year, it will be necessary to maintain a temperature of around 60°F. by day in greenhouse or frame, the latter being heated by soil wires or cables. The plants must be kept growing on without check and if correct conditions cannot be provided, it will be better to buy in one's plants from a reputable supplier at the appropriate time.

Transplanting To transplant, have the boxes or pots already filled with the J.I. potting compost and, holding the plant with the fingers of one hand, carefully loosen the roots with a piece of smooth-ended wood or cane held in the other hand. Then lift from the compost with one movement and transfer the plant to the new growing medium, inserting the roots and making quite firm. Make sure that the plants have room to develop. Water in and maintain a humid but not a stuffy atmosphere. Those plants which resent root disturbance may be grown on in soil blocks made to the formula of the J.I. potting compost, or in Jiffy pots. These are made from 75 per cent wood pulp impregnated with essential nutrients and are made round or square and 3 inches in diameter. If using boxes or clay pots, make sure they have been scrubbed clean before use.

Clean and light to handle are the Vacapots which are thin-walled containers divided into 24 detchable units, each 2 inches square and 2 inches deep so that they fit exactly into a 2 inch seed tray. The Vacapots are filled with compost and one seedling is planted in each. When ready to move to larger pots or when planting out, the plants are removed with the soil ball intact or each compartment may be detached and sold without disturbing the roots.

If planting out, do not do so until the plants have been well hardened and, so that they do not remain too long in the pots or boxes, timing is all-important. Seed is sown so that there will be time for the plants to have made substantial growth before being set out, though the length of this period will depend upon the hardiness of the plants and climatic conditions in which they are to grow. For example, northern gardeners should not plant out tomatoes until June 1st. unless they can be covered with cloches (when they may be planted three weeks earlier than if unprotected) but in either case the plants must have been well hardened. This is done by placing them towards the end of April in a cold frame to which air is admitted on all mild days. The frame should be kept closed at night until early May when the lights are raised by inserting a brick or piece of wood between the lights and the frame boards. By the month end, the lights may be removed altogether. At this time, tomato plants should be about 6 inches tall, rich green, sturdy and short jointed.

Cauliflowers and other plants raised in a warm greenhouse will be hardier and may be removed to a cold frame by April 1st. for hardening and planting out at the month end. By then, the plants should be about 4 inches tall, sturdy and bright green. They should be in the same condition if purchased from a garden shop or nurseryman. If yellowish green and too tall (drawn), this will signify that the plants have been sown too soon or may have been raised in too warm a temperature. Again, they may not have been hardened.

Early crops and plants set out in the open, may be raised in frames by sowing direct into a prepared seed bed which has been brought to a fine tilth and into which peat or old mushroom bed compost has been incorporated. Vegetable plants should be sown early in March and after hardening, may be planted out in April. In the more favourable parts of the south and west seed is sown a month earlier in frames (or under cloches) and the plants set out about April 1st; or a sowing may be made directly into the open ground early in March. For an early crop of frame cucumbers or marrows, seed is sown in spring over a hot bed made in a frame. This is made by composting straw with Adco M as used for mushroom growing, or from farmyard manure. Additional heat will be obtained if some poultry manure is added to the straw during composting. Straw will take about three weeks to compost and should be placed in the frame to a depth of about 15 inches and covered with 5–6 inches of soil to prevent loss of heat. When the temperature has fallen to 80°F., the seed is sown in the soil or in pots inserted into the soil. The frame is kept closed to maintain a humid condition and hasten germination. A mild hot bed may be used for a crop of early turnips, radishes or carrots which will be sweet and succulent. Afterwards, the compost may be used on the land.

Sowing in the open   Vegetables may also be grown entirely without any form of heat and without the use of a frame though a row of cloches will ensure earlier crops and they may be kept in use the whole year round. Cloches are like small portable greenhouses and are of many types and sizes. The Chase large barn-type is made of glass sheets, held together by galvanised wires. Being 19 inches high it is suitable for melons and marrows, tomatoes and cucumbers until they reach maturity. It is ideal for strawberries too. Low barn cloches are 12 inches high and are suitable for growing winter lettuce and early crops of turnips, radishes and beetroot. They may also be used to cover rows of early spring-sown seedlings. Later, the plants are hardened by removing the cloches on mild days and then at night, when the plants will be ready to transplant during April.

The Vitrone cloches, glass clear and made of strong Vitrone P.V.C. sheets, held in place by wire hoops which skewer firmly into the ground are unbreakable and light to handle, whilst an inexpensive tunnel cloche 35 feet long may be made from I.C.I. polythene sheeting supported by hoops and securing wires. Vitrone and polythene cloches are shatter-proof and should be used where there are low flying aircraft. Where growing under cloches, cover the ground several days before the seed is sown so that the soil is partially warm at sowing time which will ensure more rapid germination.

Always sow thinly, using pelleted seed where possible for pelleting makes small seeds easier to handle and to sow, whilst correct spacing does away with much labour in thinning and allows the plants space to develop properly. Pelleted seeds are dried to a low moisture level which causes the coating to break down more quickly.

Seeds for transplanting may be sown in drills or broadcast in prepared beds. First make the soil friable by breaking down all lumps and incorporate into the top 3 to 4 inches some moist peat or bark fibre and give a sprinkling of superphosphate to encourage root action. When the soil is in a reasonably dry, friable condition, the drills are made 1 inch deep with the back of a rake. Use a line to make them straight and if the rows are to be covered with cloches, make them of the correct width. A Chase barn cloche is 23 inches wide which will allow for three rows 6 inches apart. This will permit the hoe to be taken between the rows but where sowing in the open, slightly wider spacing will make for greater ease in hoeing.

Where growing crops which are to be grown on to maturity under cloches, the seedlings will need thinning to the correct distances apart and they will require attention as to their watering, though in showery weather, sufficient moisture will percolate under each side of the cloche and it will be necessary to move them only occasionally. If strips of black polythene are placed between the rows, they will attract and retain the warmth of the sun's rays and this will make for earlier maturity as well as suppressing weeds and reducing moisture evaporation from the soil.

Planting out   Thinning should be done with care, removing any plants where there is over-crowding and any weakly or diseased plants. After thinning, gently make firm those plants remaining. To transplant, lift when the soil is damp and with as much soil attached to the roots as possible. Brassicas should have the roots dipped in Calomel solution before replanting. Do not lift more plants than can be handled in a reasonably short time for if the roots are long exposed to sun and wind, flagging may occur from which they may take some time to recover. If possible, plant on a dull day. Plant firmly, using a trowel and insert the roots well into the ground. Make the plants comfortably firm and water in. Be certain that they are spaced correctly. Cauliflowers and cabbages may be quite small when planted but will soon grow to 2 feet or more and where there is overcrowding they will not develop as they should, whilst disease may become trouble-some through lack of a free circulation of air. This does not however mean that space should be wasted. Between the rows, crops of radish and lettuce may be grown which will have reached maturity long before the cabbages have become fully grown. Keep the plants growing during dry weather by giving the soil around the roots a thorough soaking. This is important for if only surface waterings are given, the roots will turn upwards in search of moisture and will not only suffer harm from exposure to the sun and drying winds but the plants will lack the nutrition and moisture essential for their full maturity.

After planting, keep a close look out for pests and diseases and use the spray at the first appearance. For a small garden, the ASL Cadet spray is to be recommended. It has a 4 pint capacity and gives 7 minutes of continuous spraying. It is fitted with a thumb control tap and a long reach extension arm. This model may also be used for spraying roses and fruit trees.

Highly efficient, too, is the Master pneumatic hand sprayer made of brass throughout and holding 2 pints of liquid. The spray is fine and mist–like, with trigger action giving instantaneous control. It is not usually necessary to purchase a dust spray for most powdered fungicides and pesticides are made up into 'puffer' packs.

At all times keep the hoe moving between the plants to prevent the appearance of weeds and to keep the surface broken up so that air and moisture may penetrate to the roots. The Mill-spur draw hoe made of high carbon steel is most efficient for this purpose and, among Dutch hoes, that manufactured by Wilkinson Sword has a razor edge of tempered steel.

Hoeing may be eliminated by mulching between the plants but apart from peat, mulching materials are expensive and difficult to obtain, though composted straw will serve the purpose. A mulch will suppress weeds and prevent too rapid moisture evaporation of the soil whilst certain mulches provide valuable plant food. They should be applied when the soil has warmed, about midsummer. If peat is used in quantity, additional liming may be necessary for future crops.

As they come to maturity, plants will benefit from a weekly application of dilute manure water whilst those which are making less growth than expected, possibly because of cold winds and a soil slow to warm, should be stimulated by giving a dressing of nitrate of soda, a quick acting fertiliser with a high nitrogen content. The plants will also benefit from weathered soot which, if applied early in summer, will encourage the soil to warm up and will also provide additional nitrogen.

During dry periods, all plants will appreciate a syringing of the foliage, given in the evening when the sun is going down. French and runner beans especially benefit from this and it helps the flowers to set. Certain plants will also need supporting though the introduction of varieties of more compact habit now make this less troublesome. The taller growing outdoor tomatoes, sweet corn and broad beans will require supporting and a simple method is to place stout stakes or canes at intervals along the rows and to fasten twine from stake to stake, looping it around the plants along the rows.

Earthing up will also help the taller growing plants to resist strong winds whilst leeks and celery will require earthing up at regular intervals for their satisfactory blanching, and potatoes to prevent the haulm being broken away during cultivations.

Vegetables do need some attention to get the best from them and particularly is it important to harvest them whilst still young and full of flavour. Nothing is gained by allowing them to remain too long on the plants so that they run to seed or grow too large with the resultant loss of flavour and quality. In addition, if removed when young, others are able to come to maturity and each plant will yield its maximum crop and cropping will last over a longer period. Peas should be removed as soon as the pods are well filled and runner beans when about 6 inches long, before the beans have begun to swell in the pod. Harvest marrows and cucumbers when quite small and cauliflowers before they begin to seed, whilst the heads are still white and firm. In this way the crops will be most enjoyable.

When to sow

★Sow under glass

Vegetable	Month	Depth
American cress	March, August	1 inch
Artichoke, Globe	March	1 inch
Asparagus	April	1–2 inches
Asparagus pea	April	1 inch
Aubergine★	January	Just cover
Bean, broad	October, March	2 inches
Bean, butter	May	2 inches
Bean, dwarf	May	2 inches
Bean, runner	May	3 inches
Beetroot	April–May	1 inch
Borecole	March	1 inch
Broccoli	March	1 inch
Brussels sprouts	March	1 inch
Cabbage (spring)	July	1 inch
Cabbage (winter)	April–May	1 inch
Cabbage, Chinese	April	1 inch

When to sow

Vegetable	Month	Distance Apart
Cabbage, Red	September	1 inch
Calabrese	April	1 inch
Cardoon	March	Just cover
Carrot (early)	March	½ inch
Carrot (maincrop)	April	½ inch
Cauliflower (early)	September	1 inch
Cauliflower (late)	March	1 inch
Celeriac	March	½ inch
Celery	March	½ inch
Celtuce	March–June	½ inch
Cherry, Ground	March	Just cover
Chervil	August, March	1 inch
Chicory	June	1 inch
Chinese Mustard	April–June	1 inch
Collards	April–June	1 inch
Corn Salad	September	1 inch
Cucumber (frame)★	March–April	1–2 inches
Cucumber (indoors)★	March	1–2 inches
Cucumber (ridge)	March	1–2 inches
Dandelion	April	1 inch
Endive	July–August	1 inch
Finocchio	April–May	1 inch
Good King Henry	April	1 inch
Hamburg Parsley	March, June	1 inch
Kohl Rabi	April–July	1 inch
Leek	March	½ inch
Lettuce (outdoors)	March–June	Just cover
Lettuce (indoors)	September	Just cover
Malabar spinach	April	½ inch
Marrow	March–April	1 inch
Okra	May	2 inches
Onion	September, February	1 inch
Onion, spring	August, March	½ inch
Orach	April–September	1 inch
Parsnip	March	½ inch
Pea (early)	November	2 inches
Pea (mid-season)	March	2 inches
Pea (late)	April–May	2 inches
Pepper (Sweet)	March	1 inch
Pokeweed	March–April	1 inch
Radish	March–July	½ inch
Rhubarb	March–April	1 inch
Rutabaga (Swede)	May	1 inch
Salsify	April	1 inch
Savoy	March–April	1 inch
Scolymus	April	1 inch
Scorzonera	April	1 inch
Skirret	April	1 inch
Sorrel	April	1 inch
Soya Bean	April–May	2 inches
Spinach	March–July	1 inch
Spinach Beet	April	1 inch
Sugar Pea	April	2 inches
Sweet Corn	March	2 inches
Swiss Chard	April–July	1 inch
Tomato★	January	1 inch
Turnip	March–June	1 inch

Vegetable	Month	Distance Apart	
		In rows	Between rows
American cress	April, September	9 inches	10 inches
Artichoke, Chinese	April	9 inches	18 inches
Artichoke, Globe	April	3 feet	3 feet
Artichoke, Jerusalem	March	12 inches	2 feet
Asparagus	April	9 inches	2 feet
Asparagus Pea	May	18 inches	20 inches
Aubergine	June	15 inches	18 inches
Bean, broad	March–April	8 inches	9 inches
Bean, butter	May	9 inches	10 inches
Bean, dwarf	May–June	8 inches	12 inches
Bean, runner	May	9 inches	10–12 inches
Beetroot	May	6–8 inches	15 inches
Borecole	April	2 feet	2 feet
Broccoli	April–July	2 feet	2 feet
Brussels sprouts	April	2 feet	2 feet
Cabbage (spring)	September	16 inches	18 inches
Cabbage (winter)	April–May	20 inches	24 inches
Cabbage, Chinese	July	9 inches	12 inches
Cabbage, Portugal	April	30 inches	3 feet
Cabbage, Red	March	2 feet	2 feet
Calabrese	April–May	2 feet	2 feet
Cardoon	May	18–20 inches	2 feet
Cauliflower (early)	October	20 inches	2 feet
Cauliflower (late)	April–May	2 feet	2 feet
Celeriac	May	12 inches	18 inches
Celery	June	10–12 inches	12 inches
Celtuce	April–July	9 inches	15 inches
Cherry, Ground	June	18 inches	2 feet
Chervil	March	12 inches	18 inches
Chicory	June	10 inches	18 inches
Chinese Mustard	June	18 inches	15 inches
Collards	April–July	15 inches	18 inches
Corn Salad	September–October	8–9 inches	9 inches
Cucumber (frame)	April–May	3 feet	
Cucumber (indoors)	March–April	3 feet	
Cucumber (ridge)	June	3 feet	
Garlic	October, March	6 inches	12 inches
Good King Henry	April–May	18 inches	18 inches
Hamburg Parsley	April, July	9 inches	15 inches
Kohl Rabi	May, July	9 inches	15 inches
Leek	May, June	9 inches	6 inches
Lettuce (outdoors)	April–July	9 inches	12 inches
Lettuce (indoors)	October	6 inches	6–8 inches
Malabar Spinach	April–May	8–9 inches	
Marrow (Bush)	June	3–4 feet	
Marrow (Trailing)	June	5–6 feet	
Okra	June	2 feet	
Onion	April	6 inches	12 inches
Onion, Potato	January	12 inches	12 inches
Parsnip	March	10 inches	18 inches
Pea (early)	November	3 inches	2 feet
Pea (mid-season)	March	3 inches	2 feet 6 ins.
Pea (late)	April–May	3 inches	3 feet
Pepper (sweet)	May–June	18 inches	
Pokeweed	April	3 feet	3 feet
Potato	April–May	9–10 inches	2 feet
Rhubarb	November	3 feet	
Rutabaga (Swede)	May	9 inches	18 inches
Salsify	April	8 inches	12 inches
Savoy	April–May	2 feet	2 feet
Scolymus	April	15 inches	18 inches
Scorzonera	April	8 inches	12 inches

35

When to plant

Vegetable	Month	Distance Apart	
Seakale	March–April	16 inches	16 inches
Shallot	March–April	10 inches	10 inches
Skirret	April	12 inches	12 inches
Sorrel	May	12 inches	12 inches
Sugar Pea	April–May	2 inches	3 feet
Sweet Corn	June	15 inches	15 inches
Swiss Chard	May, July	12 inches	15 inches
Tomato (indoors)	January–April	2 feet	2 feet
Tomato (outdoors)	June	2 feet	2 feet

Note: Those vegetables which will not transplant well are omitted.

When mature or ready to harvest

Vegetable	Month	Vegetable	Month
American cress	All year	Finocchio	August–December
Artichoke, Chinese	October–December	Garlic	August–October
Artichoke, Globe	July–September	Good King Henry	April–June
Artichoke, Jerusalem	September–December	Hamburg Parsley	September–April
Asparagus	May–June	Kohl–Rabi	July–March
Asparagus Pea	June–September	Leek	September–March
Aubergine	July–October	Lettuce	All year
Bean, broad	May–June	Malabar spinach	July–September
Bean, butter	September–October	Marrow	August–October
Bean, dwarf	July–August	Okra	August–October
Bean, runner	August–October	Onion	September–October
Beetroot	July–October	Onion, Potato	July–August
Borecole	September–March	Onion, spring	April–August
Broccoli	October–July	Orach	July–December
Brussels sprouts	August–March	Parsnip	November
Cabbage (spring)	April–June	Peas	June–September
Cabbage (winter)	October–March	Pepper (sweet)	July–September
Cabbage, Chinese	August–September	Pokeweed	May–June
Cabbage, Portugal	September–March	Potato	June–November
Cabbage, Red	September–March	Radish	May–October
Cardoon	November–March	Rhubarb	January–August
Carrot (early)	May–June	Rutabaga (Swede)	August–November
Carrot (maincrop)	September–March	Salsify	November–March
Cauliflower (early)	July–September	Savoy	November–April
Cauliflower (late)	October–January	Scolymus	November–April
Celeriac	October–March	Scorzonera	November–April
Celery	September–March	Seakale	November–April
Celtuce	June–October	Shallot	September–October
Cherry, Ground	August–September	Skirret	October–March
Chervil	October–December	Sorrel	June–September
Chicory	October–December	Soya Bean	September–October
Chinese Mustard	July–March	Spinach (summer)	June–September
Collards	September–March	Spinach (winter)	October–April
Corn Salad	March–May	Spinach Beet	All year
Cucumber (indoor)	July–October	Sugar Pea	July–August
Cucumber (ridge)	August–October	Swiss Chard	All year
Dandelion	April–June	Tomato	June–November
Endive	August–September	Turnip	All year

Whilst it may not be possible to use all the vegetables as they reach maturity, many can be preserved for using during winter and those crops which mature in autumn may be lifted to protect them from frost damage. Others, such as celery and leeks benefit from frost and are allowed to occupy the ground through winter, to be lifted when required, and as the weather permits.

The first vegetables to harvest and store will be French and runner beans and they should be removed before they grow old and stringy. They are placed in large glass or earthenware jars to be salted down, when they will 'keep' until the first crops of French beans are ready the following year and for as long as two years if necessary.

The beans are sliced and trimmed and a layer 3 inches deep is placed in the jar. The beans are then given a generous covering with salt; more beans are then added, and another layer of salt and the jar filled in this way as the season advances; the beans should always be young and brittle with no seeds showing through the pods.

When required for use, a quantity of beans are removed, washed free of salt and allowed to soak in cold water for an hour before cooking. The beans will be as fresh and full of flavour as when removed from the plants.

Haricot or butter beans are harvested towards the end of summer when fully ripe for it is the seeds that are stored for winter use, not the pods. The beans are removed from the plants on a dry day and are taken to a dry, airy room where they are spread out on trays or on shelves to complete the drying. The seeds are then removed from the pods and their drying completed before being placed in wooden containers to be used when required. They will store almost indefinitely.

Winter squashes or marrows which bear hard-skinned fruits may be grown for winter keeping. Unlike summer marrows, they must remain on the plants until fully matured and be harvested in autumn, before the frosts, with a portion of the stem attached. They must be handled with care for they bruise easily, and if bruised will decay in storage. They will 'keep' through the winter if stored on shelves in a dry room and will keep best in a temperature of 50° – 55°F. Place them on a layer of cotton or wood wool and so that they do not touch each other.

Storing root crops   Most root crops (and those plants with tuberous roots) can be stored for winter use, though where severe winter weather is not expected, they will retain their quality and flavour better if left in the ground, to be lifted as required. If they are to be stored, allow them to occupy the ground until mid-October when they should be lifted before the advent of the autumnal rains. If lifted when the soil is in a dry, friable condition, the operation will be more easily performed and the soil will be more readily shaken from them whilst they will store in better condition.

Lift them from the ground with care, so as not to break the tips or cut them by the careless use of spade or fork which would reduce their keeping qualities. Hold the tops with one hand whilst prising up the root with spade or fork held in the other hand. Shake away all surplus soil and if the weather is dry, allow the roots to remain on the ground for several hours to permit any remaining soil to dry off. The best way is to place the roots on sacks or canvas laid flat on the ground. Then cut away, or with beetroot screw off, the top foliage and bury the roots in deep boxes of dry peat or sand. First place a layer of peat (or sand) at the bottom of the box and on this the roots. Then cover with an inch of peat and over this place more roots until the box is filled. They should be stored in a dry, airy room but away from hot pipes.

Vegetables in cold storage   Green vegetables, including peas, Brussels sprouts, cabbage, lettuce and all salad crops may be kept fresh in cold storage for many weeks. Sprouts keep especially well under refrigeration and may be removed from the plants when weather conditions permit. They will keep fresh for several months.

The use of a refrigerator or deep freeze cabinet will ensure that the most profitable use is made of the kitchen garden and of one's labours. There will be little or no waste as is likely to occur when too many plants may have been grown and it may not have been possible to utilise all the produce as they reach maturity. Again, frozen food will be available often at a time when adverse weather makes it impossible to harvest winter greens whilst to have a supply always on hand will ensure that working people have a quick meal readily available. There will also be a substantial saving in having the produce from one's garden available, without the need to purchase frozen and canned food of proprietary brands.

Peas should be removed from the plants when in the right condition and, after removing from the pods, should be placed in thick polythene bags before consigning to the deep freeze or refrigerator where they will keep fresh for many weeks. Sprouts, too, are also improved by placing in polythene bags.

Vegetables such as asparagus, sweet corn, cauliflower and broccoli heads, spinach and young root crops will not remain fresh under refrigeration unless first blanched in boiling water for 2 minutes. This is done to retard the action of the chemical substances known as 'enzymes' which would harm the flavour and quality in storage if not controlled. The vegetables are placed in wire baskets in pans of boiling water for 2–3 minutes, are then removed and transferred to a bucket containing iced water where they remain for the same length of time. All moisture is then drained off and the vegetables are placed in plastic boxes or in polythene bags for refrigeration.

Potatoes, after cooking and mashing, and new potatoes after cooking until almost done, will freeze perfectly and will be ready to serve after reheating for 4 or 5 minutes.

Mushrooms should be frozen in the fresh condition.

Most vegetables will keep under refrigerated conditions for at least a year and only sweet corn should be thawed before cooking. Other vegetables may be cooked in the frozen state.

Vegetables for deep freeze:

	Variety	When to sow	To mature
Broad bean	The Sultan	September	May–June
Brussels sprouts	Sanda	April	September–December
Calabrese	Autumn Spear	April	September–November
Carrot	Scarla	April	September–October
Cauliflower	Early Snowball	April	August–October
French bean	Processor	May	July–August
Kale (Borecole)	Dwarf Green Curled	April	October–January
Pea	Kelvedon Monarch	April	July–August
Spinach	Greenmarket	September	April–May
Sweet corn	Golden Bantam	April	August–September

With potatoes, as with most root crops, it is necessary to exclude light when in storage, otherwise they will turn green, and green root crops are poisonous. They may be stored in sacks in a cellar, after removing all soil from the tubers. This is really done if they are exposed to the air for several hours upon lifting. They will keep better if stored when dry but they should not be placed too close to hot pipes or in a warm atmosphere.

Making a potato clamp Large quantities of main-crop potatoes may be stored in a clamp made under an open shed or in the open ground. If made outdoors, tip them as they are lifted and dried on to a raised bed so that surplus moisture will not percolate beneath them. The potatoes are placed in ridge fashion, and to keep the base rigid, fix two 6 inch boards into the ground on either side held securely by stout pegs, extending the whole length of the clamp. Make the clamp about 4 feet wide at the base and pile the potatoes as high as possible, removing all diseased tubers, and then cover them with straw or dry bracken to a depth of 6 inches. Over the straw add a 6 inch covering of soil removed from around the base of the clamp. Start at the base and work upwards, making the outside surface firm and smooth with the back of the spade so that surplus water will drain off. Be sure to give the clamp some ventilation. This may be done by inserting a drain pipe at the top or by pulling up some of the straw covering and placing the soil round it. Turnips and swedes may be clamped in the same way.

New potatoes may be preserved in tin boxes containing dry peat with which the potatoes are covered. The box is buried 2 feet below soil level, the place being marked by a stone or stick. Stored in this way they will keep fresh for 6 months or more.

Onions and shallots are harvested early in autumn when the foliage has turned yellow and begun to die back. After lifting, preferably on a dry day, spread out the bulbs on mats to dry for

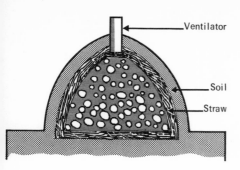

Well-made potato clamp showing the layers of insulating straw between the potatoes and the covering of soil. Note the ventilation pipe, and the shape of the clamp, which is designed to shed water.

2–3 days. Then, after removing the tops, place in string bags and suspend from the ceiling of an airy shed or room; or hang up by stringing the necks together. Onions and shallots must have a free circulation of air around them. It is also necessary to lift with care for if the outer skin is damaged, they will not keep well. Potato and tree onions may be stored in the same way. Onions are not suitable for freezing owing to their high water content; nor is it necessary to freeze them as they will last in good condition for many months without freezing.

Harvesting herbs   The harvesting, drying and storage of herbs calls for attention to detail. Under suitable conditions, it will be possible to make two cuttings of many herbs, especially the shrubby thymes and sages, the first being made about July, the second early in autumn. In this way, the herbs are cut before the flowers and leaves begin to die back, when the valuable oils return to the base of the plants and they begin to lose their flavour and smell.

Select a dry day for cutting herbs for if cut when damp, mildew may set in before the herbs can be completely dried. Dryness in their growing and harvesting is the secret of success with herbs.

The shrubby herbs are cut with a sharp knife, the stems of savory and thyme being removed about 3 inches above the base when the whole plant may be held with one hand whilst the cutting is done with the other hand, the stems being placed on sacking laid on the ground. Sage and other hard wooded plants are best cut with secateurs, whilst parsley and mints are cut with scissors. These are the herbs grown for their dried leaves and stems, to be used in stuffings and to flavour broths and soups during winter.

After cutting, allow the foliage to be exposed for an hour or so to the rays of the sun but not for longer or the herbs will lose flavour. Their drying should be completed in an airy room, fastening them into bunches and suspending them from the roof or from nails in the walls. Or they may be spread out on racks or shelves made of slatted wood which will allow a free circulation of air. The herbs should be kept away from the direct rays of the sun though the drying must be completed quickly to retain their maximum fragrance. Select an attic room or shed if possible for the sun upon the roof will enable high temperatures to be maintained and 100°F. is not excessive where drying the thick-leaved mints and parsley. The herbs should be frequently turned so that all parts become fully dry.

A rack for herb drying may be made from 1 inch timber, making trays 4 feet square with a square of hessian canvas tacked on for a base. The frames or trays are held in position by strong corner posts and about 12 inches allowed between trays. This allows room for the turning of the herbs and for the free circulation of air. A rack made 6–8 feet high will occupy only one corner of a room and will hold large quantities of herbs. Where space is at a premium herbs may be dried in an airing cupboard. If there is no ventilation, the door should be left open to allow moisture to escape.

In a warm, airy room most herbs will dry within 2–3 weeks when they should crackle and snap at the touch. They should then be spread over large sheets of brown paper and the leaves (or flowers) rubbed from the stems with the palms of the hands. Pieces of stem can be removed and the leaves then placed in a fine meshed riddle for any dust or chaff to be removed. The leaves are stored in wooden drums or boxes for wood does not absorb moisture from the atmosphere and the herbs remain dry for any length of time. Small quantities may be stored in glass or earthenware jars with tightly fitting stoppers, each being labelled and placed on a shelf away from the sun. They will store indefinitely and may be mixed and used as required.

When harvesting plants grown for their seeds, care must be taken to ensure that the seeds are fully ripe, yet to allow the seed pods to open will be to let the seed be scattered and lost. Each day the seed heads must be inspected and removed with care as soon as they reach maturity and are quite dry. Midday is the best time to cut off the pods and they should be dropped into a cardboard box and removed to a dry, airy room. The seed capsules are then placed in muslin bags and hung up to dry, after which the seed is separated from the capsules by placing them in a fine meshed riddle. They are then placed in jars or small wooden boxes to be kept in a dry place and used as required. Where the plants are wanted to seed themselves, a number of seed heads should be left on to open when ripe.

Plants like angelica, grown for the value of their stems, should be cut back at regular intervals throughout summer for it is the young stems that are required for candying and for stewing with rhubarb.

Part 2

`ABC` OF VEGETABLES

American Cress
Barbarea verna

Also known as Land Cress or Winter Cress to distinguish it from Water Cress and for which it is an excellent alternative where there is no running water. It is perennial and a bed will remain in good productive condition for several years.

The best method is to make up a bed in a position in semi shade, where the plants will be cool and shielded from the summer sunshine. The bed may be divided into two parts, one for cutting in summer; the other for late autumn and winter use.

Sowing Seed is sown mid-March in a frame or under cloches, either in shallow drills or broadcast, and in a soil containing plenty of humus. Germination will take about three weeks and, when the seedlings are large enough to handle, they are moved to a specially prepared bed and planted 9 inches apart. For the shoots to be mild and succulent, a well manured soil is necessary and one containing liberal quantities of moisture-retaining humus. The first shoots will be ready to cut towards the end of summer and in all respects resemble the better known water cress, being deep green with a similar strong and somewhat bitter flavour. It is delicious in salads throughout the year or used with cream cheese in sandwiches.

To enjoy the crop through winter, a part of the bed should be surrounded with 12 inch boards and covered with a light: only when the weather is severe should the frame be closed. Water copiously in summer but give little moisture in winter.

After heavy cutting of the sprigs, the bed will appreciate a light mulching of decayed manure placed between the plants when they will come again with renewed vigour.

Seed may also be sown during August in a frame or under cloches and the young plants moved to permanent beds the following April. Small sowings made at regular six-monthly intervals will ensure a supply of tender shoots throughout the year.

Artichoke, Chinese
Stachys tuberifera

Introduced to European gardens at the end of the 19th century, though rarely grown now because the tiny tubers are difficult to store and to clean, but have a delicious flavour when boiled or fried in batter. It is also known as Crosnes, a name used by the French.

The necklace-like tubers are planted in April and they require a rich, deeply dug soil into which plenty of moisture-retaining humus has been dug. If dry, either when in the ground or in storage, the white, finger-like tubers quickly shrivel and are useless. For this reason, seedsmen send them out packed in damp moss or peat. They should be planted in April, as soon as received.

General cultivation Plant in drills made 4 inches deep and 18 inches apart, allowing 8–9 inches between the tubers. If the soil is heavy, lay them on peat and use peat to cover over them before the drills are filled in. A warm, sunny situation should be provided.

The tubers require all the help possible to grow large and plump, and should be watered copiously whenever the soil is dry, whilst a weekly application of dilute manure water will greatly increase their size.

They will be ready to lift about mid-October when the foliage, which grows about 2 feet tall, begins to die down. In those gardens where hard frost is not experienced the tubers are best left in the ground to be lifted and used when required. If this is done they will remain plump and succulent and retain their full flavour.

They are troubled neither by pest nor disease.

Artichoke, Globe
Cynara scolymus

This is the most handsome of vegetables, worthy of a place in the herbaceous border for its foliage alone. Since the earliest times the flower heads, with their broad thickened scales, have been regarded as an epicurian's food. It is perennial, native of S. Europe and North Africa, and was prized by the Romans who may have introduced it into Britain. It is botanically related to the Cardoon, but not to the Jerusalem Artichoke.

It requires a sunny situation but one sheltered from cold winds. For this reason it used to be found in the walled gardens of manor houses where it grew to perfection, undisturbed through the years.

General cultivation A rich deep soil is necessary to produce the finest heads which must be succulent and tender, otherwise they make highly unpleasant eating. For the same reason, they should be cut and used before they become old and tough. Before planting in spring, trench the soil, incorporating whatever humus forming materials are available, together with some decayed manure. Cow manure suits this plant well but if not available, old mushroom bed compost is ideal, or seaweed (for this is a a maritime plant) augmented by 2 ounces of Kainit and 2 ounces of superphosphate per square yard. In a well manured soil the plants will remain productive for at least five years, especially if given a mulch of strawy manure each autumn. More succulent heads, however, may be obtained by renewing every 2–3 years, using the suckers or shoots produced around the crown of the old plant.

Planting The suckers are detached with a sharp knife when about 6–8 inches high and a few roots should be removed with them. Plant them deeply, allowing 3 feet between each, for they will eventually grow 4 feet tall and wide. After planting, tread in firmly, water well and shade from sunlight until established. If the suckers are removed in autumn, it is advisable to plant them in pots and winter in a cold frame until April when they can be planted out.

The plants must be kept moist at the roots during summer and the main heads will grow larger if the lateral heads are removed from the main stem. If removed when about walnut size, they may be fried whole in butter.

If it is not intended to use the main heads at once, they should be cut with a length of stem and stood in water in a cool shady room until used. In this way they will remain tender. After the heads have been removed it is advisable to cut down the main stems of several plants to within 12 inches of soil level. The plants are then mulched and well watered when a number of new shoots will arise. When about 2 feet tall these are tied together with raffia and earthed up like celery. From mid-September to the end of October, the blanching will take place when the stems will be ready to remove and use as a vegetable. These are known as 'chards' and are cooked like cardoons, cutting them into 6 inch lengths and removing the outer skins before simmering until tender.

Globe artichokes are obtainable in two varieties, 'Green' and 'Purple Globe', both bearing heads up to 4 inches in diameter and both are a great delicacy when boiled until tender and served with butter. The small pointed tips should be removed from the scales before cooking .

Exhibiting It is rarely shown but whenever it is, it always commands attention. The heads should be removed when little larger than cricket ball size and if cut some days before the show, the stems should be placed in water until required. To transport, wrap each in a muslin cloth and lay flat in a deep box with the stems still attached. These are cut off at the base of the head just before arranging on the dish.

Pests and Diseases
ARTICHOKE LEAF SPOT This may occasionally attack leaves in a damp, humid summer causing grey blemishes on the leaves which then turn brown at the margins and wither, the plants dying back often to ground level. Spraying with half strength Bordeaux Mixture before the heads form will give control.

Cockchafer It is the grubs of the common cockchafer beetle which do the most damage, feeding on the roots. The grubs are fat and dirty greyish-white in colour whilst the adult beetles may feed on the leaves of the plant. Treating the ground with Gammexane or Aldrin dust before planting will exterminate the pest.

Artichoke, Jerusalem
Helianthus tuberosus

This has nothing to do with the Holy Land nor is it in any way related to the globe artichoke. Its nearest cultivated relative is, in fact, the sun flower, though its yellow, sun flower-like blossoms are only produced after a long, hot summer. It is native of North America and we first obtained them from the French who brought them back from Canada. It grows beneath the soil, like a potato and is equally nourishing, which is why it was so highly prized by the early settlers in Virginia. The reason for its neglect by modern gardeners is perhaps because the rough nobbly skins prove difficult to clean in the kitchen, but its unique flavour should ensure its greater popularity.

General cultivation It prefers a light sandy soil into which some decayed manure has been deeply worked. Just before planting give a dressing of 2 ounces per square yard of superphosphate and the same of sulphate of potash.

As the tubers begin to grow early, plant during the first week of March in the south; the month's end in the north. Small tubers are the best, of about walnut size. They should be planted in narrow trenches and about 6 inches deep. Allow 12 inches between the tubers in the row and make the rows twice that distance apart. If the ground becomes dry, water copiously and give a weekly application of dilute liquid manure from early May. This will help to increase the yield as will earthing up the rows after the manner of potatoes.

Harvesting The roots are lifted at the end of October, as soon as the tops have begun to die down and before the soil becomes saturated with winter rains. They may be stored in boxes of dry sand and used when required. However, since they have a better flavour when fresh and are perfectly hardy, they may be lifted from early September onwards until Christmas, when any remaining roots are lifted and stored. If alternate roots are lifted first, this will allow those remaining more room to develop and make larger tubers.

It should be pointed out that the plants will make considerable top growth. This must be supported by inserting two stout stakes at each end of the rows and running parallel lengths of wire between them, the top growths being supported between these wires. If the stems are broken by strong winds, smaller tubers will result. Before lifting commences, the stems should be cut away a few inches above ground.

The silver-skinned artichoke is the finest, being hardy and mild of flavour. The tubers should be partially boiled in their skins, then have the skins removed before baking; or they may be sliced and fried in batter.

They are troubled by no disease and only one pest.

Pest

ROOT APHIS   It also feeds on the roots of lettuce, severing them and causing the plants to wilt. Watering the ground before planting with liquid Lindex will bring about its extermination.

Asparagus
Asparagus officinalis

One of the most delicious of vegetables, yet rarely grown, possibly because it is necessary to wait 3 years before cutting the first 'sticks'. A well-prepared bed will, however, continue to yield for 20 years with the minimum of attention and will repay its planting costs a hundredfold. Plants may be raised from seed, like rhubarb, but will take longer to come into bearing than if 2-year roots are planted.

Sowing   Early April is the time to sow seed which is done in a bed brought to a fine tilth and enriched with some old mushroom bed compost. If the soil is heavy, work in some coarse sand or grit and if gardening near the sea, dig into the ground some chopped seaweed. Asparagus is a maritime plant and will crop heavily if provided with those things found along the sea-shore, namely sand, salt and seaweed. It was Samuel Pepys, of diary fame, who introduced plants bearing the familiar thick 'sticks'. These he found growing on the North Sea coast of Holland three centuries ago.

Sow only fresh seed for quick germination and never seed which is more than 2 years' old. The seed is large and easy to handle and should be planted singly, spacing it 1 inch apart, in drills made 1 inch deep and 9 inches between each other. The seed may take a month to germinate and, so that the ground may be kept clear of weeds during this time, it is advisable to sow a small amount of radish seed in the drills before covering them in, the radishes being removed as soon as the asparagus has germinated. At all times, the soil should be kept moist or germination will be delayed.

The young asparagus plants should remain in the rows which must be kept free of weeds until the following spring, and when growth recommences, carefully lift and plant into permanent beds.

Planting   Whether planting home-raised seedlings or 2–3 year roots obtained from a specialist grower, soil requirements will be the same and the ground should be prepared well in advance of planting. Remember when making up the bed (and asparagus seems to do better in a raised bed if the soil is heavy) to do it well, for the plants will be expected to crop for at least 20 years. Make the bed flat and 10–12 inches above the surrounding ground. If the soil is light, planting may be done on the flat.

When the soil is free from frost, remove all perennial weeds then, early in March, make the trenches 8–9 inches wide and allow 2 feet between each. Make the trenches 9 inches deep and at the bottom provide a layer of drainage materials such as shingle or crushed brick. Above this, is placed a layer of decayed cow manure. Hop manure or old mushroom bed compost is equally suitable. This is then covered with a layer of screened soil. If the soil lacks lime, give the ground a light dressing before the trenches are made.

Early in April, the roots or 'crowns', as they are called in the trade, are planted and as a further precaution against excess winter moisture causing the crowns to decay, plant them over small mounds of soil and about 4 inches below the top of the trench, spreading out the claw-like roots evenly.

General cultivation   The secret of growing quality asparagus is threefold:

(a) To obtain a good strain;
(b) To make up the bed correctly; and
(c) To allow the crowns ample room to develop.

The latter is probably the most important rule and for this reason the French, specialists in asparagus culture, allow 2 feet between the crowns in the rows. Commercial growers plant 18 inches apart to crop the ground to the maximum but 2 feet is to be recommended, for if the roots are not allowed room to develop over the year they will not obtain sufficient nourishment and moisture from the soil and will produce only thin weakly 'sticks'.

Some commercial growers plant in the ridge system as for potatoes, planting the crowns 2 feet apart in the rows. Here, seed is sown in two's and three's at intervals of 2 feet, the strongest seedling from each group being retained. Seedling plants will usually prove to be more vigorous than older transplanted roots. To maintain vigour and so that the ground may be kept clean and well nourished, specialist growers retain the crowns for no more than 6 years when they are destroyed and fresh plantings made. This practice also allows the sticks to be cut more heavily during the final year of the crop.

After planting, cover the crowns as quickly as possible so that they are not harmed by long exposure to cold winds. Into the soil used for filling in the trenches, incorporate 2 ounces per square yard of superphosphate and 1 ounce of sulphate of potash. Pack the soil carefully around the crowns and leave the surface of the bed quite level. Always avoid planting crowns older than 3–4 years which will be then have become acclimatised to the soil into which they were originally planted and may show little vigour when moved to fresh ground.

By mid-May, the shoots will be seen pushing up through the soil but no cutting must be done for their first 2 years. Instead, the shoots are allowed to make fern (foliage) which dies back in autumn to provide the roots with nourishment needed to

Top The annual herb Dill derives its common name from the Saxon verb *dilla*, to lull. The soporific seeds used to be given to children to make them sleep. The leaves are now used in fish sauces, or boiled with new potatoes or peas, but should be used sparingly.

The perennial herb Rue, though traditionally the herb of repentance because of its bitterness, takes its name from the Saxon *ruth*, meaning pity. Grown for its blue-grey foliage, the leaves are delicious in sandwiches with cheese, lettuce or cress.

Tree Onions. This unusual onion is hardy and easy to grow. The onions, which are about the size of small shallots, are carried at the top of 3 foot stems. They may be pickled or dried and used in stews, or chopped for use in salads or sandwiches.

build up a sturdy plant. Limited cutting may begin in their 3rd year.

Asparagus loves salt, and early in May each year give the beds a 2 ounce per square yard dressing of common salt, or give a dressing of nitrate of soda early in April at a similar strength and preferably on a rainy day. Though the plants must not be allowed to set seed, the foliage should not be removed otherwise the plants will be weakened.

Harvesting Cutting the shoots from an established bed will begin about mid-May and for the first season this should be finished by early June, removing no more than 2 sticks from each plant and allowing the other shoots to make foliage. The following year, cutting may continue until mid-June or even later, but on no account should any cutting be done after the month end. The later shoots which form must be allowed to produce fern to maintain the vigour of the plants.

During summer, never allow the plants to lack moisture and as soon as cutting has ended, mulch the bed with decayed manure or with material from the garden compost heap. Clearings from ditches are of value, in fact anything to conserve summer moisture. Those living near the sea may cover the beds with seaweed, taking care not to damage the fern. This is the best of all mulches for asparagus.

Another aid to obtaining large thick sticks is to give the beds a weekly application with dilute manure water from early July until the foliage has died back and is removed.

When cutting from an established bed, remove every stick until late in June when the newly formed shoots are allowed to make foliage. Cut the 'sticks' when about 6 inches above the surface of the soil using a special asparagus knife with its saw-like blade for the shoots are extremely tough to cut through. The blade is inserted 2–3 inches below soil level but care must be taken that the shoots newly forming around the crown are in no way damaged, nor the tips of those shoots which are removed for this is the most succulent part and is easily broken off.

The commercial grower will grade his 'grass', as the 'sticks' are called, into 'specials' and 'ordinary' and tie them into bundles of selected thickness. The blanched ends of the shoots are then made level to improve the appearance. They are placed in a wooded 'cradle' for the ends to be cut and are then tied into bundles with raffia. This is left in place during cooking which is done by standing the bundle upright in 2 inches of water. In this way the purple-green tips are only steamed and retain their full flavour. The sticks are served piping hot with melted butter.

Where exhibiting, gently wash the sticks in cold water then tie them in bundles, keeping the tips level and cutting the ends in line with each other. The sticks should be as near as possible of the same thickness throughout the bunch and, when ex-

hibited, the bundles should stand erect.

Forcing Asparagus responds well to forcing and if a bed is made up to the measurements of a garden light, frame boards 12 inches deep may be fixed around the sides and the crowns planted 18 inches apart. Around the frame boards on the insides, a 9 inch wide trench is made and early in March this is filled with composted straw or farmyard manure and well trodden down to retain its heat. The frame lights are then placed over the bed which should not be forced until its 3rd year. The warmth generated by the compost and aided by the spring sunshine is sufficient to bring about mild forcing and the first 'sticks' will be ready to cut before the end of April or by the middle of the month in the more favourable parts of Britain. Cutting may continue until the first of the outside shoots are ready.

Pests and Diseases

ASPARAGUS BEETLE If unchecked, the grubs will feed on the foliage during summer, often stripping a bed with the resulting loss of vigour of the plants. For prevention or cure, spray the foliage during July and August with derris, either in solution or as powder.

ASPARAGUS FLY This is rarely troublesome but is more difficult to eradicate as the grubs burrow into the shoots near the base, causing them to turn yellow and die back. Where small puncture marks are observed, make a slit in the stem with a sharp knife and flick out the grub with the end of the blade.

RUST This appears on the foliage early in July, shortly after the last 'sticks' have been cut. It has close affinity with summer blight on potatoes. It is controlled in the same way, by spraying at fortnightly intervals until early September with Bordeaux Mixture. This is made by dissolving 1 pound of quicklime and 1 pound of copper sulphate in 12 gallons of water.

Varieties 'Connover's Colossal.' An old American variety, still unsurpassed for earliness and for quality. Ready before all other varieties, a good strain will produce a high average of thick, straight greenish-white shoots.
'Mary Washington.' This variety has proved highly resistant to rust disease and is the best for canning and quick freezing. The shoots are thick and uniform, dark green in colour, with tightly closed tip scales.
'Purple Argenteuil.' The most popular French variety and the best for late cutting so that it should be planted with one of the early American varieties to extend the season. The flavour is outstanding.

45

Asparagus Pea
Lotus tetragonolobus

'Alike as two peas' is a frequently heard saying but this is a 'pea' unlike any other. It is not, in fact, a pea at all but is of the trefoil family, closely related to the clovers. It comes by its name because it is pod-bearing and has a flavour exactly like that of asparagus. With its clover-shaped leaves, it is a handsome plant, growing about 18 inches tall and almost as bushy, its reddish-purple flowers followed by deeply grooved pods which are borne with great freedom. The whole plant is most ornamental. It requires a sandy, well drained soil and an open, sunny situation for it is native of Southern Europe and crops well only in a warm summer or in the milder parts of Britain.

Sowing   The plants are best raised under glass, in a frame or greenhouse, sowing the seed early in April and planting out the seedlings mid-May when large enough to handle. Allow 18 inches between each plant and incorporate plenty of humus into the soil to retain summer moisture. Peat, fortified with nutrients, such as Acta-bacta or Bio-humus is suitable or straw composted with an activator. Keep the soil moist throughout summer and remove the pods when about 2 inches long, whilst still succulent. They should be steamed whole with a piece of butter for about five minutes and eaten on their own with brown bread, so that their unusual flavour may be enjoyed without competition.

During a warm summer and if the soil is kept moist, the pale green pods will appear in rapid succession from mid-June until the beginning of September when the plants are taken up and burnt.

Neither pest nor disease will trouble it.

If sowing directly into the open ground, sow early in April, in rows about 20 inches apart and thin to 18 inches in the rows. No staking is required.

Aubergine
Solanum melongena

From its egg-shaped fruit, this is also known as the Egg Plant. Though native of Mexico and the Southern United States, it will fruit in the British Isles with the minimum amount of heat. It is, incidentally, a close relative of the potato. An ounce of seed will produce more than two thousand plants and in the John Innes compost, it will germinate rapidly in a greenhouse heated to 56°F. Sow early January, just covering the seed and, to hasten germination, cover with a sheet of glass.

When the seedlings are large enough to handle, move to small pots containing the John Innes potting compost and again, to larger pots 3–4 weeks later. When the plants are established, nip out the growing point to encourage bushy growth and by this time, artificial heat will no longer be necessary. The plants will now require copious amounts of water and ample ventilation. Early in May they may be transferred to a frame or set out under barn-type cloches. The plants love the sunlight and should be kept as close to the glass as possible, syringing the foliage whenever the days are warm.

General cultivation   Aubergines may be grown outdoors in the milder parts of Britain, planting out early June 15 inches apart after hardening off. When planting in their final pots or in the open, they require a well drained porous soil, enriched with decayed manure. Cow manure is ideal or old mushroom bed compost.

Gentle syringing will help the fruit to set and when the first fruits have formed, feeding with dilute manure water will increase their size and quality.

During the season, each plant will yield a dozen or more fruits which, when fully developed, may weigh more than a pound each. They should, however, be picked off before they become too large and exhaust the plant. They are at their best when the skin has a brilliant gloss. To serve, cut into halves, remove the seeds and serve cold with salad oil or grill for a few minutes and serve with butter.

From a sowing made in gentle heat, plants in pots under glass will begin to fruit within about 70 days and will continue until the end of summer or when cut down by frost if growing outdoors.

During dry weather, the plants must not be allowed to lack moisture or the skins will split as with tomatoes. Wherever they are to be grown, they require an open, sunny situation.

Diseases   Aubergines suffer from the more common diseases of the tomato, though the newer hybrid varieties show considerable resistance to Fusarium and Bacterial Wilt. For preventive treatment, see under Tomato.

Varieties   'Burpee's Hybrid.' Disease resistant, this variety grows 3 feet tall and does best under glass, producing a continuous supply of oval, medium-sized fruits of dark crimson-purple with a high gloss and a delicious flavour.

'Early Beauty.' This will come into bearing within 65 days and though the fruit is not large, it is most prolific and is of delicious flavour. The dark purple egg-shaped fruits are held above the ground on plants that grow almost 2 feet tall. The flesh is especially firm.

'F_1 Hybrid Long Tom'. An early maturing Japanese hybrid, the cucumber-shaped purple-black fruits measure 6 to 7 inches long and about 2 inches in diameter. A single plant will produce as many as fifty fruits in a season.

'Jersey King'. A hybrid that is later to mature and bears large numbers of cylindrical dark purple fruits which have an attractive green calyx. It makes a spreading bush.

Bean, Broad
Vicia faba

Broad beans bridge the gap in the kitchen garden between the late spring greens and the first of the summer crops and with their rich earthy flavour are welcome at this time. They are appetising when steamed until tender and served with parsley sauce. Introduced into Britain by the Romans, they were grown by all poor people as they were particularly rich in protein and salts and were most sustaining during a hard day's work.

Sowing Broad beans like a deeply worked soil, and one which has been manured for a previous crop. If this is not so, work into the soil some well decayed manure or old mushroom bed compost. They like an alkaline soil, one which has been well limed.

In a sheltered garden, a sowing may be made early November and left unprotected during winter. When gardening in colder parts, it is advisable to cover the young plants with cloches during severe weather. A second sowing is made early March to mature when the early sown crop is finishing.

It is usual to sow in a double row 8–9 inches apart, so that both rows may be covered by a barn cloche. Allow the same distance between the beans in the rows. Plant the seeds singly, about 2 inches deep. It is preferable to use a trowel rather than a dibber for the seeds are large and if the hole is not made large enough, the seeds may be held against the sides. If the soil is of a heavy nature, it is advisable to assist winter drainage by planting on a layer of peat or sand.

General cultivation When the plants begin to make growth in spring, hoe between the rows and earth up the base of the plants. If the garden is exposed, support the plants by placing canes along the rows at regular intervals on each side of the plants and fasten twine about 12 inches above soil level and again when the plants are about 2 feet tall. Support may also be given by inserting short branches into the soil between the rows and on the outer sides. This is done when the plants are about 2 inches tall and also gives protection from cold winter winds if cloches are not available. The 'Longpod' varieties are the hardiest and most prolific; the 'Windsors' have the besy flavour but should be sown only in spring.

After cropping, pull up the plants and move the haulms and roots to the compost heap for they have a valuable nitrogenous content. Or cut off the stems at soil level and dig in the roots.

Pests and Diseases
BLACK FLY   By far the most troublesome for the broad bean. It attacks the blossom causing deformed beans and greatly reduces the crop. It rarely attacks autumn sown plants and as it normally congregates at the top of the plant, if this is pinched out early in spring when a fair crop has set, this will greatly discourage the pest. This will also make for early maturity of the pods. The pest may also be kept under control by spraying the plants from mid-April with derris solution.

CHOCOLATE SPOT   This occurs as light brown spots on the leaves and stems which, if not controlled, may cause the plant to die back. The disease is most prevalent in a cold, wet spring and in a soil deficient in potash. Spraying with Bordeaux Mixture will give control.

RUST   This is due to the fungus *Uromyces fabae* and appears on the foliage as whitish spots, later turning brown. Unless the weather is cold and wet the disease is rarely serious. There is no known cure and any affected plants should be destroyed.

SLUGS   These pests can devour a row of succulent plants in one night, and before sowing it is advisable to water the ground with Slugit and again early in spring.

Varieties
'BUNYARD'S EXHIBITION'   One of the best longpods, being the first to mature from a late autumn sowing. The pale green seeds are of delicate flavour.

'FENLAND GREEN'   A longpod variety containing 7–8 beans to a pod, of excellent flavour and a heavy cropper.

'GILLETT'S IMPERIAL GREEN LONGPOD'   For exhibition, this is the finest of all broad beans, the elegant straight pods measuring up to 14 inches long and containing 8–9 beans, evenly sized.

'GREEN WINDSOR'   A prolific bearer, the beans remain green after cooking and have a delicious mild flavour.

'PROLIFIC LONGPOD'   One of the finest maincrop beans for general cultivation bred to give the heaviest possible crop of medium-sized pods of excellent flavour and uniformity. Reliable in all districts: good on heavy soils.

'LONGFELLOW'   This has received an Award of Merit and is one of the finest all-round broad beans ever introduced. It has tremendous cropping powers whilst the long straight pods contain 8–9 beans.

'RED EPICURE'   The beans are of an unusual chestnut-red colour with a flavour unrivalled amongst broad beans. It is hardy and an excellent cropper.

'RYDER'S BROADSWORD'   A most reliable cropper, the long pods being broad and shapely, containing 8–9 beans of delicious flavour.

'THE MIDGET'   Also known as Dwarf Bush, this grows only 15 inches high and each plant produces 3–4 stems, each bearing a cluster of beans up to 6 inches long. It is best planted as a single row as each plant grows 18 inches across. It does well in poor soils.

'THE SUTTON'   Similar in habit to Dwarf Bush, this variety is extremely hardy, the white-seeded pods maturing early. It is best sown in a single row.

Bean, dwarf French
Phaseolus vulgaris

One of the most prized of all summer vegetables, this is suitable for growing in the smallest of gardens, and in tubs or in window boxes where there is no garden. Dwarf, or Bush beans as they are called in America, will provide a succession of food for the epicure from June (or earlier where grown under glass) until late autumn and will yield a larger amount of edible green for the area of ground they occupy than any other crop. Neither do they require staking nor any considerable labour in their culture. They are Dwarf beans and to call them French beans is an anachronism for they reached Europe from North Africa. For this reason, they are tender and unless sown in a frame or beneath cloches, they should not be planted out in the more exposed parts of Britain until May so that when the seed germinates, there will be no fear of damage from frost.

As to be expected, the plant requires a light, warm soil and an open, sunny situation. As for all legumes, lime is an essential part of their diet and 4 ounces per square yard should be applied to the soil during winter. The soil, too, must be friable and well drained and plenty of humus should be incorporated at this time such as hops, cow manure or old mushroom bed compost. The plants will begin to crop within eight weeks of the seed being sown and will continue to bear for the same length of time. The seed may be sown between rows of lettuce or cabbage or on soil thrown up from celery trenches and which will not be used for earthing up until the beans have finished cropping.

Sowing the seed   The first sowing, under cloches, may be made early in March, though plants raised in gentle heat and set out under cloches towards the month end will give more reliable results. Beans transplant well and it is usual to sow seeds under cloches or in a frame to fill in any spaces in the rows which may occur with outdoor sowings. Some growers do not sow directly into the open ground but raise their plants in deep boxes under glass and plant out when in their second leaf.

The first outdoor sowing is made about mid-April in the south, a fortnight later in the north and at monthly intervals until mid-July, to give a succession of beans until the end of September. For early sowings use a quick maturing variety such as 'Sutton's Premier' or 'The Prince' and plant with a trowel, 2 inches deep and 8 inches apart in the rows. If sowing a double row, plant 12 inches apart and stagger the planting to allow each room to develop. Or plant the seeds 4 inches apart and remove alternate plants when large enough to handle, transplanting them into nearby ground which may only then have become cleared of other crops.

After germination, keep the hoe moving between the rows and tread in any plants blown over by strong winds. In dry weather, water copiously otherwise the beans will grow hard and stringy, and to prolong the crop, give an occasional application with dilute manure water.

Harvesting   Care is necessary when picking the crop so as not to loosen the roots of the plants when removing the beans, which should be harvested whilst young and succulent. If allowed to remain too long on the plants they will deteriorate both in quality and flavour, whilst the total weight of the crop will be greatly reduced. They mature rapidly and from early July it is advisable to look over the plants daily. The beans should break with a snap when pressed, hence their name 'snap' beans.

Under glass culture   French beans are one of the easiest of vegetables to force well. A temperature of 65°F. is all that is required and constant syringing to keep the plants free from Red Spider. Use 10 inch pots, sowing 3–4 seeds in each and an open, friable compost containing a small quantity of decayed manure. As the plants make growth, insert a few twigs around the side of the pot to keep them upright and if the sun causes a rise in temperature, admit plenty of fresh air. At all times, the plants should be kept comfortably moist at the roots whilst they will benefit from an occasional watering with dilute liquid manure.

Seed is sown in early January under glass when the plants will begin to crop towards the end of March. They are generally grown on benches, beneath tomatoes or cucumbers and the two best varieties for forcing are 'Masterpiece' and 'Canadian Wonder'.

Exhibiting   The dwarf French bean takes a minor place on the show bench in comparison with the runner bean for it is less imposing when displayed. Where showing, it will be necessary to keep the beans from touching the soil by inserting twiggy sticks about the plants. Remove the beans with a length of stem attached and place in a bowl of water to keep fresh until ready to transport to the show ground. It is preferable to remove the beans by cutting the stalks with scissors and they should be taken to the show in boxes lined with damp cotton wool. For exhibition, 'The Prince' is outstanding with its graceful wafer-thin pods of emerald green colouring.

Pests and Diseases

ANTHRACNOSE   The beans may become infected by dark brown sunken spots scattered over the pod which will eventually damage the seeds. The disease rarely attacks outdoor plants except in damp, humid seasons. If observed, spray the plants up to flowering time with half strength Bordeaux Mixture.

BLACK FLY   This aphis will occasionally trouble the dwarf bean but may be controlled by dusting the plants with derris powder as for broad beans.

HALO BLIGHT   A bacterial seed-borne disease which

will produce a stunted or yellow plant which soon dies. It appears on all parts of the plant as pale brown spots with a transparent halo-like margin from which may ooze a slimy liquid. Spraying with weak Bordeaux Mixture gives control.

RUST This is to be found on dwarf and runner beans throughout the world, though is now rarely troublesome owing to the introduction of rust-resistant varieties. In an outbreak, the leaves become covered on both sides in brown coloured pustules which later turn black. There is no cure and infected plants should be pulled up and destroyed.

Varieties

'CANADIAN WONDER' An old favourite, early and prolific which does especially well under glass.

'DUPLEX' Noted for its heavy cropping and resistance to all diseases. The beans are long and straight and are entirely stringless, whilst the flavour is all that could be desired.

'EARLIGREEN' The first to mature, often coming into bearing 10 days before any other variety. Of compact habit, it bears long straight pods, often 6 inches long, which are fleshy and easy to slice.

'MASTERPIECE' Probably the best dwarf bean ever introduced, cropping abundantly, the long green pods being of crispy texture and of delicious flavour.

'PROCESSOR' Outstanding for freezing, the rounded pods being smooth and brittle, shorter than most but of fine flavour whilst it is a heavy and consistent cropper.

'SUTTON'S PREMIER' The beans are broad and tender and it is the first to mature under cloches.

'TENDERPOD' An all-American winner and one of the best for bottling and freezing. It matures early and is productive over a long period, the curving green pods being smooth and stringless.

'THE PRINCE' With its long thin pods of brilliant green, crisp and stringless, it is outstanding for exhibition. The pods often measure up to 12 inches long.

Various other types

'DEUIL FIN PRECOCE' An outstanding dwarf bean of French origin, maturing early and cropping heavily. The dark green pods are long and thin and heavily mottled with violet. It is of delicious flavour.

'KINGHORN WAX' A golden bean with slender pencil-like pods which are smooth and stringless. It is without rival for freezing and canning. The Waxpod beans should be steamed whole and not sliced.

'MEXICAN BLACK' It is the seeds that are black and when dried and used in sauces, they have a flavour similar to that of a field mushroom. The same flavour is to be enjoyed when the beans are sliced and simmered in the usual way.

'PENCIL POD WAX' The pods are deep yellow, as round as a pencil and half-moon shaped. They grow 6 inches long and are fleshy and stringless and of delicious flavour.

'ROYALTY' A purple-podded bean which is hardier than most and does well in all soils. The long purple pods become dark green when boiled whilst they possess outstanding flavour.

'SPECKLED CRANBERRY' A most unusual variety, cropping heavily and bearing stringless pods speckled with red and more than half an inch wide.

Bean, runner
Phaseolus coccineus

Runner or kidney beans follow the early summer French beans, being at their best during late summer and autumn. The runners are more demanding as to their culture for they will reach a height of 8–10 feet in a single season and are in every way heavier than other climbing beans. They require a rich soil and efficient staking, and are best grown against rows of laths which have one end inserted into the ground and the other held in position by strong wire or twine fastened to stout stakes at each end of the row.

The ground should be trenched where the plants are to grow and before fixing the laths in position. The trench is made 10 inches deep and to the width of a spade and at the bottom is placed material from the compost heap which is limed and well trodden down. Over this is spread a layer of soil and decayed manure which is then allowed to settle. The trench is filled up with sifted soil to which is added 1 ounce of superphosphate and ½ ounce of sulphate of potash per yard of trench.

The stakes are then inserted at intervals of 9 inches and are tied in place to a stout wire stretched 4–5 feet above the trench. Canes may be used instead of laths but the plants do prefer to twine about the rough square laths and this way pull themselves up more quickly and more securely. Tying at intervals will also keep the plants tidy and prevent them from growing into each other. It must be remembered that when in full leaf and bearing, the plants will be of considerable weight and must be well supported.

Sowing One seed is planted at the foot of each stake. This is done by using a trowel and planting the seed 3 inches deep. It is usual to plant a dozen or so seeds at the end of the row to fill in any 'misses'. Mid-May is the best time to plant for runner beans will be damaged by frost if they appear above ground before June 1st.

General cultivation As soon as the plants begin to form their first beans, they should receive an application of dilute liquid manure once each week until early in August; they will also benefit from a mulch of strawy manure. Above all, the plants must not be allowed to suffer from lack of moisture at the roots, otherwise the buds and beans may fall and the older beans will mature tough and stringy. Regular spraying of the foliage will help the flowers to set and will keep the plants free from red spider. When the plants reach to top of the stakes it is advisable to remove the growing points so that they may concentrate their energies on the production of beans rather than in making more growth.

Where space is limited, runners may be grown against stakes fixed in tent fashion and tied at the top, with the bottom of the stakes 2 feet apart. Though no trenching will be done, the soil should be made rich and friable before planting the seed. Dwarf runner beans, supported by twiggy sticks and started under cloches will also crop heavily in a confined space.

Exhibiting This is one of the most satisfactory crops for the show bench, being at its best when the shows are most prolific and the size of the beans command attention. To obtain the finest beans, grow the plants in the cordon system as for sweet peas, trenching the ground and growing against laths or canes but pinching out the side growths at one or two leaves. As they make growth, water copiously and be generous with liquid manure feeding. Then nearer show time, thin out each group to no more than two beans, selecting the best for the show.

Runner beans suffer from neither pest nor disease which cannot be prevented by the normal precautionary methods. Slugs must be guarded against and red spider, by frequently syringing the foliage during dry weather or if growing close to a wall. It is possibly the most trouble-free of all crops.

To enjoy beans through winter, a quantity of young beans should be salted down during the season when they will retain their flavour and quality for two years if necessary. Use an earthenware jar or a glass jar with a screw top. Place in a layer of sliced beans, then a covering of salt and so on until the jar is filled. When required, wash free of salt and soak for an hour before cooking.

Varieties
'CRUSADER' An exhibitor's favourite for its beans will grow 18 inches long yet remain straight and slim. It also does well in all soils and in all weathers and does not drop its buds at the least provocation. Also excellent for the table.
'DOBIE'S YARDSTICK' A leading exhibitor's bean, it bears an abundance of succulent pods up to 20 inches long and crops over an extended period.
'GIRAFFE' The tallest growing of all beans, reaching a height of 10–12 feet and bearing an abundance of large, brittle pods until the end of autumn.
'GOLIATH' It will produce pods up to 20 inches long in an ordinary soil whilst they remain brittle and supple with the mild flavour of the French beans.
'HAMMOND'S DWARF' A dwarf form of the long established 'Prizewinner' and growing only 18 inches tall. The 8 inch long pods are produced over a period of 10–12 weeks and are tender and sweet if not left on the plant too long. It may be grown

under barn cloches for an early crop, the seed being sown late in April and the cloches removed mid-June.
'LONG AS YOUR ARM' Received an Award of Merit, and is to be recommended for exhibition and kitchen use. An immense cropper, it bears pods up to 18 inches long under ordinary soil conditions.
'PRIZEWINNER' This bears an enormous crop and is early to mature, its long slim pods forming in large clusters. Excellent for exhibition or culinary use.
'STREAMLINE' An outstanding exhibitor's bean. The 18 inch long pods grow straight and slim, whilst they are borne in large trusses right through the season.

Beans, butter
Phaseolus lunatus

These are also known as Lima or Madagascar beans and are grown for their seeds which are removed from the pods when dry and mature, to be used as a winter vegetable. There are two forms, dwarf bush and climbing (or pole) which are grown as described for climbing French beans. In America, the early pods are cooked whole, like Waxpods and those maturing later are saved for winter use.

Butter beans mature late, and for the seeds to attain their maximum size, they should be allowed to remain on the plant until early autumn when they should be removed and spread out on benches in a dry airy room to complete their ripening. They are then removed from the pods and should be stored in a clean cardboard box provided with air holes. If placed in a tin, they will sweat and deteriorate. It is the white and cream coloured varieties that should be used for drying as the black and brown seeded kinds are too hard for cooking. Even the pale seeds will require soaking in water for at least two hours before cooking.

Varieties
'BURPEE'S FORDHOOK' The best of all dwarf haricot beans for it crops profusely, the 4 inch pods containing four large plump beans which, when cooked, have a mealy, chestnutlike-flavour.
'COMTESSE DE CHAMBARD' This bears heavily and though the seed is small, its skin is extremely thin, thus requiring little soaking and the minimum of cooking whilst the full flavour is retained.
'PRIZETAKER' This climbs rapidly and bears its 6 inch long pods in clusters, each being filled with four giant seeds which possess excellent flavour.

Beetroot
Beta vulgaris

There is now a golden beetroot to add to the ever popular red varieties and which is a valuable dual-purpose vegetable for the tops may be screwed off and cooked like spinach whilst the roots are boiled and used in salads when cold. Or they may be preserved in malt vinegar to be used when required.

Red beetroot was a popular vegetable in Tudor times. Gerard in his Herbal mentions the Great Red Beet, first given to him by 'Master Lete, a merchant of London who obtained seed from the Mediterranean regions. It is a maritime plant, requiring a sandy soil and one containing some salt. Before sowing the seed, dress the ground with 1 ounce per square yard of common salt and the same amount of superphosphate and sulphate of potash mixed together.

Sowing The seed is sown about mid-April in the south; early May in the north—for the young plants may be harmed by frost if they appear too early. Sow in drills 1 inch deep and 15 inches apart. An ounce of seed will sow a 30 yard row.

Beet seed is now packeted in pelleted form whereby each seed is covered with a coating of plant food. This gives protection from disease whilst it awaits germination and gives the seedlings an extra boost when germination has taken place. The coating is pre-programmed to break down quickly when sowing has taken place.

Pelleted seeds are more easily sown individually and may be spaced at distances which will later avoid the need for thinning, thus saving time, energy and money.

Onion, lettuce and parsnip seed is, incidentally, also obtainable in this pelleted form.

Beet is best grown in a friable, well nourished soil which has been manured for a previous crop. If not, work in some peat or leaf mould, together with a small amount of decayed manure. Old mushroom bed compost is ideal for this crop whilst anything of an organic nature may be dug in to lighten the soil and to help to retain summer moisture. This is a crop that must never lack water or the roots will grow coarse and 'woody' whilst the plants will run to seed prematurely in warm weather if deprived of moisture.

Germination is rapid if the seed has first been 'rubbed'. When large enough to handle, thin out the seedlings to 4 inches apart. Give a mulch between the rows towards the end of June to suppress weeds and to help retain moisture. Alternatively strips of black polythene may be placed between the rows and held in place by stones. The polythene will serve the same purpose as a mulch.

As the roots make growth, remove alternate plants when reaching tennis ball size, to use in summer salads after boiling. This will allow the remaining roots to grow on to a larger size for winter use.

The plants will benefit from a ½ ounce per square yard dressing of common salt given in July, preferably during showery weather.

Harvesting A second sowing may be made during June to provide additional roots for winter storage.

When lifting, great care must be taken to ensure that the roots are not in any way damaged for with many varieties, the smallest cut or bruising of the skin will cause the roots to 'bleed' so that when pickled, they will turn pale pink and will have lost much of their flavour.

Lift the roots in October, before the frosts, and while the soil is still dry and friable. Always twist away the leaves rather than cut them off with a knife for twisting will reduce bleeding to a minimum. Then place the roots in boxes of dry sand or peat in a frost-proof room for use as required.

Exhibiting To grow top quality beet for exhibition, it will be necessary to trench the ground. First remove the soil to the width of a spade and 12 inches deep, placing at the bottom of the trench, material from the compost heap. Over this, place a layer of soil which has been fortified with inorganic fertilisers as suggested previously and at the same time incorporate some decayed manure. Then sow the seed singly, at intervals of 6 inches in a double row.

Where growing 'long' beet for exhibition, the holes in which the seeds are to be sown should be made with a crowbar and at least 3 feet deep. These are then filled with compost similar to that described. The seed is sown 1 inch below the top of of the hole. Several sowings should be made throughout spring and early summer so that there will be a succession of roots for exhibiting at the late summer and early autumn shows.

When preparing for show, after lifting the roots with care (and this is especially vital when removing 'long' beet from the ground), wipe away the soil with an old sponge and trim off any fibrous roots with a sharp knife. The tap root, however, must be retained. To keep them fresh whilst transporting to the show ground, lay the roots on sheets of damp newspaper and pack damp wood wool around them.

Diseases
DOWNY MILDEW This occasionally troubles beetroot, appearing as a white powder on the underside of the leaves. It may be controlled by spraying the seedling plants with a weak solution of Bordeaux Mixture.
PHOMA LINGHAM This causes the young beet seedlings to turn brown and decay. It is a seed-borne disease, for which reason seedsmen now market Thiram-soaked seed which will guard against an outbreak.

Beetroot

Varieties

'AVON EARLY' The best beet to sow early for it does not readily 'bolt', showing remarkable resistance in the N.I.A.B. trials whilst it produces roots of uniformly good size and shape and of good colouring. Produced at the National Vegetable Research Station, Wellesborne, primarily as an early bunching variety.

'BOLTARDY' A beet which has proved itself almost completely free from 'bolting' (running to seed prematurely) in hot weather. It should be grown in southern gardens or in the drier parts of Britain. The roots are of globular shape and of deep crimson colouring throughout.

'BURPEE'S GOLDEN' Introduced in 1970 by the American seed house of W. Atlee Burpee, it is an entirely new colour break and is a vegetable of the first importance for exhibition and culinary use. The roots develop rapidly and are ready to use within 60 days of sowing, the skin being deep golden-yellow whilst the flesh has a mild, sweet flavour. There is no 'bleeding' as with most of the red varieties.

'DETROIT GLOBE' An old favourite and possibly the best all-round beet ever introduced. Perfectly globular, the skin is deepest crimson, the flesh free from any paler 'rings' when cooked. The flesh is crisp and sweet.

'EXHIBITION CRIMSON' The finest 'long' beet ever introduced, the root gradually tapering to a point and retaining its crimson colour throughout. Where grown well, it rarely becomes 'woody'.

'RED BALL' A Burpee introduction, this matures within 60 days when the globular roots will be of tennis ball size, of darkest crimson throughout and free from any paler zones inside. Sweet and mild, the colour is retained after cooking.

'SPANGSBJERG CYLINDER' May be classed as an intermediate variety, the roots being cylindrical in form, of deepest crimson, the flesh of fine-grained texture.

Borecole
Brassica oleracea

It takes its name from the Dutch *Boerenkool* which means 'peasant's cabbage', for it was originally grown in humble cottage gardens. We know it better as cole or kale and, in spite of its modest associations, it is one of the most useful of vegetables, succeeding in poor soils and possessing extreme hardiness. The kales will bear through the severest weather when the broccolis may have been frosted. They also provide plenty of 'green' when vegetables are most scarce.

Soil preparation The plants will grow well in soil which has been well manured for a previous crop, provided it does not lack lime, and the addition of 1 ounce per square yard of superphosphate and sulphate of potash given in mixture at planting time is all that is necessary to grow bushy plants. If planting in poor soil, work in some decayed manure or garden compost and provide the inorganic fertilisers at the same strength.

Sowing This is done early in April, sowing thinly in a prepared bed or in shallow drills and setting out the plants early in June, 2–3 feet apart. Plant firmly and as the plants make growth, keep the soil well trodden around them so that they will not heel over in the autumn winds. To ensure a bushy plant, which is essential with borecole, it may be advisable to transplant the seedlings to a bed containing peat or leaf mould and a little decayed manure where they are set out 6 inches apart. When moved to their permanent quarters, trim back the tap roots and in this way a bushy plant will result.

The handsome curled leaves should be removed whilst young and tender, simmering them rather than boiling them to bring out their delicate flavour and to preserve their rich protein and vitamin content.

The borecole is rarely troubled by pest or disease but precautionary measures should be taken as for other brassica crops.

Varieties

'ASPARAGUS KALE' This needs rather different culture, the seed being sown in shallow drills and thinned to 2 feet apart, for it resents transplanting. It is ready to use in spring, the long thin shoots stewed in butter having a flavour similar to that of asparagus.

'COTTAGER'S KALE' Taller growing than the others, it produces an abundance of curled leaves for use in late winter and spring.

'DWARF GREEN CURLED' This is a hardy variety with extremely curled leaves and, being dwarf, is most suitable for an exposed garden. A handsome plant, the leaves resemble those of parsley.

'LABRADOR KALE' Very dwarf, this produces mats of curled shoots during the severest weather.

Broccoli, Large-heading
Brassica oleracea

There are two forms, the large-heading (winter cauliflower) and the sprouting, both valuable crops for winter and spring use, though by planting several varieties or strains, it will be possible to bring the large-heading varieties to maturity almost thoughout the year.

To withstand a severe winter, the large-heading must be grown well from the time the seed is sown. As the plants normally take exactly twelve months to reach maturity, those required for March cutting should be sown the previous March; those to be cut in May being sown the May before and so on. Of numerous strains, several are bred only for the Cornish growers for it is from there that most of the large-heading broccolis come, severe winter frosts being almost unknown in the Penzance area. It is therefore necessary to obtain a strain sufficiently hardy to withstand the type of winter usually experienced in that part of the country where they are to be grown. The commercial grower must also satisfy himself that the strain he is using will produce a close, refined head (or curd), uniform in size, if grading is to be done to obtain market prices.

Sowing Seed is sown in a frame or in specially prepared outdoor beds and, to have a sturdy plant capable of withstanding a hard winter, overcrowding must be prevented. Sow thinly and remove any seedlings at an early date after germination, should they appear to be growing too closely together. Plants which become 'drawn' and 'leggy' will never recover.

Seed may also be sown in shallow drills made with the back of a rake and here again, thin sowing is desirable, thinning out if necessary. In this way, transplanting is not done, the plants being set out into the open ground when large enough to move. If raising plants in boxes under glass or over a hotbed, transplanting into boxes or frames will be necessary.

Requiring a long season to mature means that the plants must receive sufficient nourishment to form large heads and this should be made available over a long period. At the same time, an excess of nitrogen will cause the plants to grow 'soft' and they may be damaged by frost and cold winds.

Planting If possible, plant in a well drained soil which has been manured for a previous crop and augmented by a 2 ounce per square yard dressing of hoof or horn meal given just prior to planting. Where growing in land which has not been previously manured, work in a slow-acting nitrogenous fertiliser such as wool shoddy or decayed manure, supplemented by a dressing of bone meal whilst, to build up a 'hard' plant, work into the soil 1 ounce per square yard of sulphate of potash given at planting time.

As with sprouts, firm ground is essential for the formation of a tight head. Set out the plants 2 feet apart and insert the roots well into the ground, making the soil quite firm. Planting should be done during showery weather but not when the soil is sticky. Late spring and early summer is the usual time, those late to mature being planted out in July.

General cultivation After planting, keep the hoe moving along the rows and water copiously during periods of drought. Should the weather be unduly severe in winter, the heads may be protected by bending over them the long leaves which surround them. This is done by breaking the mid-rib at a point level with the top of the curd. This will also keep the head clean.

The heads are cut as soon as they reach maturity before they begin to go to seed. A good head should be pure white and round with the curd tightly formed. Several of the smaller leaves should surround the head. Where growing for market, the heads are packed in special wooden crates of two dozen.

Pests and Diseases

CABBAGE CATERPILLAR   It is the grub of the Cabbage White butterfly which lays its eggs on the brassicas and in a few days small cream coloured grubs hatch out. They proceed to devour the leaves and penetrate to the centre of the head. They are eradicated only by immersing the head in salt water for an hour before cooking. To control, dust the plants with derris powder once a fortnight from early June until September.

CLUB ROOT   Also known as 'Finger and Toe', it attacks all the brassicas, the roots becoming swollen and knobbly. It is caused by a slime fungus which lives on decayed vegetable matter in the soil. Well limed land which is adequately drained will rarely support the disease and as a further precaution, dust the roots of all brassicas with Calomel before planting.

DAMPING OFF   This is due to a water-borne fungus and affects seedlings at an early stage, causing them to turn black, wilt and die back. It chiefly attacks the roots and stems at soil level. As it may be present in all soils which have not been sterilised, and as there is no known cure, it must be prevented by watering the soil with Cheshunt Compound when the seeds are sown.

FLEA BEETLE   This is a black and shiny beetle, with two yellow stripes down the outer edge of its back so that it is often mistaken for the Colorado beetle. It attacks swedes and all brassica crops, devouring the leaves and often severing the stems at soil level. Treating the soil with Aldrin dust before planting will prevent an outbreak or, after planting, dust the plants with Lindex.

SLUGS   These may prove troublesome in damp weather, attacking and severing the young plants at ground level and often devouring large numbers of plants in a single night. To prevent an outbreak, water the soil after planting with Slugit and again four weeks later. 1 ounce dissolved in 1 gallon of water will treat 10 square yards.

Varieties for succession

'ASMER JUNO'   An outstanding late variety for cutting in June and July, the pure white heads being uniform in size and of good quality. One of the latest to mature.

'CLUSEED ST. GEORGE'   An outstanding variety for early spring use, the firm white curds being ready in April.

'DOBIE'S MATCHLESS'   A valuable variety to cut in July, forming a large, tight head of pure white, at its best when all others have finished.

'EARLY PENZANCE'   Maturing late in autumn, it is the first variety to cut, forming firm white heads of medium size (autumn).

'KNIGHTS PROTECTING'   Hardy and self-protecting, it is possibly the best April-maturing broccoli for

53

the home grower. It forms a solid head of purest white.

'LEAMINGTON' A top quality broccoli of proven merit for cutting April and May, the heads being large and of firm texture.

'MARKANTA' Of recent introduction, it matures in May and is remarkable for the uniform high quality of the heads.

'ROYAL OAK' This makes a dwarf compact plant and matures early in June, the pure white heads remaining firm in the hottest weather.

'SNOW'S SUPERB WINTER WHITE' Extremely hardy, the large white heads stand for several weeks. (Early Winter).

'SUTTON'S EARLY ROSCOFF' The first to mature of a range of white heading varieties especially raised for the Cornish growers, the large white curds maturing in December.

Broccoli, Sprouting
Brassica oleracea

For the home grower, there is no more valuable plant for both the white and purple-sprouting varieties possess extreme hardiness and may be grown anywhere in the British Isles to provide a succession of shoots for boiling or braising from early spring until the end of summer. It comes into full cropping when the equally hardy Brussels sprout is finishing.

As the sprouting broccoli grows tall, it should be given protection from strong winds. As it is semi-perennial, it will occupy the ground for several years, at the end of which time it will have become most unsightly. It should, therefore, not be given a too prominent place in the vegetable garden.

General cultivation With its continuous cropping sprouting broccoli requires a rich, deeply worked soil, into which plenty of decayed manure, garden compost or shoddy has been incorporated. The plants will also appreciate a mulch of strawy manure during winter which should be forked in around the plants early in spring.

From an April sowing, the seedlings will be ready to plant out 3 feet apart, in May. As with sprouts, firm planting is essential, otherwise the mature plants may be blown over by strong winds. As they make growth, the soil around the plants should be trodden whenever it is friable.

The shoots are removed when young, whilst they are tender and mild of flavour. If left un-gathered, they will run to seed, especially in warm weather when they will not only be useless for cooking but will rapidly exhaust the plant. If the shoots are continually removed, others will take their place.

Varieties

'EARLY PURPLE SPROUTING' From a March sowing, there will be a regular supply of purple shoots from Christmas onwards.

'LATE PURPLE SPROUTING' This comes into use in April when the 'Early Purple' is past its best.

'NINE STAR PERENNIAL' One of the most useful of all vegetables for, with good cultivation, it will continue to produce its small cauliflower shoots almost indefinitely, coming into bearing in March each year and producing 8 or 9 heads from each plant during spring and summer. To maintain productivity, the plants should be given a liberal dressing of nitrogenous manure each winter.

'SUTTON'S WHITE SPROUTING' This possesses extreme hardiness and begins producing its tiny cauliflower curds from January onwards.

Brussels sprouts
Brassica oleracea

The most important of winter vegetables for it begins to crop in October and continues until March, spanning the six coldest months of the year. It is extremely hardy and will continue to bear sprouts no matter how severe the weather.

To have firm sprouts which retain their shape after cooking, the plants must be grown well. They should be sturdy and compact and be grown in firm ground. A long jointed plant growing in loose soil will produce a large, open sprout lacking in all those qualities which go to make up a vegetable of refinement, especially when steamed in butter or margarine, rather than boiled in water.

Sowing Brussels sprouts require a long season, so make two sowings, one about September 1st to come into bearing in the autumn of the following year and another in March to crop during the latter weeks of the following winter and through spring.

If the seed is sown thinly in a frame or in drills transplanting will not be necessary, though where growing for exhibition, transplant into specially prepared beds before moving the plants to where they are to crop.

As they crop over a long period, a rich well prepared soil is necessary, one which has been worked in winter and has been given a generous application of hydrated lime. The soil should be allowed to 'weather' and in spring, when free from frost, work in some well composted strawy manure or wool shoddy, both of which will release their nitrogen steadily and over a long period. Just before planting fork in 4 ounces per square yard of hoof or horn meal and 2 ounces per square yard of superphosphate and sulphate of potash mixed together. This will help both to build up a sturdy plant and with the formation of hard, crisp sprouts.

General cultivation Plant early in April, 2 to 3 feet apart depending upon variety and make the soil firm about the roots. Grown well, the plants (at 2 feet apart) will yield 4 tons per acre or rather more than 1 pound per plant, though the amateur devoting greater attention to details will obtain twice the weight.

After planting, keep the hoe moving between the plants and, as they make growth, tread the soil around the roots so that when in bearing the heavily weighted plants will not blow over. A late summer mulch of strawy manure will assist the plants in their cropping whilst they must not be allowed to lack moisture during summer.

Early in autumn, remove any decayed leaves and begin to harvest the sprouts before they become large and coarse. If they do, they will lose flavour and will prevent the later forming sprouts from reaching maturity. To remove the sprouts, snap them from the main stem, gathering one or two from each plant as they reach about an inch in diameter. In this way, the plants will continue to crop right through winter and when all the sprouts have been gathered, the tops may then be cut and used as 'cabbage'.

Exhibiting   No winter 'green' is more useful to the exhibitor for there will be few days when there will be no sprouts to harvest. After removing the sprouts, trim the stems with a sharp knife and carefully cut away any yellowing leaves which are sometimes to be found at the base of the sprout. If these leaves are still green, do not remove them. So that they are quite clean, wash the sprouts in cold water or wipe them with a damp cloth and remove any that have opened.

Pests and Diseases

CABBAGE ROOT FLY   This is the most serious pest attacking Brussels sprouts and indeed all brassica crops. The flies lay their eggs in the soil and white maggots eat the roots, causing the plants to wilt and die back. To prevent an attack, spray the soil around the base of the plants with Lindex solution and as a further precaution, dip the roots before planting into a paste made up of Calomel and water. Dusting the plants with Lindex at regular intervals throughout summer will also prevent trouble from aphides which winter on the plants, sucking the leaves and causing them to wilt.

CLUB ROOT   The swollen roots contain spores of the disease which will pass into the soil to attack later crops. Calomel dust applied to the roots before planting will prevent an attack.

DOWNY MILDEW   This attacks all brassicas, especially the Brussels sprout, including the young seedlings and also the sprouts, covering them with a grey mould. It also attacks cabbage and it is possible for the fungus to remain alive on decaying leaves in the soil for several years. It may also attack the heads of savoys during the latter weeks of winter. Regular spraying with Bordeaux Mixture will prevent an outbreak.

WIREWORM   This pest may prove troublesome to brassica crops and is often prevalent in newly dug soil. It is the grub of the click beetle, being thin and wiry and orange in colour. It will sever and devour the roots of many plants. Treat the soil before planting with Aldrin dust or Gammexane at a strength of 1 ounce per square yard or with napthalene at double the strength. These preparations will also exterminate leatherjackets and millepedes.

Varieties

'AVON CROSS'   An F_1 hybrid which begins to form its sprouts early in autumn, producing even sized sprouts of firm, smooth texture. Unpicked sprouts hold their quality without deterioration.

'CONTINUITY'   A compact grower, this is an extra early cropper, producing masses of dark green sprouts from August until the year end. It is excellent for a wind swept garden.

'IRISH ELEGANCE'   Tall growing, it bears an extremely heavy crop of firm, medium sized sprouts over a long period which will mature in the severest weather.

'JADE CROSS'   An F_1 hybrid, it is early to mature but continues throughout winter, its jade green sprouts being even in size and shape and packed in tight rows on plants which grow 22 inches tall.

'PEER GYNT'   An F_1 hybrid, it is outstanding in every way for it is a plant of compact habit for the small garden, whilst the medium sized sprouts of emerald green are packed so tightly on the stems that it is impossible to place a finger tip between them.

'THE ARISTOCRAT'   The sprouts are of medium size and are firm and heavy and this quality is maintained throughout winter.

'WROXTON'   An old favourite and still the best for late maturing. Of very dwarf, compact habit, it shows extreme hardiness and is best sown in spring for later cropping.

'RUBIN'   This resembles the red cabbage in the colour of its sprouts which are small and tight and of bright crimson colouring. They possess a flavour all their own and should be half cooked, adding a little vinegar to preserve the colour. Then drain away the moisture and steam in a casserole with butter or margarine.

Cabbage
Brassica oleracea

This is one of the indispensable vegetables for all gardens, with its extreme hardiness and ease of culture. By planting varieties to mature at various times, it is possible to have cabbages for cutting all the year. There are varieties (a) for spring and early summer; (b) for autumn and (c) for winter use.

For spring and summer   These will be ready to cut during the sparse late spring and early summer months when the Brussels sprouts have finished and when there are few other vegetables available. The plants never attain the large size of the winter varieties and maturing quickly, remain sweet and tender, never becoming coarse or strongly flavoured.

With spring cabbage, timing is all important for the plants have to be large and strong enough to withstand severe winter weather and yet must not have been grown 'soft' otherwise they are liable to be damaged by hard frost. Again, if too advanced before winter, the plants may 'bolt' before they are ready to use if the early spring weather is dry and warm. Sow those varieties with large pointed hearts which are better able to withstand adverse weather.

General cultivation   In the south, a sowing is made late in July; in the north, at the beginning of that month. Sow thinly in shallow drills made 9 inches apart or sow broadcast in a prepared seed bed. Keep the soil moist to hasten germination and move the plants to their permanent quarters early in September. The ground should have been well manured for a previous crop. If not, dig in some well decayed manure; old mushroom bed compost is ideal for this crop and give a 2 ounce per square yard dressing with basic slag at planting time.

Plant 16 inches apart, for spring cabbages retain their compact habit and never grow as large as others. Except for keeping the hoe moving between the plants, they will require no attention other than to give a $\frac{1}{2}$ ounce per square yard dressing of nitrate of soda between the rows, preferably on a rainy day, as soon as growth commences early in spring.

To have spring cabbage at its best, cut off the heads before they become too large and rather than boil in water, steam them in butter. If the stems are left in the ground, a succession of small succulent heads will form where the cabbage head was cut away. These may be used early in summer.

Varieties
'CHOGO'   Raised by Sakata & Co. of Yokohama, it should be planted 18 to 20 inches apart for it has F_1 hybrid vigour and makes a larger head than most spring cabbages. The head is ball-shaped with cup-shaped leaves and it comes very uniform in size and weight, averaging 3 to 4 pounds each.
'DURHAM ELF'   Raised by Clucas & Co., this variety is of very compact habit and makes a small pointed heart, dark green in colour and sweet and succulent when cooked.
'EARLY OFFENHAM'   Early to heart, this variety has great uniformity of size and shape which for long has made it a market favourite.
'FLOWER OF SPRING'   Making a compact plant, it matures early, the medium sized heads being firm and pointed.
'GREYHOUND'   Very early to mature, it makes a large pointed heart with few outer leaves and possesses good flavour.
'UNWIN'S FOREMOST'   One of the best of all spring cabbages, the large pointed hearts are of dark green with few outer leaves and they possess excellent flavour.

For autumn   To continue the supply when the spring cabbages finish early in June, a number of quick maturing varieties should be ready to cut. For tenderness and mildness of flavour, they may be said to come somewhere between the spring and winter cabbages.

Seed is sown in a frame in September or early in March, the plants being moved to the open ground in April. By August, they will have formed well-hearted heads for cutting until the winter varieties are ready towards the end of the year.
'GOLDEN ACRE'   Of compact habit, it makes a small rounded head and with the stem being short, appears to sit on the soil like a football.
'PRIMATA'   This is ready a few weeks after Primo, making a medium-sized ball-shaped head with few outer leaves and with its high sugar content, the flavour is exceptional.
'PRIMO'   Extremely early, it makes a small ball-shaped head which is ready to cut 5 months from sowing.
'STANDFAST'   A remarkable cabbage, forming a solid heart with few outer leaves and ready late autumn. If not cut then, it will stand until after Christmas without losing condition.
'TOZANDA'   An F_1 hybrid which at the 1970 Scottish Horticultural Research Institute trials, out-yielded all other autumn varieties and gained first place for uniformity. It is ready early October when it will have formed a solid, flat head of blue-green with an ice-white centre when cut. The average weight is about 3 pounds.
'WINNINGSTADT'   The first of the early autumn cabbages, ready late July when it will have formed solid pointed hearts which are mild and succulent.
For winter   For cutting during winter, sow the late maturing cabbages in April and plant out when large enough to handle. Allow 20–24 inches between the plants for they make larger heads and occupy the ground longer. For this reason, the soil must be well supplied with shoddy or decayed manure whilst town garden soils should be given a 4 ounce per square yard dressing of nitro-chalk before planting.

Owing to the frequency of club root amongst cabbages and all brassicas, dipping the roots in Calomel solution before planting will give control but as an extra precaution, the plants should be given fresh ground every year on a 4-year rotation.

Exhibiting   The smaller ball-headed autumn varieties are those most wanted for the show bench and harvest festivals. They should be cut at soil level and taken to the show with as great a length of stem as possible to conserve their freshness. Before exhibiting, cut the stem close up to the lower outer leaves which should be removed if yellow or dirty. Before displaying, spray the heads with cold water to preserve their freshness.

Pests and Diseases
BLACK ROT   This may attack plants growing in a

warm, humid climate. It enters through the water pores at the leaf edges when a network of black veins may be observed. This eventually spreads down to the upper part of the stem which then decays and the head falls over. The disease is rare but should it have been observed, grow only resistant varieties such as 'Tokyo Pride' which is also resistant to Black Speck.

BLACK SPECK   This is caused by a virus and is recognised by tiny black spots which appear on the surface of the leaves. There is no known cure but as it is transmitted by aphides, their control is essential.

CABBAGE CATERPILLAR   This is the caterpillar of the Cabbage White butterfly which lays its eggs on the leaves of cabbage and cauliflower. In a few days these hatch out to creamy white grubs. If unchecked, they will rapidly devour the leaves and penetrate to the heart of the plants making them unfit for use. To prevent an attack, dust the plants with derris once a fortnight throughout summer.

CABBAGE ROOT FLY   This is the most destructive of pests. For treatment see under Brussels sprout.

DARK LEAF SPOT   All parts of the plant may be attacked, the fungus appearing as dark brown spots which will greatly harm the appearance of the cabbage whilst, if growing for seed, it will attack the pods and later the seed. Harvesting is done as early as possible but regular spraying with Bordeaux Mixture will usually keep the plants clean.

Varieties

'EMERALD CROSS'   This is a large ball-headed variety, uniform in size and in its maturing.

'FILLGAP'   This matures between the autumn and winter varieties, making a small globular solid head with smooth outer leaves. It will hold its head for many weeks if not cut as soon as ready.

'SENTINEL'   This is one of the largest of all cabbages, an average head weighing more than 6 pounds. It is a handsome variety with a mild flavour, blue-green in colour with waved outer leaves.

'TOKYO PRIDE'   An F_1 hybrid, this variety matures early in winter and is highly resistant to Black Speck and Black Spot. The plant grows about 24 inches across and forms a solid heart of about 5 pounds weight which is crisp and in no way stringy.

'WINTER KEEPER'   The value of this variety lies in its keeping qualities. The solid pale green hearts will be ready in November and, if cut, may be stored in perfect condition in a cool shed for the whole of the winter.

Cabbage, Chinese
Brassica pekinensis

This is also known as Pe-Tsai and originated in the East, being similar to a cos lettuce in its appearance and with greater heat resisting qualities than the ordinary cabbage. It is a dual-purpose vegetable and may be used in a salad during autumn as a substitute for lettuce, or steamed and used as an accompaniment to meats. It has a milder flavour than ordinary cabbage.

The Chinese cabbage requires the same culture as endive, a medium rich soil containing plenty of moisture-retaining humus. If not, the plants will run to seed before reaching maturity. For this reason also, do not sow the seed before early July. Sow broadcast and thin out to 9 inches apart for, like endive, it seems to resent transplanting. Keep the hoe moving between the plants and water copiously in dry weather. Again, like endive, it is usually more troubled by dry conditions than by pest or disease.

Varieties

'LOOSE-LEAVED CHOY'   This is ready within 50 days of sowing and it is of quite different habit, forming bunches of 10-12 greenish white stalks, resembling celery. The stalks grow 9 inches tall and are topped by green spoon-shaped leaves. The whole plant is crisp and succulent and with a mildly pungent flavour. Use cooked or grated in salads.

'MICHIHLI'   This makes a larger head and grows taller than most. In the formation of its dark green leaves it resembles a cos lettuce.

'SAKATA'S F_1 HYBRID 15'   Introduced in 1970, it withstands hot weather well. The large heads of tightly folded crinkled leaves average 4 pounds in weight. It is late to mature.

'TROPICAL PRIDE'   This is ready to cut within 60 days of sowing when the almost globular heads will weigh 3-4 pounds. When cut, the large heart is a mass of creamy-yellow leaves tightly packed together.

Cabbage, portugal
Crambe maritima

Also known as seakale-cabbage, it is rarely grown, the reason being that it occupies considerable space in the garden.

The seeds are sown early in April in shallow drills and covered with cloches. As soon as large enough to handle, the seedlings are moved to their permanent quarters and planted 3 feet apart. They require a rich, deeply worked soil and protection from strong winds. Keep the plants well watered during summer and cut the outer leaves when mature. The white midribs may be cooked as seakale and the 'green' part as cabbage.

Cabbage, red
Brassica oleracea

This is a most valuable vegetable for pickling but of all cabbages it is the most difficult to grow well. To be successful, it must be given a long growing season, seed being sown in shallow drills early in September and the plants remaining in the rows during winter.

Calabrese

In spring, the plants are set out 2 feet apart into a rich soil which has previously been well limed. Just before planting, work into the top soil a 2 ounce per square yard dressing of superphosphate and sulphate of potash and plant firmly. A sprinkling of sulphate of ammonia around the roots towards the end of spring will enable the plants to get away to a good start. 'Early Blood Red' will have formed a large head of deepest crimson by the autumn and is delicious cut into shreds and used raw in a winter salad.

Calabrese
Brassica oleracea

This is unknown to many gardeners but is a most valuable vegetable, closely resembling the sprouting broccoli, which it precedes in its cropping. It grows erect and for about 10 weeks in autumn bears tight central clusters of green buds with the appearance of a head of green cauliflowers. It retains its colour and flavour after quick freezing.

Sow the seed early in April and set out the plants mid-May, 2 feet apart. Firm planting and a well manured soil are necessary for heavy cropping. Treat as for sprouting broccoli, though it will occupy the ground for only 8 months and a winter mulch is not necessary.

Varieties

'EMERALD CORONA' A main crop hybrid maturing early in winter, being the last of the calabrese family to mature. It makes a dwarf plant and bears a compact head of deepest green. It is especially recommended for quick freezing.
'EXPRESS CORONA' A hybrid variety, coming to maturity within 7–8 weeks of planting with the formation of a central head of deepest green. After its removal, numerous side shoots will form so that cutting may continue throughout autumn.
'GREEN COMET' An F_1 Hybrid, this is ready for cutting in July. It is a single-head type forming few side shoots, the deep green curds retaining their shape longer than any other variety. Each head will weigh about a pound and will be ready to cut within 6 weeks of planting.

Cardoon
Cynara scolymus

This is closely related to the globe artichoke and is equally handsome with its silvery fern-like foliage, but whereas the globe artichoke is usually propagated from suckers (offsets), the cardoon is always raised from seed. It is grown for its succulent stems which are blanched like the chards of the globe artichoke and the stems of celery.

The plant requires the same culture as celery, including a deep trench, at the bottom of which is placed a layer of decayed compost and into which the top soil is mixed with some well decayed manure. Like celery, the cardoon requires a moist, rich soil so plenty of humus forming materials should be incorporated. The trench is made 12 inches deep and 18 inches wide and 2 feet should be allowed between the trenches.

Sowing The seed is sown in a greenhouse or frame, the young plants being set out early in May, 20 inches apart; or the seed may be sown in 'two's' directly into the trench, allowing the same distance between each group, one seedling being removed when large enough to handle. To hasten germination, the trenches may be covered with cloches which should be left in place until the end of May, to protect the plants from frost.

Like celery, cardoons require a long season of growth, whilst through summer the plants must be kept moist with copious waterings during dry weather. The regular use of liquid manure from the end of June will ensure large, tender stems.

Blanching The plants will continue to grow until the end of September when they will be ready for blanching. The method is to tie together the fern-like foliage, using fresh raffia and making the tie neither too tight nor too loose. The soil is then heaped along the row. Bracken is placed around the plants and more soil is thrown over the bracken to keep it in place. By early November, the stems will have blanched and will be ready to use during winter, the bracken affording protection from hard frost until the plants are to be used.

The outer stems may be tough and should be discarded but the inner hearts, stems and leaves may all be used, cooking them as for celery. To keep them white, add a few drops of lemon juice to the water.

Exhibiting The heads should be large and solid, the leaf stalks well blanched and free from blemish. Any with pithy stalks and which have not been well blanched should be discarded whilst those exhibited should be as uniform in size as possible.

The plants are troubled neither by pests nor diseases.

Variety
'IVORY WHITE' A cardoon of Spanish origin, hardier than the French variety and therefore better suited to the English climate. The stems should be blanched until the mid-ribs of the inner leaves are crisp and tender.

Carrot
Daucus carota

Though native of the British Isles, it was not until the arrival of the Hugenot refugees who taught us how it should be grown and cooked, that the carrot became an important part of our diet. The most delicious carrots are those grown over a gentle hot bed early in spring, the seed being sown in February, in a frame. If a frame is not available, make a sowing over a hot bed made in a shelted sunny corner about mid-March when the roots will be ready to use at the end of May.

Sowing   The seed is sown broadcast into a finely screened soil, radishes being sown at the same time for they will be removed long before the carrots mature. The bed should be kept comfortably moist and whilst the frame must be kept closed when the weather is cold, admit plenty of fresh air on mild days. The young carrots will be ready to pull early in May, the smaller roots being left to mature later in the month. One of the shorter rooted varieties should be grown for forcing such as 'Sweetheart' or 'Early Gem'.

For the maincrop, the ground should be friable and well drained and, as for all roots, should have been manured for a previous crop. Bring the soil to a fine tilth and sow early in April, in shallow drills made 10 inches apart. On land which tends to be heavy, sow the short-root varieties.

General cultivation   As soon as large enough, the seedlings must be thinned to 2 inches apart in the rows, later removing alternate plants to allow the roots 4 inches in which to mature. Another sowing is made early in June to provide a winter crop.

Carrots are not improved by frost and any still in the ground should be lifted before the end of November and stored in boxes of sand in a shed or cellar.

Raw carrots chopped or grated with salad are delicious or, steamed and served with white sauce they are sweet and tender, but pull them before they become hard and woody.

Exhibiting   With their orange-red flesh and handsome feathery foliage, well grown carrots correctly presented are amongst the most attractive of vegetables for the show bench. For exhibition, the long-rooted varieties should be grown like parsnips, in boreholes filled with suitable compost whilst the stump and intermediate rooted varieties may be sown along the top of ridges of prepared soil. Yet another method is to prepare a trench 12–14 inches wide and to sow a double row 10–12 inches apart. Successional sowings will provide roots from early summer until the year end.

During dry weather, keep the plants growing by regular waterings and give the plants an occasional application of dilute liquid manure. Frequent dustings of weathered soot on either side of the rows will encourage early maturity and assist in the control of pests.

As the plants reach maturity, make certain that the tops are not out of the ground and exposed to sunlight, for this will cause them to turn green. They should be lightly earthed up to prevent this condition or give a mulch of strawy manure.

Pests and Diseases

CARROT FLY   The most troublesome of carrot foes, the flies laying their eggs in the soil when the yellow larvae will burrow into the 'carrots' causing considerable damage, and making them virtually useless for any purpose. Dressing the seed before sowing, with Dieldrex 'B' (one-sixteenth of an ounce per one ounce of seed) or dusting the soil with Lindex at sowing time and the seedlings when they appear will give complete control. The presence of the pest may be detected by the yellowing of the foliage.

DOWNY MILDEW   This may attack the upper surface of the leaves causing them to shrivel and decay. Appearing as blackish-brown spots on the leaves, it is controlled by dusting with a copper fungicide.

FLEA BEETLE   This occasionally attacks the foliage of root and all brassica crops causing the plants to die back but may be controlled by dusting with Lindex as for Carrot Fly.

SCLEROTINIA ROT   This is caused by a fungus which makes white fluffy growth on the carrot causing rapid decay and the formation of hard black bodies which winter in the soil and germinate the following season, attacking not only carrots but turnips, artichokes and dahlia tubers. There is no cure but any roots found to be infected when lifting must be destroyed.

SPLITTING   A common trouble with carrots but it is non-parasitic, being a functional disorder by which the root splits lengthwise. It may be caused by heavy rain following a long period of drought during which time the plants should be watered artificially. A soil deficient in potash may also cause this trouble.

Varieties

'CHANTENAY'   Though early to mature, it stores well and is the best for late summer sowing, being a stump-rooted carrot of first class flavour and good texture.

'EARLY GEM'   Outstanding for forcing and early sowing, it is extremely short-rooted with a small core.

'EARLY NANTES'   This forces well, the long, tubular roots being uniform in size and shape whilst the quality and flavour are outstanding. Known in America as Nantes Half-long.

'GOLDINHART'   This grows 6 inches long and is 2 inches thick at the shoulder, tapering to a stumpy point. Its orange flesh continues through to the centre with almost complete lack of core, making it outstanding for freezing and canning.

'JAMES' SCARLET INTERMEDIATE'   A good all-purpose variety, being an excellent keeper with a mild flavour.

'SCARLET PERFECTION'   A long stump-rooted variety with flesh of excellent quality, this is an excellent keeper for winter use.

'SWEETHEART'   A valuable forcing carrot, the intermediate roots being uniform in size and of deepest orange with a small core.

Cauliflower
Brassica oleracea

The cauliflower has been in cultivation for a very long time indeed. It is mentioned in John Parkinson's 'Paradisi in sole Paradisus terrestris', the first English dictionary of gardening. The title, incidentally, is a pun on Parkinson's name, meaning 'The earthly Park of Park-in-sun'. As illustrated in that work, it has a head no larger than a golf-ball, surrounded by thick, tall leaves. Since then the cauliflower has been improved out of all recognition, the plants now having large compact heads and few leaves whilst several varieties will give a succession of heads for cutting.

Sowing For an early summer crop, seed is sown in a cold frame or under cloches early in September, and in October the young plants are pricked out into another part of the frame where they remain until April. The seed bed must not be too rich but it must not lack lime. After sowing, water with Cheshunt Compound, 1 ounce dissolved in 2 gallons of water, to prevent the seedlings being attacked by Black Leg, but water as little as possible during winter.

General cultivation After hardening, set out the plants early in April, spacing them 2 feet apart. The early varieties will begin to form heads in July and these are followed by plants obtained from a sowing made outdoors in spring, certain varieties being sufficiently hardy in sheltered gardens to mature during the early months of winter.

Cauliflowers require a soil rich in humus and plant food for they will not make large compact heads if these requirements are lacking. The land must first be well limed, then dig in some strawy manure and material from the compost heap. Hop manure is excellent for cauliflowers whilst northern gardeners will find wool shoddy readily obtainable and a valuable source of nitrogen and humus.

To make close compact heads, the plants also need potash which should be given as sulphate of potash at the rate of 2 ounces per square yard just before planting. At the same time give a similar dressing of superphosphate of lime which will help to promote vigorous root action. Should the spring be cold and the plants slow to start growing, dust around each a sprinkling of nitrate of soda given on a rainy day.

As the heads quickly run to seed, especially during dry weather, it is preferable to grow small numbers of plants for succession rather than to make a large sowing of a particular variety which will mature at the same time. When the heads begin to form, cutting should commence before they reach their best, otherwise those left until later may have started to 'bolt'. Firm planting will reduce the tendency for the plants to go to seed prematurely.

Harvesting If there are more heads than can be used maturing together, they may be kept in condition by lifting the plants with their roots, and after shaking away surplus soil, tying the stems with twine and hanging them head downwards in a cool, airy shed. Spray with water regularly to maintain their freshness.

There are numerous ways of cooking and serving cauliflowers, none being more tasty than when braised and served with cheese sauce; or after steaming, dipping the 'flower' in the yolk of an egg and browning in the oven.

Exhibiting To protect the curds (heads) from dirt and strong sunshine, fold over one or two of the outer leaves as the heads begin to form and so that they will be clean and white when cut for showing. To keep them fresh, lift the head with the stem and roots attached and, after shaking away the soil, stand the roots in a bowl of water until show day. Then cut away the head with its leaves attached and carefully wrap in clean paper before placing in an open crate so that the heads cannot shake about but not packing so tightly as to cause bruising.

Pests and Diseases
BROWNING A condition which attacks the cauliflower rather than the cabbage and is caused by a lack of the trace element, boron. In this instance, the leaves grow narrow and may turn brown whilst the curd is bitter and unpalatable. In cabbage, the leaves curl at the edges and there is cracking of the stems. It is corrected by manuring with borax at the rate of 1 ounce per 60 square yards, merely a trace.
CABBAGE CATERPILLAR The small grubs hatch out from the eggs of the Cabbage White butterfly and penetrate to the centre of the curds and if left unchecked, they will devour whole fields of plants in rapid time. To prevent an attack, dust the plants with derris powder from early June, before the curds begin to form.
CABBAGE ROOT FLY This may attack the roots causing wilting and the formation of mis-shapen heads. The pest will be kept from the plants by dusting the roots with Calomel before planting.
CLUB ROOT The fungus attacks the roots causing swellings from which oozes a slimy liquid and infected plants soon die back. An attack may be prevented by dipping the roots in Calomel solution before planting.

Varieties
'ALL THE YEAR ROUND' This may be sown any time for frame culture and open ground planting for it will mature throughout the year depending on date of sowing. It forms large milk-white curds protected by large green leaves.
'DWARF MONARCH' Of compact habit and ideal for a small garden, its small white heads are ready to use early September from a late spring sowing.
'EARLY SNOWBALL' Of dwarf, compact habit it may be grown in a frame to mature early in spring or from an early sowing, it will mature early in

Carrot 'New Scarlet Intermediate'. A main crop carrot with long, uniform roots. The flesh is firm and sweet, and has very little core. The best carrots are grown on a light soil that has been very deeply dug and well manured the previous season.
Courtesy of W. J. Unwin Ltd.

Cabbage 'Emerald Cross'. An F$_1$ hybrid, 'Emerald Cross' is a large, ball-headed cabbage producing a smooth, solid head and small outer leaves. The remarkable uniformity in size, form and maturing make this variety popular with commercial growers.
Courtesy of W. J. Unwin Ltd.

summer, its close firm heads being of medium size.

'POLAR BEAR' Raised in Australia, it matures very late from a spring sowing being at its best in October. The large white heads will be protected by the equally large leaves.

'SNOW KING' An F₁ hybrid, maturing 3–4 months after sowing in March. The solid, well rounded pure white heads are uniform and of outstanding quality.

'SOUTH PACIFIC' This variety matures late, forming its heads from late October onwards and being extremely hardy may be grown in the most exposed parts.

'SUTTON'S SUPERLATIVE' The huge white heads of this variety are at their best in November when the incurving foliage gives complete protection against frost.

'UNWIN'S SNOCAP' This follows 'Early Snowball' in its season, its tight heads being of purest white and even in size.

'VEITCH'S SELF-PROTECTING' The hardiest of all, its large incurved leaves affording protection to its milk-white curds until early January when the broccolis are ready to cut.

Celeriac
Apium graveolens var. *rapaceum*

One of the most delicious of winter vegetables, it is rarely grown and all too rarely served at table. Where celery proves difficult to grow, celeriac should be planted instead: it has a similar flavour. It may be used grated in a winter salad or stewed and served with cheese or parsley sauce.

Celeriac is planted on the flat. It requires no blanching, and no earthing up, nor does it suffer as does celery, from lack of moisture during dry weather. It is a variety of celery grown for its swollen base rather than for its stems. It resembles the turnip in its habit of growth and a well cultivated root will weigh 3–4 pounds.

Sowing It requires a long growing season to reach its best, seed being sown early in March, in a frame over a hot bed or in a greenhouse with a temperature of 60°F. When large enough, transplant the seedlings to boxes or a cold frame and when hardened, plant out towards the end of May. Plant into rich, deeply cultivated ground, in rows made 18 inches apart and allowing 12 inches between the plants. It is important not to bury the bulbous-like root which should sit on top of the soil.

Keep the ground comfortably moist, watering with dilute liquid manure once every 10 days from early July and as the root swells, pull back the soil and remove any lateral shoots with a sharp knife. Only the main stem should be allowed to grow up.

Harvesting The turnip-shaped roots will be ready to lift about mid-October and they are always better when used fresh from the ground. Unless the

garden is adversely situated as to climate, cover the roots with bracken or straw and lift as required. Those gardening in the colder parts should lift in November and store the roots (after removing the foliage) in boxes of sand or peat in a frost free room. Trim off the roots before using.

Varieties

'GIANT PRAGUE' Extremely hardy, this makes a large succulent root of splendid flavour.

'MARBLE BALL' It makes a solid globular root of medium size, entirely without pith and of excellent flavour.

Celery
Apium Graveolens

Two sowings should be made, one of the self-blanching to use from the latter weeks of summer until the late autumn; another of the ordinary white or pink variety to use through winter. This will be crisp and tender only after hard frost. It requires more labour in its culture than the self-blanching type.

(i) Self-blanching The culture of this type of celery has greater appeal to the amateur as it does not require trenching. It is grown on the flat in a soil which has been deeply worked and well manured, decayed strawy manure being most suitable, whilst any other materials which will enable the soil to retain moisture should be provided.

The plants are set out early in June about 9 inches apart. Plant firmly and never allow them to lack moisture or they will grow tough and stringy. Early in September the first roots will be ready to lift and should be used as soon as possible. Eaten raw or braised, this celery has a mild, nutty flavour and, if grown well, the sticks will be crisp and tender.

Varieties

GOLDEN SELF-BLANCHING This is the best to grow, the heart being of purest white and self-folding. However, it should be said that where the sticks are required for eating raw, they will be more succulent if pieces of cardboard are fastened round the stems about three weeks before they are to be used. The lengths of cardboard should be cut beforehand to the requisite size and be tied in place with raffia near the top and bottom of the stalks. Earthing up is not necessary for with close planting and being self-folding, they will blanch themselves but will be made more tender if light is excluded for several weeks before lifting.

'GREENSLEEVES' This requires no earthing whilst the lime-green sticks are solid and free from fibre with the flavour outstanding.

'GREENSTICK' Developed in the U.S.A., this variety requires no earthing up and makes a large head with sticks 10–12 inches long, greenish-white in colour

61

with plenty of deep green foliage. It is crisp and nutty when eaten raw.

Non self-blanching This is the more familiar ordinary celery, mostly cultivated by market gardeners to supply the wholesale markets during winter, though with the greater economy of the self-blanching type, whereby three times the number of plants may be grown to the acre, more growers are now planting the self-blanching type.

Most celery is grown in the black fenland soil of East Anglia, elsewhere it requires a heavy loam retentative of summer moisture. It also needs to be grown in trenches which should be enriched with decayed manure, augmented by garden compost or peat. As the trench is prepared, the humus materials should be well trodden down for firm planting is essential. Make the trench 12 inches deep and if it is made sufficiently wide, a double row should be planted so as to obtain the most economic use of the compost.

Sowing To be successful, celery must be grown well from the beginning and raising the plants demands some attention. Should the seedlings be left too long before transplanting, they will become 'hard' and may run to seed if the summer is dry and warm. Taking 3 to 4 weeks to germinate, the seed must be sown early enough to have made good sized plants to set out early in June. This means sowing in a frame over a gentle hot bed about mid-March, St. Patrick's Day being the time usually chosen by the fenland growers.

Sow thinly and as soon as the seed has germinated, admit fresh air whenever the days are mild. The seedlings are transplanted to frames or are set out in rows beneath cloches, setting them 2 inches apart and here they remain until ready for the open ground about June 1st. They should not be planted out until they have been gradually hardened off.

Plant out on a dull, showery day and moisten the roots before doing so. If the trench is filled in to within 3 inches of the top, this will enable the plants to receive moisture from the surrounding soil and will make it easier for earthing up. Plant 10 inches apart in a double row, but allowing 12 inches for the most vigorous varieties such as 'Lancashire Prize Red'. Keep the plants damp by frequent waterings whilst an occasional watering with dilute liquid manure from early July will help to build up plants of exhibition quality.

Blanching This calls for some care. In late July, when the plants are about 12 inches high they should be earthed up at the base as for potatoes, but full blanching should not be done until the plants have stopped growing. A second earthing up is done at the end of August and again a month later whilst the soil is still friable. At this time, the plants are tied at the top with strong twine or with raffia to prevent the soil reaching the heart. This may be done by using a long length of twine and looping it around the top of each plant in the row without cutting the twine. More soil may then be earthed up and by early November, the plants will be comfortably blanched.

Harvesting Celery is not lifted before the first sharp frost which is considered necessary to improve its quality, ensuring that crispness which is the hallmark of good celery. Take care when lifting, that the soil does not reach the heart, which will prove difficult to clean if it does. Begin lifting at the end of the row, first pulling back the soil and pressing the fork well into the ground so that the plant may be lifted without damage to the stems. Then trim off the roots and wash free of soil.

Exhibiting With celery, a large root usually signifies tender stalks, the reverse of most vegetables when size generally stands for coarseness. To have the stalks free from soil, blanching may be done by the cardboard method but it is important to allow the plants to mature fully before blanching commences.

When lifting for exhibition, leave the roots on, carefully shaking off the soil and, until ready to take to the show ground, leave the cardboard on for this will keep the sticks clean. Stand the plants upright in shallow water to give them a long drink then, several hours before exhibiting, remove the cardboard and wash the stems, the leaves being left on. After washing, allow excess moisture to drain away then wrap the plants in muslin and pack close together in a long box provided with air holes.

Pests and Diseases
CELERY FLY It lays its eggs on the foliage during the mid-summer months, the larvae attacking the leaves causing them to blister and decay. The blisters may be pinched to kill the maggots but to prevent an attack, spray the foliage during June and July with quassia solution which will prevent the flies from laying their eggs. As the flies will lay several times, it is necessary to repeat the spraying at intervals of 3 weeks.
HEART ROT It involves the heart leaves and eventually spreads along the stalks causing decaying at the centre. It may occur on land which has an excess lime content, and is controlled by spraying with Bordeaux Mixture.
LEAF SPOT This attacks the foliage, especially in damp, humid weather, first as small brown spots on the leaves. These rapidly increase in size and under magnification will be seen to be covered with black dots which are the fruiting bodies. Soon the foliage will turn brown and die. Spraying with Bordeaux Mixture shortly after the plants are set out and again before earthing up will prevent an outbreak. It is also advisable to sow seed which has been treated for Leaf Spot as recommended by the Ministry of Agriculture.

Varieties

'BIBBY'S DEFIANCE' One of the best varieties which does well in all soils, making a large plant with the 'sticks' crisp and sweet where grown well.

'CLUSEED DWARF WHITE' An interesting celery for a small garden for it grows only half the height of ordinary varieties and makes a large, solid heart. It is late to mature and improves with the frosts.

'ICE WHITE' Growth is vigorous and compact with numerous 10–12 inch sticks on each plant entirely free of fibre and pithiness.

'LANCASHIRE PRIZE RED' This makes a large solid plant, ideal for exhibition, the sticks being pale red and with outstanding flavour.

'RYDER'S EXHIBITION PINK' This makes a handsome root of brightest pink, the sticks being crisp and tender.

Celtuce
Lactuca sativa angustana

A dual-purpose vegetable, all parts of which are nourishing and full of flavour, the young leaves having four times the vitamin C content of ordinary lettuce. The leaves may be eaten raw in salads or stewed as for spinach whilst the central heart or stem is used for grating into salads or may be cooked as for celery.

Seed is sown in spring and at fortnightly intervals until early July, to provide a succession of plants which may be used when young and succulent. Sow in shallow drills made 15 inches apart and thin out the plants in the rows 9 inches apart.

The soil should be friable and have been manured for a previous crop or dig in some old mushroom bed compost or hop manure before sowing.

Keep the plants well watered, otherwise they will grow hard and stringy and keep the hoe moving between the rows. The young leaves may be used as they are forming and the central core afterwards, pulling up the plant and trimming off the roots.

Cherry (ground)
Physalis pruinosa

This interesting plant, which is variously known as the 'Strawberry Tomato' or the 'Dwarf Cape Gooseberry', is grown for its fruits, which may be eaten raw but which are usually boiled and used in stews, sauces and preserves. It is often confused with the 'Tomatillo' or 'Jamberry' which is in fact *Physalis ixocarpa*. Both need similar culture. Like their well-known decorative garden relative *Physalis alkekengi*, the Chinese lantern plant, the fruits are contained inside an inflated calyx: the fruits are edible, the calyxes are not.

The plants may be grown under glass in pots or raised in gentle heat and, after hardening, may be planted out when fear of frost has passed.

Sowing Sow the seed in boxes of John Innes compost early in the year and, to hasten germination, provide a temperature of 60°F; or sow in a frame in spring. When the seedlings have formed their second pair of leaves, transplant to small pots containing a slightly richer compost and keep them growing near the glass until ready for larger pots. They may be brought into fruit in a 48-size pot containing a compost made up of 2 parts fibrous loam; and 1 part each coarse sand and decayed manure.

If growing outdoors, prepare a trench and at the bottom place material from the compost heap, then fill up the trench with a mixture of loam and decayed cow manure or old mushroom bed compost. Give a dusting of superphosphate to assist root action, and set out the plants at the end of May. They require copious amounts of moisture during dry weather whilst an occasional feed of dilute liquid manure will enhance the size and quality of the fruits.

Chervil
Anthriscus cerefolium

The bulbous-rooted chervil has been a favourite vegetable on the Continent from earliest times but has remained comparatively neglected in Britain. It belongs to the umbellifer family and grows 3 feet tall with parsnip-like roots which, when cooked, are floury and sweet with an aromatic flavour.

A biennial, seed is sown in August or in April, in drills made 15 inches apart, the plants thinned to 12 inches apart. The soil should be rich and friable, preferably having been manured for a previous crop.

Whilst growing, keep the plants well watered during dry weather and keep the hoe moving between the rows. The roots will be ready to lift when the foliage dies down in autumn but if left in the ground until required, their flavour will be better retained.

Do not peel the roots but wash them and steam for about an hour, then serve with butter or white sauce. They make a pleasant addition to the winter diet.

Chicory
Cichorium intybus

No vegetable is more easily managed nor so little grown. It is a native British plant which the countryman knows as Succory and at one time was grown in most cottage gardens for its 'greens' yet it is far more appetising when forced and blanched.

Sowing It requires a rich, well manured soil containing plenty of humus and the time to sow the seed is early June. If sown earlier, the plants may run to seed, especially if the summer is warm and dry. Sow in rows made 18 inches apart and thin the plants to 10 inches apart when large enough. Being deep-rooting plants, a deeply dug soil is necessary and throughout summer the plants should be kept free from weeds and comfortably moist. By early November, the foliage will have died down and the roots, which by then will be as thick as a man's wrist, are dug up, trimmed of any small shoots and made ready to force.

Forcing This may be done in a cellar, shed or garage, preferably where there is some slight heat to protect a car for it is desirable to bring on the shoots in 3–4 weeks.

One method is to fill an orange box to a depth of 6–8 inches with freshly composted manure and over this is placed fine loam to a similar depth. Remove all leaves immediately above the crown and plant closely together. Water thoroughly and provide complete darkness, or cover the top of the box with sacking to exclude light.

With the slight warmth from the compost, the roots will be ready to use within 3 weeks. They will be quite white and about 8 inches long when they are broken off. The roots are left undisturbed, to bear a second crop of smaller shoots in 3–4 weeks time.

The roots may be forced in a kitchen cupboard, being planted into 9 inches of loam mixed with old mushroom bed compost. The warmth of the kitchen will force them into growth and have them ready in about the same time.

The shoots are best left until shortly before they are required for cooking. This is done by removing the outer leaves and boiling the shoots for a few minutes in salt water. Then place them in a pan, cover with butter and cook slowly for an hour until tender right through. Serve with melted butter or with a sauce to one's liking. Or pull them apart and use raw in winter salads.

Exhibiting The shoots, known as chicons, may be displayed at the late autumn shows when they should be cut as near to show time as possible, wiped clean and wrapped in tissue paper for transporting. They should be placed flat in wooden boxes and made secure, so that they will not shake about and bruise. The heads (chicons) should be long, solid, crisp and tender and well blanched.

Variety
'GIANT WHITLOOF' The best known variety, the heads being large and uniform and pure white when forced. It makes sweet and tender eating.

Chinese chives
Allium tuberosum

Scarcely known in this country, but an important vegetable in parts of eastern Asia, this close relative of the leek may be grown in any friable soil and is resistant both to heat and to cold. It bears large,

flat dark green leaves which have a strong flavour, resembling that of garlic. They are useful for flavouring meat dishes, soups and stews. The leaves should be cut off as required, as with chives. Plant 15 inches apart in spring and increase by division of the roots.

Chinese cabbage
Brassica chinensis

Though known as Chinese cabbages these vegetables are in fact far more closely related to swede and rape than to what are known as cabbages in Europe and America. They do not form a heart, as does a cabbage, but grow rather more like spinach, for which they make an excellent substitute. The leaves can be eatern raw in salads, or cooked as 'greens'. They have been grown for centuries in eastern Asia and are now beginning to become popular in the western world. Several varieties are well-adapted to the British climate.

Sowing Like miniature Swiss chards in appearance, the plants are left to mature where the seed is sown. April is the best month to sow, the seed being sown in shallow drills 15 inches apart, the plants being thinned to 18 inches in the rows.

The plants require a friable soil containing some decayed manure and throughout summer should not be allowed to lack moisture otherwise the leaves will grow tough and flavourless. The quality will be improved by an occasional watering with dilute liquid manure. Highly resistant to cold and slow to run to seed, several sowings should be made for a succession of leaves, the variety 'Mizuma' being grown for a winter crop.

The leaves are removed before they grow too old while they are sweet and succulent and others will mature in rapid succession. They are troubled neither by pests nor disease.

Varieties
'CHINESE PAC-CHOI' A compact variety like a small Swiss chard, with thick glossy crinkled leaves which are tender and delicious when cooked.
'FORDHOOK FANCY' Sow in June and plant at the end of July for winter use. The deeply curled dark green leaves curve back like ostrich plumes and, when used young are tender and mild of flavour.
'JAPANESE WHITE' Known as Celery Mustard for the leaf stems are pure white, like sticks of celery, whilst the dark green leaves are spoon-shaped and are thick and glossy.
'MISUMA' Vigorous and highly resistant to cold, it is a valuable winter vegetable, with slender white stems and narrow dark green leaves, fringed at the edges.
'MUSTARD SPINACH' The leaves are deep green, round and smooth, resembling those of spinach.

They are tender and mild-flavoured when cooked. It quickly makes leaf and, being extremely hardy, the plants may be used the whole year round.

'SEIKO PAC-CHOI' The dark green leaves grow 12 inches tall and have wide greenish-white ribs. An early variety, it quickly matures.

Climbing French bean
Phaseolus vulgaris

Also known as the Pole bean, this combines the delicate flavour of the French varieties with the heavy cropping of the runner beans. They may be grown against trellis or netting as for runners or against a sunny wall. They may also be grown up twiggy branches 5–6 feet tall and made to form a hedge, like sweet peas. In the Channel Islands, the variety 'Tender and True' is grown in this manner for the London Market for the islanders consider it superior to the runner bean in its flavour and cropping powers.

Sow in April 12 inches apart and nip out the growing point when the plants are 6 inches tall. This will encourage the side shoots to form. Plants may also be raised in small pots under glass for planting out in May or they may be grown entirely under glass and brought into bearing in a temperature of 60°F. Sow one seed to a 6 inch pot containing an open, friable soil enriched with some decayed manure. Grow them up 4 foot canes and stop the plants when 6 inches tall and again when they reach the top of the canes. Spray frequently during warm weather and keep the compost comfortably moist.

Varieties

'AMATEUR'S PRIDE' This is a climbing form of 'The Prince', possessing all its good points and bearing even more heavily over many weeks.

'BLUE COCO' A climbing bean, the flowers, stems and pods being of purple-blue and with a flavour surpassing all others. Of rapid growth, it matures early and continues to crop for 10–12 weeks.

'BLUE QUEEN' This variety makes rapid growth and is a heavy cropper producing deep purple pods which are tender and stringless and of excellent flavour.

'BURPEE'S GOLDEN' It begins to grow like a bush bean and sets its first pods early, close to the ground. Then the runners shoot upwards and continue to crop for many weeks. The golder-yellow beans grow 6 inches long and 1 inch wide and, though meaty, are tender and stringless in all stages of growth.

'KENTUCKY WONDER' A dual purpose bean for the seeds make delicious eating on their own. It climbs well and bears a heavy crop of large green pods 8–9 inches long. They are straight and stringless and are excellent for quick freezing.

Collards
Brassica oleracea

Georgia collards or coleworts are non-heading cabbages, producing numerous tender rosettes of blue-green leaves at the top of the plant. Hardy and quick to mature, the plants will be ready to cut from the beginning of winter from a late spring sowing. They require a well nourished soil when they will continue to bear their cabbage-like sprouts all winter. Plant 15 inches apart and make firm after frost and winds. To continue the supply through early spring, make a second sowing in July. The plants grow upright, taking up little space and bear their rosettes at the top. They should be cut frequently when other sprouts will form. If this is done they will never become coarse and bitter.

Corn salad
~~*Lactuca sativa*~~ Valerianella Locusta.

This is also known as Lamb's Lettuce for it is at its best during the latter weeks of winter, at the start of the lambing season. It was introduced, so Gerard tells us, by the Hugenots during Elizabethan times for in France and the Low Countries it was widely grown as a winter salad crop.

Unlike most salad crops, it requires an open, sunny position and a dry, sunny soil. Only to assist the seed to germinate and the seedlings to begin growing is artificial watering necessary. The plant is extremely hardy and the severest winter weather will not harm the foliage. A few leaves may be taken from each plant to be used as required.

Sowing Sow the seed in August, in shallow drills made 8 inches apart, thinning the plants to the same distance in the rows. They will produce their leaves through winter and if a second sowing is made mid-September, the plants will continue to provide 'greens' throughout springtime.

Making rapid growth, the plants may be picked over when they have formed their fourth leaf, the 'green' being delicious used with winter radishes and with hamburg parsley or celeriac grated raw.

At the end of winter, dig in any remaining leaves to provide humus.

Cucumber
Cucumis sativus

Where a cold frame or barn-type cloches are available, the frame cucumbers may be grown; where there is no glass then one may still enjoy summer cucumbers by growing those known as ridge cucumbers. These are the hardiest of all the forms, those for frames being also suitable for growing in a heated greenhouse. For flavour and tenderness the frame varieties are the equal of greenhouse cucumbers and as they are most prolific and easily grown they should be more widely cultivated. Even more delicious is the apple cucumber, which is so mild and tender that those who suffer after-effects from other varieties will suffer none from this unique variety. It is about this type that Parkinson says, 'in many countries they do eat cowcumbers as we do apples, paring them'. It was for that reason that these ball-like fruits came to be called apple cucumbers.

With all types of the cucumber we usually allow them, as we do most other vegetables, to grow too large before removing them. This not only greatly reduces the quality but also the cropping capacity of the plant. No member of the summer salad is more appreciated than those tender slices of the frame or apple cucumber, and their value is that they may be grown in a sunny corner of any back garden, taking up but little room in comparison with the size of the crop they yield. And how inexpensive they are compared with the greenhouse varieties so often offered soft and pulpy, or far too big.

Frame cucumbers These are prolific, and grown and marketed attractively will be the equal in appearance of greenhouse grown fruits, and have very much better flavour. If they have a disadvantage it is that being in frames through the summer, the plants will require detailed attention as to watering and ventilation. But the trouble is well worth while for they will continue to fruit until well into October—even in the north—and where one is away all day at some other occupation, then the care of the frames could be undertaken by the housewife. For this reason 4 feet by 4 feet frame lights should be used, so that a woman can easily handle them.

Though frame cucumbers may be grown quite cold in a well manured bed, growing over a gentle hot bed will result in an earlier crop and so give an additional month's fruiting. Cucumbers, like tomatoes are required as soon as the weather becomes warm and are more appreciated in July and August, than in September when we are thinking of warm food again. So use a hot bed wherever the compost can be obtained or artificially prepared.

Sowing The hot bed should be made up at the end of March, the compost being placed 18 inches deep in the frames and covered with 5–6 inches of soil. When the bed temperature has fallen to just below 80°F. the seed is sown. As cucumbers resent root disturbance, the seed is best sown where the plants are to grow rather than in small pots as for marrows. Where two, 5 feet × 4 feet lights are together, the frame will accommodate three plants, two seeds being sown close together in three parts of the frame, the strongest plant in each group being retained.

If no hot bed is being used, then the soil should

be thoroughly enriched to a depth of 6–8 inches with well decayed strawy manure. The seed is sown early in April and being slower to germinate owing to lack of bottom heat, the plants will bear fruit a month later. If two frames are available, it is better to delay planting the seed until early May so that the plants will be bearing their largest number of fruits when the hot bed plants have passed their peak.

After sowing the seed into soil made damp, cover with the lights and place sacking over them at night to retain as much heat as possible. Keep the frames closed to maintain a warm, damp atmosphere until the seed has germinated. The sacking should be placed over the lights each night until the end of May, for hard frosts are often experienced until that time. Should the temperature of the frame be falling due to the hot bed losing its heat, fresh compost should be placed round the frame boards to give additional warmth, especially at night. In the south this should not be necessary.

Keep the plants comfortably moist but not wet, and always use slightly warm water for spraying and watering. Until the end of May any damping down should be done before mid-day, so that the moisture will dry off the plants before the cooler temperature of night. But regular spraying must be done to keep down red spider; cucumbers must be given a humid atmosphere and a high degree of moisture at their roots. If the plants are kept too dry they will never be a success. Attention should be given to watering throughout the life of the crop.

General cultivation As the plants grow they should be trained about the frame, spacing out the shoots and carefully pegging them down so that each has room to develop. The laterals should be stopped at the second leaf, the sub-laterals being trained about the frame as they grow, and if the frame becomes too crowded, should be removed altogether. It is important to remove the fruits before they become too large for they will not only lose texture and flavour, but will crowd the frame, at the same time taking too much out of the plants.

As the plants make growth the soil should be kept quite moist which, during a sunny period may mean watering twice daily, also syringing the plants to guard against red spider. Ventilation now calls for attention as the early summer sunshine gathers strength. It is essential to keep as even a temperature in the frames as possible, so that the plants are not wilting in considerable heat by day and then having to endure greatly reduced temperatures at night. So ventilate freely whenever the day is warm. Hand pollination of the flowers is not necessary with cucumbers.

Before the frame becomes too full of plant growth it is advisable to give a light top dressing around the roots, using finely sifted loam to which has been added a small quantity of decayed manure. This will provide any surface roots with nourishment, and will act as a mulch in keeping the roots cool and moist. Some peat may also be added or used instead of the manure.

Watering with dilute liquid manure when the first fruits begin to form will result in a vigorous plant and in the ultimate formation of a large crop. As the fruits have a tendency to decay as they come into contact with the soil and they may also grow slightly mis-shapen, each fruit should be carefully placed on a flat piece of wood until it has matured and been removed. Glass is used for this purpose but tends to hold moisture, and the fruits may decay on the side next to the glass especially if the weather is dull and the fruits are slow to mature.

For exhibition the fruits must be fresh and pale green, straight, and of uniform thickness. Yellow crooked fruits with long necks are not required, and the same may be said for those fruits that are being marketed.

Growing under cloches Cucumbers do well under barn-type cloches. Ground the width of the glass should be well enriched with decayed manure to a depth of 12 inches. This should be done during March, the glass being placed in position for a full week before the seeds are sown at the end of April. They are best planted 4 feet apart. Planting in this way gives protection from stem rot. At all times the plants from the seedling stage should be kept well watered, a humid atmosphere being created exactly the same as when growing in frames.

The plants should be stopped at the fourth leaf, two laterals only being allowed to develop, which in turn should be stopped at the fifth leaf. A mulch of peat and soil, regular syringing during hot weather, and placing narrow pieces of wood beneath the fruit to mature, should be done during the life of the crop. If the plants should make too much foliage as the season advances, defoliation must be done with care and by degrees, so as not to upset the balance of the plant.

Varieties (frame)

'BUTCHER'S DISEASE RESISTING' Very hardy and of vigorous constitution. Possibly the best variety for the north.
'CONQUEROR' A splendid cucumber for a cold frame, long and even in shape with a handsome dark green skin. Does better when given hot-bed cultivation.
'EVERY DAY' A valuable variety in that it will set its fruits well even in a dull summer. The fruits have a smooth dark green skin and are of excellent flavour, whilst they are unsurpassed for exhibition.
'FEMINA' An F_1 hybrid, producing almost all-female flowers and so crops heavily and continuously. The smooth fruits are free from bitterness.
'LOCKIE'S PERFECTION' Not so well known as it should be. With its black spines this is a handsome cucumber, of richest flavour.
'ROCHFORD'S MARKET' Excellent for cold frame

culture. The fruit is large and extremely prolific and has a rough spiny skin.
'TOPNOTCH' An F_1 hybrid bearing a large crop of slender, dark green cucumbers. The skin is thin, the flesh white and of excellent mild flavour. Suitable for a greenhouse or frame, with or without heat.

Ridge cucumber Where there is neither frame nor cloches available, then the ridge cucumber should be grown, for it is hardy and in an average season will grow well in the north. No plant is more prolific, in fact where cultivations have been generous it will be necessary to look over the plants almost daily so quickly do the fruits form.

Select a sunny, open position but one where the plants may be given some protection from strong winds. In a walled garden they crop abundantly and are quite as richly flavoured as the frame varieties. On the balcony of a flat they may be grown and will prove most attractive with their handsome foliage. All that is required is a box filled with decayed manure and loam, the seed being germinated by covering the box with a sheet of clean glass.

This is also the method by which the seed is germinated outdoors; if no cloche is available construct a miniature frame with bricks, and cover with a sheet of glass. A miniature hot bed may also be made by removing 2 square feet of soil and filling this to a depth of 9 inches with prepared manure. This is covered with 3 inches of soil which is made level with the surrounding soil. Similar hot beds can be made at intervals of 4 feet keeping them in line to help with cultivations. Bricks are placed round each, two seeds sown, 1 inch deep, the weaker of the two plants being removed. All cucumbers resent transplanting and this is a better method than growing in pots. Simply set the seed where the plants are to fruit.

Should the garden be in any way exposed, the plants should be grown between ridges which will provide protection from cold winds, but the soil should be light and friable enabling excess moisture to drain away. Should water collect in the trenches, stem rot may result. Neither should planting be done on the top of the ridges, for in a dry summer the plants would seriously lack moisture.

The seed must not be sown before early May, for the plants should not be exposed to the elements before the beginning of June. In the south, sow a week earlier for there should be no fear of frost after the end of May.

When the plants have formed two or three leaves they should be stopped to encourage the formation of the lateral shoots which will carry the crop. No further restriction will be necessary, but to ensure a heavy crop give a mulch around the roots either of decayed lawn mowings, or with well rotted manure and never allow the plants to lack moisture, otherwise fruits will cease to form. During a dry period and where growing in a light soil, copius amounts of water will be required daily. If the plants are given this attention and the fruits are constantly removed before they become over-ripe, they will continue to bear well right into autumn.

Varieties

'BEDFORDSHIRE PRIZE RIDGE' Long fruited and a heavy cropper, it is very hardy and crops well in all soils.

'BURPEE HYBRID' An F_1 hybrid from America bearing handsome dark green fruits in great abundance and in all seasons. The skin is smooth and thin, the flesh crisp and white.

'HAMPSHIRE GIANT' A splendid hardy cucumber, the fruits are more than 12 inches long, the skin pale green, the flesh never coarse, even when left too long on the plants.

'KING OF THE RIDGE' A well grown plant will bear fruit up to 15 inches in length, almost free of spines and of exceptional flavour. Possibly not quite as hardy as 'Stockwood Ridge', but otherwise one of the best.

'STOCKWOOD RIDGE' Extremely hardy and prolific this variety bears long, well shaped fruits over an extended period.

'SUTTON'S PROLIFIC' Very hardy and of compact habit, making it popular for small gardens. The medium sized fruit possesses excellent flavour.

More hardy cucumbers of interest

'APPLE CUCUMBER' Of all cucumbers this, in the opinion of connoisseurs of good food, is the most delicious. It is listed by few seedsmen, and rarely found growing in any gardens. The fruits are like pale yellow apples, oval in shape and they should be gathered and used when they have reached the size of small apples, for the plants bear abundantly, and over a long period. Whilst the fruits possess the true refreshing cucumber flavour, they are much more juicy and yet the flesh is crisp.

'GHERKIN' This is a ridge cucumber which bears short, spiny fruits which if removed before they become too large, are excellent for pickling, no larder should, in fact, be without at least a few jars. They have very tender skin and are also delicious eaten fresh, especially if allowed to become slightly more mature.   The fruit is borne in profusion, and should be gathered every day or so when at the height of the season. The plants require the same conditions as for other ridge cucumbers, but where manure is scarce they will also crop abundantly if planted in friable soil, which has been well manured for a previous crop. Work in small quantities of manure and after giving the plants a mulch as the season advances, give frequent applications of manure water.

'JAPANESE CLIMBING' A valuable variety which may be classed somewhere between the frame and ridge type, and where space is strictly limited may be grown in an upright position, a trellis being ideal. Or it may be grown up wires against the side of a sunny wall. It is of the same hardiness as the other ridge cucumbers, and bears fruit about 9–10 inches long and of even thickness. The plants will continue to fruit as long as there is no frost, but where growing against a wall, it is imperative to give the foliage a daily syringe to guard against red spider. The roots will also require watering copiously every day, for there is little moisture beneath the eaves of a house. Frequent mulchings with strawy manure and lawn mowings will help to keep the roots moist.

'WEST INDIAN GHERKIN' I have not grown this interesting variety in the north so cannot be certain of its hardiness, but in the south it bears an abundance of prickly fruits, about the size of a half crown and possessing so rich a flavour that they should be used all the year round, either fresh or preserved. They should be given exactly the same culture as the ordinary ridge varieties.

'WHITE CUCUMBER' Possessing almost the same delicate flavour and juiciness of the 'apple cucumber', it is surprising that this excellent variety has never become popular. It makes a handsome decoration with red tomatoes and green salads, an adornment to any summer table. The fruits are equal to the best ridge varieties, long and evenly shaped, the skin being of a bright creamy-white colour. On the Continent they are greatly prized, and with the 'apple cucumber' are eaten to the almost complete exclusion of the green varieties. For marketing they have never been popular but might be tried again on a small scale. As with all vegetables, size is the criterion of a good vegetable with the British public, and so these delicately flavoured cucumbers remain in obscurity. For those who suffer from indigestion, this is the cucumber to eat. In fact the flavour is so delicate and the flesh so juicy that this variety is always the choice of discerning salad eaters, even where the other types are also available.

The habit of the plant being more compact than for other ridge cucumbers, this is an excellent variety for a small garden. The plants should be given exactly the same treatment and culture as for the ordinary ridge varieties, but it is noticeable that the 'white cucumber' is happier in a cold frame in the north where it should be given hot bed or cold frame treatment. In the south it is perfectly hardy and quick to mature, but the plant is sufficiently accommodating to adapt itself to both frame and open ground culture. The fruits are peeled and cut into slices, but to preserve the crisp, juiciness, serve the fruits whole, to be cut the moment they are eaten with salad. Or peel and stew, and serve with white sauce.

Greenhouse culture Cucumbers are grown up the greenhouse roof and though heat is necessary for an early crop, tulips or French beans may be forced on the bench at the same time. To have the crop reaching maturity early in June with the arrival of warm weather, seed must be sown, one to a 3-inch pot, early in the year. But this means employing a minimum temperature of 68°F.

during the coldest weather.

The sowing compost should be made up of 2 parts fibrous loam, 1 part each peat and sand and to each barrowful of the mixture 2 ounces of super-phosphate of lime to encourage root action. Plant the seed 1 inch deep on its side. Water thoroughly and raise the temperature to 75°F. to hasten germination. Covering the pots with glass or plastic sheeting will also help with germination. In 3 weeks, the seedlings should be large enough to move to 60 size pots containing a compost made up of fibrous loam, peat, decayed manure and sand in equal parts by bulk. Do not make the compost too compact. Reduce the temperature to 70°F. and keep the compost comfortably moist. By mid-March, move to larger pots in which the plants will fruit and into a similar compost. As the plants make growth, fasten to wires stretched across the greenhouse roof at intervals of 9 inches and maintain a moist atmosphere by frequent syringing and damping down. It may not be necessary to admit ventilation until the fruits have formed and then only on mild days. Allow the main stem to grow up the roof but 'stop' the laterals at the second leaf, also any sub-laterals. It is here that the fruits are formed, any flowers being removed from the main stem. Give a top dressing of decayed manure or feed with liquid manure from early June, once every 3 weeks.

Varieties

'BURPLESS GREEN KING'   Raised by Sakata & Co, it should be grown by all who find cucumbers acid and difficult to digest. The fruits grow long and slender and should be picked when young and tender when they may be eaten in the hand, like celery. It is resistant to Powdery Mildew, Bacterial Wilt and Mosaic.
'PEPIMEX'   An F_1 hybrid, this bears a heavy crop of dark green fruits of medium size: it is highly resistant to Spot disease. The fruit is of mildest flavour and the long straight shape of it is an additional selling point.
'SIMEX'   An F_1 hybrid and like 'Femina', bears few male flowers and so crops heavily. Highly resistant to Spot disease, the fruit has a mild flavour and thin skin.
'TELEGRAPH'   For years, one of the most widely grown of all for it crops heavily, the fruits being deep green and even in size and shape.

Pests and Diseases

GUMMOSIS   The fungus causes grey spots on the leaves which burst open whilst they may also occur on the fruits when they will exude a gummy liquid. It occurs mostly in dull wet seasons but may be kept under control by dusting the plants regularly with flowers of sulphur. Soil which has grown infected plants should be treated with formalin (1 part to 100 of water) about a month before planting.
LEAF BLOTCH   Small pale green spots appear on the upper surfaces of the leaves. They continually increase in size and later turn grey and then brown before falling away to leave holes in the leaves. The fruits may also be attacked. Infected leaves should be removed and burnt whilst spraying with liver of sulphur solution should give control.
POWDERY MILDEW   This may attack plants growing under glass where there is insufficient ventilation. It is recognised by the white mildew-like growth on the leaves and shoot tips. There are now resistant varieties but to control, spray with Shirlan to which is added the spreader Agral N.
ROOT-KNOT EELWORM   The pests attack the roots and in a severe attack will devour them entirely, causing the plant to collapse. There is no cure but raising the young plants in sterilised compost will usually prevent a serious outbreak.

Dandelion
Taraxacum officinale

For long a favourite summer vegetable of the cottage gardener for its leaves, eaten raw in a salad are both tasty and nourishing. The roots, which should be lifted in autumn for this purpose, can also be roasted and ground to make 'dandelion coffee'— said to be indistinguishable from the real thing. It is perennial and comes into leaf in spring, before lettuce is ready. It is also little troubled by pest or disease. It requires a rich soil, containing some decayed manure or old mushroom bed compost for the richer the soil the more tender will be the leaves.

Seed of the thick-leaved variety is sown early in April in semi-shade. A position where little else will grow is suitable. It is usual to sow in clumps or circles of about 18 inches diameter and 5 or 6 plants are allowed to remain in each. The following year after they are established, the plants are covered with a rhubarb forcing pot or with a box which is put into place as soon as the plants begin to make leaf. After about 10 days, the leaves will be completely blanched. They are then removed and used in salads whilst other plants are covered to maintain the supply. No blanching should be done after mid-June to allow the plants to recover; they will be assisted in this if given a thick mulch.

Endive
Cichorium endivia

Native of the Mediterranean regions and the Near East, this has been used as a salad crop since earliest times. It is mentioned by Ovid and may have been introduced into Britain by the Romans. Either cooked or eaten raw it has a most delicate flavour and, where grown well, a crispness which is unusual with summer salad crops.

Endive grows best where it is to mature for it will run to seed quickly if transplanted and also if

Endive there is not sufficient humus in the soil to retain summer moisture. If manure is scarce, dig in some hop manure, peat or decayed leaves, or garden compost for it demands a cool, moist soil which does not dry out quickly in hot weather. For this reason, a heavy soil lightened with humus, produces better endive than does a light soil.

Sowing It is not advisable to sow the seed before July 1st for the plants will mature better in the cooler conditions of early autumn whilst July is often a month of wet weather which enables the plants to start well.

Sow thinly, in shallow drills made 15 inches apart and when large enough, thin out the seedlings to 10 inches. If possible, select a position in semi-shade or ground facing north or east for, though native of the warmer parts, endive prefers cool conditions.

General cultivation Water whenever the ground is dry and, early in August, give the plants a weekly application of dilute liquid manure which will greatly improve the quality. If a second sowing is made late in July and the plants covered with barn cloches about mid–October, it will be possible to enjoy endive until Christmas for the plants will withstand several degrees of frost. If straw is placed around the cloches, the plants will withstand more prolonged frost.

Blanching is the most important part of its culture. Raffia is tied around the top of the plants as soon as they reach maturity. This should be done when the plants are quite dry. The tying must be done carefully, so as not to cut through the succulent leaves. After 3 weeks, the plants will be blanched and crisp at the centre, a mass of curled leaf and in perfect condition for an autumn salad. After blanching, the acrid flavour departs and the foliage becomes sweet and tender.

Varieties
'BATAVIAN WHITE' The best flavoured of all endives, making a large full heart of heavily curled leaves which are crisp and tender.
'GIANT FRINGED OYSTER' This makes a large head 15 inches across, filled with rich green lacinated leaves which blanch to creamy white at the centre.

Finocchio
Foeniculum vulgare var. *dulce*

A native of Italy, also known as Florence Fennel, this is a quick growing annual, the swollen stem base being used as a vegetable, either raw in a salad or boiled. The leaves which have an aniseed flavour may be used in soups and stews.

Seed is sown in early spring, thinning out the young plants to 12 inches apart. They must never lack moisture and grow best in a soil containing plenty of humus and a little decayed manure. Water heavily in dry weather and as the oval leaf-

bases begin to grow, they should be blanched by lightly earthing up.

When ready, remove and cook the basal stems as for celery, either stewing or steaming and serve with a favourite sauce.

Garlic
Allium sativum

The ancient Egyptians held garlic in as great esteem as the onion, whilst the conquering armies of ancient Rome were supported by its health-giving properties and probably introduced it into Britain. Although it is rich in alkaline salts and in the blood purifying sulphur compounds, garlic has fallen from favour in Britain but in Europe is considered indispensable to add piquancy to many dishes.

Native of the near east, the plant requires a light soil and a position of full sun. A soil which has been manured for a previous crop will be suitable. The cloves, as the offsets are called, are planted either late in October or in March. They are separated from the bulbs and planted in drills 2 inches deep, spacing them 6 inches apart and allowing 12 inches between the rows. The soil should be in a loose condition, this being one of the few plants requiring such a soil.

Cloves planted in October will be ready to lift early the following August or a month earlier if required; those planted in March will be ready in October. They are lifted as soon as the leaves turn yellow, the bulbs being dried in an open shed. They are then strung together and hung up in a dry, frost-free room for use when required.

Good king henry
Chenopodium bonus-henricus

A British native plant, also known as Mercury or Wild Spinach, grown in cottage gardens since a very early stage in our history. A perennial, it grows 2 feet tall with long-stemmed arrow-shaped leaves, waved at the edges and frosted on the underside.

A rich soil will produce juicy young shoots and seed is sown in April in shallow drills. Transplant the seedlings when large enough to handle, spacing them 12 inches apart; or established plants may be lifted and divided in spring when growth commences.

From May until the end of June the young shoots are cut and boiled and served with butter and make a pleasant alternative to asparagus. Earthing up the young shoots will bring about blanching at the base and increase their tenderness. The shoots are cut when 5–6 inches long. Later, the shoots which resemble kale may be removed and cooked in the same way.

If established plants are mulched in autumn, they will begin to make new growth early in spring and if divided in alternate years will be a valuable addition to the vegetable garden.

Hamburg parsley
Petroselinum crispum var. tuberosum

This interesting vegetable, though widely grown in continental Europe, has never really caught on either in Britain or in the United States. It is indeed a parsley as its name suggests, but it is not for the leaves that it is grown but for its turnip-like root hence its alternative common name, 'Turnip-rooted Parsley'. The roots grow more than 6 inches long and are about 2 inches thick at the neck. They have a parsley-like flavour when used raw or grated in salads, but a flavour more like celeriac when cooked.

Plants are grown in the manner of parsnips and the seedlings transplant more readily than those of any other root crop. They require a long growing season and seed is sown mid-March, in ground previously manured for another crop. Bring the soil to a fine tilth and sow in drills 1 inch deep, in rows 15 inches apart. Thin out the seedlings to 9 inches apart. A second sowing should be made in June to mature early the following spring. Keep the hoe moving between the rows and the plants watered during dry weather.

The roots will be ready to lift at the end of October and may be used throughout winter and spring. When lifting, insert the fork deeply down so that the ends of the roots are not broken.

Kohl-rabi
Brassica oleracea

This may be said to resemble a cross between a turnip and a swede, though it is really a swollen-stemmed cabbage. Abercrombie in the 'Gardener's Dictionary' called it the 'Turnip Cabbage'. It forms a large turnip-like globe on the stem, several inches above soil level and if used when about 3 inches across has a mild, sweet turnip-like flavour. It grows quickly, the 'globes' being ready to use within 10 weeks of sowing.

Kohl-rabi requires a light, sandy soil, enriched with some decayed manure. Old mushroom bed compost is ideal, whilst any materials which will enable the soil to retain moisture should be dug in.

Sowing Make the first sowing early in April, in drills made 15 inches apart and thin out to 9 inches in the rows. Sowings may be made once each month from April until early July so that the early 'globes' can be used when small whilst those from later sowings may be left to stand over winter.

Do not peel them, merely trim off the roots and remove the leaves; then cook as for turnips or swedes. They should never be allowed to grow too large or coarse.

This is a plant which is never troubled by hot,

dry conditions and when the turnip is often fibrous and unpleasant, the kohl-rabi retains its delicate and agreeable flavour. It requires no special care in its culture and is troubled neither by pest nor disease.

So quickly does it mature that an early crop may be obtained by sowing in March over a mild hot-bed in a frame when the 'globes' will be ready to cut before the end of May, when fresh vegetables are usually scarce.

Exhibiting Fresh, tender, small-leaved 'globes' are required, about tennis-ball size and free from blemishes. If the leaves are large and the 'globes' more than 4 inches in diameter, they will often be coarse and will by then have lost quality. It is also important that the skins are without cracks.

Varieties
'EARLY PURPLE VIENNA' This takes slightly longer to mature than 'Early White' and stands better over winter. The 'globes' have a purple skin whilst the flesh is greensih-white, being tender and mild of flavour.
'EARLY WHITE VIENNA' Quick to mature, this variety has a smooth pale green skin and a creamy white flesh which is sweet and mild.

Leek
Allium ampeloprasum var. porrum

Native of Southern Europe and the Near East, the leek is believed to have been introduced into Britain by the Romans and is mentioned in Saxon writings as being a most valuable food. To the Egyptians it was almost a sacred plant and all bulbous plants were given the same name in its honour. It was a plant of the humble cottager and has remained so, especially in the north for it is tolerant of extreme cold.

To grow leeks well, the soil should be trenched and heavy soils should be lightened by incorporating some peat or garden compost and a quantity of grit or boiler ash. Excessive manuring is not desirable and leeks are best planted in ground which has been manured for a previous crop.

Where trenching, remove the soil to the width of a spade and 10 inches deep and at the bottom place some garden compost. This is covered with friable soil in good 'heart' into which some peat has been incorporated, together with 1 ounce per square yard of superphosphate and a half ounce of sulphate of potash. An idea is to throw up the soil on both sides of the trench so that the fertilisers may be added to the soil on one side which is replaced, whilst the soil on the other side is used for blanching the leeks as they grow.

Sowing Seed is sown about mid-March in shallow drills and covered with cloches to hasten germination, or sow in frames for the leek requires a long growing season to produce a large succulent 'stick'. Keep the seed moist when it will soon germinate and the plants will be ready to set out before the end of June. This is essential if large 'sticks' are to be obtained.

When planting, make a hole 6 inches deep with a dibber, into which the plants are dropped. Do not fill in the hole with soil but when planting is complete, water well in. A double row should be made in the trench, planting 9 inches apart and staggering the plants with the rows about 6 inches from each other. When planting, allow the wide part of the leaf, the blade, to fall along the row rather than across it.

Like celery, leeks are lovers of moisture and must be kept well provided with it. If lacking, the leeks will remain small and will be tough and woody after cooking, being almost uneatable.

Blanching Early in August, corrugated paper held in place with a rubber band is placed around the lower part of the plant. This will help to 'draw' it and at the same time will blanch the stem. From then onwards as the plants make growth, the soil thrown up on one side of the trench is placed around the plants to complete the blanching. As with celery, this earthing up must be done with care so that the soil does not enter the folds of the leaves.

Feeding with a weak solution of dried blood or liquid manure during autumn will help to build up large, succulent 'sticks' which will catch the judges' eye on the show bench.

An additional help to forming a large, well blanched 'stick' is to clip back the large leaves to half their length, at regular intervals from the time the plants are set out. If not done, the plants will form excess leaf at the expense of stem which is the edible part. The plants will continue to grow until mid-November when the first liftings are made with a fork and the soil washed away. Further liftings will take place during winter when required for no matter how severe the weather, the plants will suffer no harm.

Exhibiting To grow the finest 'sticks', the seed may be sown in gentle heat or over a mild hot bed, in February. When 3 inches high, the plants are moved to small pots containing John Innes potting compost and kept growing in a frame during spring when, after hardening, the plants are set out into trenches, planting them with the stems well into the soil. Before planting out, remove the leaf tips to encourage stem formation and begin the blanching, as described, at an early date.

When exhibiting, it is usual to allow the white roots to remain though shortening them if unduly long. The stem and roots are washed clean of soil and the green top leaves tied back with raffia. The blanched part should be covered with brown paper to exclude light or the stems will begin to take on a green tinge which will spoil their appearance. They should be at least 6 inches in circumference, solid

and well blanched, of uniform thickness top to bottom with the blanched portion 12–14 inches long. There should be no tendency to bulbing at the base whilst the skins should be clean and unblemished.

Pests and Diseases

EELWORM Many bulbous plants are attacked by this pest, a nematode which lays its eggs in the bulbous root, the young, upon hatching, feeding on the living cells and causing the leaves to turn yellow. If an attack has been noticed on plants previously occupying the same ground, treat the soil with Jeyes Fluid (2 tablespoons to a gallon of water) several weeks before the leeks are planted. As a protection against seed-borne eelworm, most seedsmen fumigate the seed with methyl bromide before packeting.

WHITE TIP A fungus which attacks the leaf tips, causing them to turn yellow, then white with the leaf finally entering a state of decay when the plants will fall over at soil level. If caught in time, the disease will be arrested by spraying the plants with weak Burgundy mixture or with a copper fungicide applied as a dust.

Varieties

'CLANDON WHITE' An early leek, producing large 'sticks' in autumn from a February sowing. The foliage is dark green, the stems of great length and of sweet, mild flavour.

'EVEREST' Outstanding for exhibition, the solid white stems may be blanched for 15 inches yet remain succulent and mild of flavour.

'MARBLE PILLAR' This produces the longest blanched stem of any variety and is ideal for exhibition, being pure white when blanched and of mild sweet flavour.

'MUSSELBRUGH' One of the hardiest of leeks, bearing large thick stems which may be blanched to 14 inches.

'ROYAL FAVOURITE' Raised at the Royal Gardens, Windsor this is an early variety of mildest flavour with dark foliage and long, milky-white stems.

'THE LYON' An old exhibition favourite, producing solid, thick stems free from any coarseness and with large dark green leaves.

'YATE'S EMPIRE' A late variety which will stand until April, the leaf blades broad and dark green, the stems long, thick and sturdy, snow-white when blanched.

Lettuce
Lactuca sativa

This is one of the most rewarding of all crops, whether grown for home use or for the market, for it is the backbone of salads throughout the year, and a continuous supply of crisp, home-grown lettuce is one of the gardener's greatest delights.

More than almost any other crop it requires a well nourished soil enriched with plenty of decayed manure. Old mushroom bed compost is especially suitable or used hops obtainable from a brewery and as much humus as can be obtained should be dug into the soil which must be retentive of summer moisture to grow good lettuce.

Equally important is a well limed soil for one of an acid nature, however slight will, in damp weather, cause the plants to grow limp and slimy. If peat is used, and it is an excellent provider of humus: take a soil test and if it shows an acid reaction, give additional lime.

Those who possess a cold frame or cloches will be able to have an all the year round supply, the seed being sown at frequent intervals. By using a small part of a frame in which the seed is sown broadcast, or by sowing in shallow drills under cloches in autumn, a spring and early summer crop may be enjoyed. By sowing in the open from spring until early autumn, lettuce may be cut from mid-summer until Christmas whilst in the more favourable parts, unprotected sowings can be made in the open to provide an all the year round supply.

Sowing The seed is sown in a prepared seed bed and the young plants are moved to where they are to mature, as soon as large enough to handle. If a sowing is made outdoors in March, the plants will have hearted by the beginning of June when the usually warm weather brings with it a greater demand for salads.

The secret of growing good lettuce is to keep the plants on the move by giving them a well prepared soil, yet they must always be grown 'hard' otherwise they will readily fall a victim to mildew. Artificial fertilisers should not be used, apart from sulphate of potash which will encourage the plants to grow 'hard'. At planting time, 2 ounces per square yard should be raked into the soil.

If possible, transplanting should be done in showery weather for the plants may not recover if moved when the ground is dry. The seedlings should be moved early, before they form a tap root but if transplanting is delayed, cut off the tap root before replanting. The plants will heart more quickly if this is done.

Plant on the flat, spacing out to the requirements of each variety for some grow dwarf and compact, whilst others such as 'Webb's Wonderful', make hearts 18 inches across. They may be set out between rows of dwarf peas or beans, or inter-cropped with late maturing 'greens' such as cauli-flower or cabbage so as to make full use of the ground.

So that the plants do not run to seed before they can be used, begin cutting the heads when they start to form hearts and to keep them crisp, place them in a refrigerator for an hour before use. If this is not possible do not cut off the heads but pull the plants from the soil, shake away the soil and place the roots in a bowl of cold water until required.

Growing under glass For a winter crop, sow the seed early in September and transplant to a frame in October. If the frame soil is heated by cables or if the plants are to be grown over a hot bed, they will quickly grow and heart up and will have made sizeable plants for cutting by the year end. The soil should be friable but not too rich in nitro-genous manure otherwise the plants will be liable to suffer from mildew. Keep the soil on the dry side, giving only sufficient moisture to maintain plant growth. Plant 8 inches apart and to guard against mildew and dust the plants with flowers of sulphur once each fortnight until they begin to heart.

If the frame is heated, ventilate on all suitable days but where the plants are grown cold, the minimum of ventilation (and moisture) should be permitted. During periods of hard frost, cover the lights at night with canvas or sacking which is removed during the day unless the weather is especially severe. Where growing in a Dutch-light house, the plants will require similar culture and where grown cold, they will not be ready to cut until March.

A frame may be used to protect the plants during winter. They should then be moved to the open ground in March after hardening. From a sowing made early in October, plant the seedlings 2 inches apart in the frame, ventilate on all suitable occasions and keep the plants dry. If planted out towards the end of March, the frame may be used for tomatoes or marrows whilst the lettuce will be ready to cut early in May.

The introduction of 'Cheshunt Early Giant' in 1932 revolutionised the forcing of lettuce in glass-houses for it was the first to heart well in the short days and low light intensity of wintertime in the British Isles.

The plants are set out into prepared beds from late September until the year end to maintain a succession. In a temperature of 50°F., which should be kept as constant as possible, plants set out on October 1st should be ready to cut on January 1st which is when the demand for winter salads really begins. Plant 16 inches apart, in rows 6 inches apart and stagger the plants so that the maximum number may be planted in a given area. The plants should be given sufficient moisture to keep them growing and to prevent the leaves from becoming limp and lying on the soil. Ventilate freely, so long as the temperature does not fall below 45°F.

Exhibiting The two outstanding exhibition varieties are 'Webb's Wonderful' in cabbage lettuce and 'Giant Perfection' in cos lettuce for not only do they grow large but they retain their freshness longer then any other varieties. Lift the plants as near as possible to the time of showing, shake away the soil and around each wrap damp tissue paper. Around the roots tie damp moss which will help to maintain their freshness. At the show ground, cut off the roots and sprinkle the heads with water to keep them fresh.

Lettuce

The modern cos lettuce is self-blanching or self-folding and there is no need to tie the heads with raffia as of old in order to induce them to form a solid heart.

Pests and Diseases

BOTRYTIS   This appears on the leaves as a grey mould causing them to decay and is most prevalent amongst plants growing under glass and during damp, humid summers. Dusting young plants with Orthocide Captan dust will normally prevent an outbreak.

DOWNY MILDEW   This mostly attacks plants growing in frames or under cloches, appearing as a white powder on the underside of the leaves. There are a number of resistant lettuce varieties, but an outbreak may be prevented by dusting plants growing under glass with a mixture of equal parts lime and sulphur.

MILLEPEDE   This is the most troublesome of lettuce pests, attacking the roots of young plants causing them to wilt. The pest is almost black in colour and moves slowly. When touched, it rolls itself up into a ball. It may be exterminated by treating the soil with Aldrin dust or Gammexane at the rate of 1 ounce per square yard when the beds are prepared.

MOSAIC   This is a virus transmitted by lettuce seed and almost all reputable seedsmen now sell only mosaic-tested seed which is guaranteed to contain less than one infected in every thousand. The first symptom is for the leaf veins to appear more prominent, then the leaf becomes yellow and brown at the edges. There is no known cure and infected plants should be destroyed.

RING SPOT   A fungus which also attacks the endive and which is prevalent in damp, humid summers. It attacks first the stem, then the underside of the midribs and appears as light brown spots. Later, the leaf tissue is attacked and falls away, leaving numerous tiny holes. There is no cure when once the plants are infected but seed steeped for 6 hours in bleaching powder mixed with 10 times its weight of water and dried before sowing will give control.

ROOT APHIS   This attacks the roots of plants both under glass and outdoors, causing the leaves to turn yellow and the plants to wilt. It may be prevented or exterminated by watering the soil before planting or later, if proving troublesome, with Lindex solution.

Varieties for succession   For winter and early spring (Outdoors):

'ARCTIC KING'   For autumn sowing, a cabbage lettuce forming a large solid head with few outer leaves.

'SUTTON'S IMPERIAL'   This variety should be sown only in autumn to mature outdoors in spring in those parts enjoying a mild winter climate. A cabbage variety, it forms a large succulent head.

'WINTER DENSITY'   The best cos for autumn sowing, making a large dark green head with a good heart.

'WINTER MARVEL'   Sow in autumn and in spring the large cabbage-like heads will be filled with wavy wax-like leaves which make delicious eating. For winter and early spring (under glass):

'CHESHUNT EARLY GIANT'   For a warm frame or for glasshouse culture, it is the best for mid-winter cutting and makes a medium-sized heart which is crisp and mild.

'SPRING MARKET'   An Asmer introduction which may be allowed to mature in a cold frame or can be planted out in March to cut in May. It makes a large solid heart with the minimum of outer leaf.

'SUZAN'   One of the best for frame culture, this variety matures early and makes a large dense heart with crisp outer leaves of emerald green.

'TOM THUMB'   An excellent lettuce for a cold frame or cloche culture: may be sown all the year round. The hearts are of cricket ball size, sweet and succulent.

'TROCADERO'   An outstanding frame lettuce of medium size, its outer leaves being free from any red tinge, its heart golden yellow and extremely brittle.

For spring and summer sowing (outdoors):

'AVON CRISPY'   Resistant to Downy Mildew, this makes a medium-sized solid heart of emerald green which stands well in hot weather.

'BUTTERCRUNCH'   A cos though with something of the cabbage varieties, the leaves being olive green, the heart crisp and succulent and never becomes bitter.

'CONSTANT HEART'   Excellent for successional sowing from spring until late summer. It hearts well in all weathers, forming a large solid head of brilliant green.

'HISTON CRISPIE'   A cos lettuce of excellent qualities and attractive appearance, with pale green crinkled leaves, firmly folding into a large heart of delicious flavour.

'SALAD BOWL'   A richly flavoured American lettuce of endive type, forming a large flat rosette of crinkled fern-like leaves which remain crisp in the hottest weather.

'SIMPSON'S LOOSEHEAD'   Neither a cos nor a cabbage, forming masses of loose cos-like leaves within six weeks of sowing. The broad light green leaves are frilled and crumpled and may be removed as required.

'SUGAR COS'   May be said to be a cross between a cabbage and a cos and is outstanding in every way, forming an erect head of medium size which hearts well and which, for its rich sweet flavour, has no equal.

'WEBB'S WONDERFUL'   The finest summer lettuce ever introduced, highly resistant to disease, the enormous hearts remaining crisp and succulent through the hottest weather whilst it does not easily run to seed.

Marrows, Pumpkins and Squashes
Cucurbita spp

These terms are all fairly much interchangeable, for the marrows, pumpkins and summer squashes are all varieties of *Cucurbita pepo*. The winter squashes, however, are varieties of *Cucurbita maxima,* while the Cushaw pumpkin is *Cucurbita mixta*. The last, while popular in the United States is not a success in Britain, taking too long to mature.

Marrows should be planted in full sun and where they may be sheltered from cold winds. They resent root disturbance, so must be grown in pots from the beginning. One method is to raise the plants over a hot bed made in a frame and sowing the seed at the end of March. Over the compost is placed 3 inches of fine soil and into this is pressed 2½-inch pots touching each other. The pots are filled with John Innes sowing compost, in which peat is substituted by well decayed manure, old mushroom bed compost being ideal.

The seeds are pressed into the compost, their pointed end towards the top and just covered with the compost. The pots are given a thorough soaking and the frames are kept closed until germination has taken place, watering whenever necessary. To prevent the pots drying out too quickly, damp peat may be pressed around them as they are placed in the frame. During the first 3 weeks of April the frames should be covered with sacking at night if frost is expected.

Early in May, when the plants have formed their second pair of leaves, they will be ready for removal to a cold frame for hardening. This is done by first leaving off the glass during the day-time, then gradually at night, so that by the month end the plants will be ready for planting out.

Soil preparation When manure was plentiful, one would plant marrows on mountains of compost, and how well they grew. Today these mountains have been reduced to minute hillocks and the plants make little headway, especially in a warm, dry summer which should suit them well. The reason is not that they lack nourishment but moisture, these little mounds drying out too readily which is fatal to the marrow, for it requires plenty of moisture about its roots.

With the shortage of compost, it is better to plant on the flat, into a soil containing plenty of humus—some decayed manure, peat, spent hops, even decayed leaves or bark fibre being incorporated. If the soil is heavy or the ground low lying then make a raised bed, but work in the same quantity of humus.

Set out the plants at the end of May allowing 3–4 feet for the bush varieties, and 5–6 feet for the trailers. Where growing under barn cloches (and this is an excellent crop to grow under glass) make the beds to fit the cloches and plant out early in May. The glass may be removed mid-June, when the plants will have made considerable growth.

If no frame is available, the plants may be grown entirely under cloches and, though the crop will not be so early to mature, it will prove much earlier than where the seed is sown in the open. Plants sown over a hot-bed will be showing fruit before seedlings raised in the open have made their second leaves.

Those able to obtain manure could raise an early crop by making up a hot-bed in the open early in April, covering with 6 inches of soil and sowing the seed under a barn cloche, covering the ends with glass to retain the warmth.

Plant firmly and press the small pot into the soil about 2 inches from the plant, water being given through the pot when required. Before knocking the plant from the pot, first give it a thorough watering to bind the roots so that there is almost no root disturbance.

When the plants have made about 18 inches of growth, pinch out the leader shoots to encourage the formation of side shoots, and to ensure a heavy crop which will set well. Under glass, give daily syringing to flowers and foliage whenever the weather is warm, and those growing in the open should be kept free from weeds and heavily watered during dry weather. A mulch of peat and decayed strawy manure will be appreciated, so will regular watering with liquid manure from the time the first fruits form. This will be about July 1st from early sown seed in the south; 3 to 4 weeks later in the north.

The fruits should always be removed when they have attained a reasonable size: to allow them to remain on the plants until they have become too large will not only reduce the quality but will also reduce the crop. Removing the fruits quickly will enable others to form.

Care must be taken in removing the fruits or the plants may be damaged. Cut away the marrow where it lies rather than lifting it first, for this will disturb the plant. At the same time carefully remove and dead foliage. The fruits should be handled carefully so as not to cause bruising.

Pollinating This is in many instances done by insects, especially during dry, sunny periods but more so in the south than the north. However, the plants will begin to fruit earlier and bear heavier crops with artificial pollination.

This may take place in two ways, either by dusting the male flowers and transferring the pollen to those of the female, or by removing the male flower entirely, folding back its petals and pressing it into the female flower. This should be done only on a dry day, when the pollen is dry, and only when the flowers are open and the pollen ripe. Plants growing under glass will benefit most by this artificial pollination.

No difficulty should be experienced in telling which flower is the male and which the female, for the latter has a tiny marrow-like swelling of the

75

stem immediately beneath the flower. The male is without this swelling.

Pests and Diseases

MILDEW This also attacks cucumbers growing outdoors and appears as a white powdery mildew on the underside of the leaves. If unchecked, the foliage will turn brown and fall off. Routine spraying with weak Bordeaux Mixture will prevent an outbreak; or spray with liver of sulphur (1 ounce to 3 gallons of water). The disease may be encouraged by dryness at the roots.

Varieties

'AVOCADELLA' This is a summer marrow of bush habit bearing at the centre of the plant small fruits about the size of a large orange but deep green in colour. The fruits ripen early September. It is also known as the Argentine Marrow, and is popular in that country served cold, as it should be. A delicious way of serving it is to boil for half an hour, then allow to become quite cold, cutting the marrow in two, removing the pulp and placing in a refrigerator for an hour. Remove half an hour before using and fill the centre with whipped cream. Add sugar and a little oil and eat with a spoon. The flesh is pale pink.

Northern gardeners are advised to grow this marrow under barn cloches or in a frame, watering and ventilating liberally. It is a good winter keeper.

'BANANA ORANGE' Of trailing habit and though not one of the easiest to grow, it should be attempted in all gardens for the fruit will keep well into winter. The rich orange coloured flesh is firm and sweet with the attractive flavour of ripe bananas, though it is from its long, slightly curved marrows that it takes its name.

'BOSTON PIE PUMPKIN' This is the old American pumpkin pie marrow, with orange skin and flesh, the fruits often weighing up to 8 pounds. It is also known as the Sugar Pumpkin on account of its sweetness. It is of trailing habit and like most of the winter-keeping squashes and marrows, the fruits are never at their best until late autumn, when the 'keepers' should first be used, served with eggs, onions and other winter vegetables. The 'Hubbard Squash' is almost identical except that its skin is deep green.

'BUTTERNUT' Of trailing habit this is one of the most delicious of marrows. It keeps well into winter, the fine-textured flesh being at its best when baked. The fruits attain a length of 12 inches and are as thick as one's forearm.

'CASSERTA' A grand marrow of the bush type and where the plants have been raised early it will come into bearing mid-July in the south being first of them all, yet it will continue to bear right through summer. Remove the fruits when quite small, cook for an hour and serve cold, or hot filled with one of the suggested French (dwarf) beans which have also been cooked. Serve with mayonnaise if cold; with white sauce if hot.

'COCOZELLE' The Italian marrow. This is a semi-trailing variety, to be eaten during August. Removed from the plant when 9 inches long, it is delicious filled with peeled tomatoes, after cooking and cooling and served cold with salad oil or mayonnaise. Dark green with yellow stripes, the marrows will reach 2 feet in length but will be past their best for eating if allowed to grow so large.

'GOLDEN DELICIOUS' A trailing variety bearing large globular marrows of deep orange with bright yellow fibreless flesh. It is a good winter keeper.

'GOLD NUGGET' An American introduction, each plant bears 6–8 marrows of deep golden yellow striped with white and of the size of a large orange. They make for delicious eating and store well. It is a bush marrow of compact habit.

'LITTLE GEM' A South African marrow of trailing habit and bearing small dark green fruits of orange size and shape. Cook young, whilst still green, cut into halves and scoop out the succulent flesh.

'MOORE'S CREAM' Of trailing habit it may be used through autumn and if carefully stored will keep well into winter. The fruits are small, oval and pale cream and are delicious baked in the skin which should be oiled, then with the pulp and seeds removed, it should be filled with cooked tomatoes, beans and mushrooms, being re-heated in its skin and served hot.

'ROTHERSIDE ORANGE' A richly flavoured little marrow, bearing fruits the size of a large grapefruit and of the same colour. It is a trailer for summer use and is almost like a melon. It should be cooked, then cooled in a refrigerator and served with sugar or ginger. Add cream or oil to suit one's taste.

'ROYAL ACORN' This variety will store well and makes an appetising meal around Christmas time. It forms a long fruit, though small in comparison with the ordinary vegetable marrow, the flesh remaining thick and firm in storage. It is of trailing habit, but where space is limited there is a bush form, which also keeps well and has a firm, sweet flesh.

'SOUTH AFRICAN MARROW' Similar to 'Avocadella' but easier to grow in the north. It makes a neat plant though of trailing habit, the fruits ripening to the size of a large orange and of the same colour. Though ready for use towards the end of August, the fruits will keep well into winter.

'SUMMER CROOKNECK' Of a bright yellow colour with pale cream coloured flesh, this American squash is more delicious than its name suggests. The fruits should be removed when 9–10 inches long. The flesh remains tender and sweet even if the marrows attain a weight of 3 pounds or more. It is of semi-trailing habit.

'SUTTON'S SUPERLATIVE' A bush marrow, tender and delicious. The fruits are of bottle-green colour, the flesh deep orange and sweet. Though it will grow to exhibition size, the fruits should be used when quite small.

'TABLE DAINTY' One of the earliest marrows to fruit, it is most prolific. The fruits are small, deep green, striped with a paler green. It is a summer

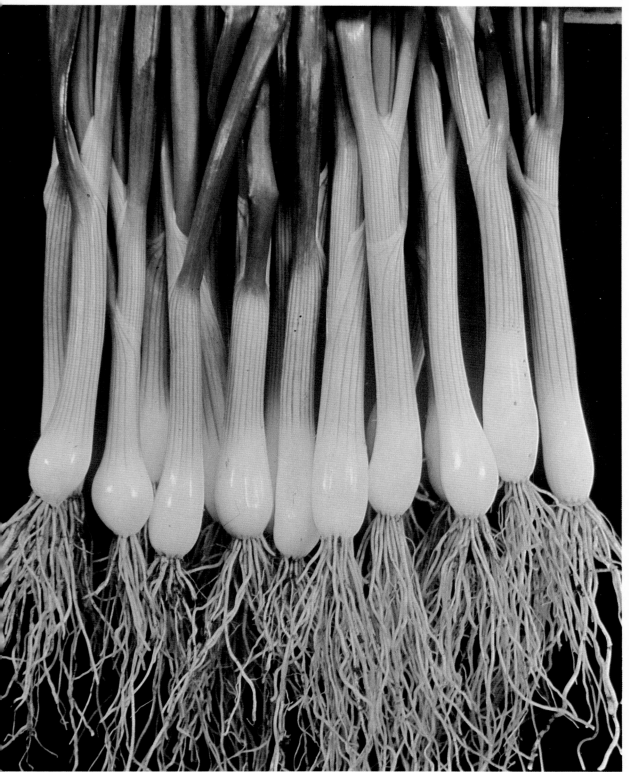

Onion 'White Lisbon'. One of the best of the so-called
spring onions. It has firm, crisp flesh and a good strong
flavour. Like all onions, it needs a deep, well cultivated
soil. Seed sown in March will produce plants ready for
pulling by early summer.
Courtesy of W. J. Unwin Ltd.

Cos Lettuce 'Giant Perfection'. A cos with an enormous heart of perfect form, yet as tender as many smaller-heading cos lettuces. It seldom runs to seed and is an excellent variety for the amateur, for commerce and for exhibition.
Courtesy of W. J. Unwin Ltd.

Broccoli 'Cluseed St. George'. An April-cutting broccoli of immense size, producing firm, solid heads of the purest white. Like all the brassicas, broccoli needs a deeply dug and well-manured soil, and should not be allowed to dry out in summer.
Courtesy of W. J. Unwin Ltd.

Cauliflower 'Unwins Snocap'. One of the largest heading of the very early cauliflowers, this variety makes compact, even growth. The head is of close, firm texture and exceptionally white. A reliable variety, suitable for forcing or for early outdoor growing.
Courtesy of W. J. Unwin Ltd.

Cabbage Lettuce 'Suzan'. An ideal lettuce for early frame, cloche or cold greenhouse cultivation, being virtually immune to damping off or for outdoor cultivation. It makes even, compact growth, hearts early and is slow to bolt.
Courtesy of W. J. Unwin Ltd.

Club Root, also known as 'Finger and Toe', attacks all the brassicas. It is caused by a slime fungus. The disease seldom occurs on well-limed, well-drained land, and may be prevented by dusting the roots with Calomel powder before planting out.

Top left Mushrooms. Grain spawn, available in cartons of various sizes, is a fairly new innovation. It may either be scattered over the surface, or a dessertspoonful dropped into holes 1 inch deep. It must be used when fresh and soon loses its vigour.

Bottom left The walnut-sized pieces of spawn should be inserted into the compost about 1 inch below the surface as soon as the temperature falls to 70°F. 'Casing' (covering the compost with a layer of soil) should not be done for a further three weeks.

Top right Pure culture spawn, the best for general use, comes in cylindrical lumps. These must be broken up into pieces each about the size of a walnut. This spawn, which is sterilised and vigorous, should be purchased in advance, though it must be still fresh.

Bottom right The finished product: a magnificent cluster of mushrooms grown by an amateur in an old garden shed. Although many people think that there is some secret to growing mushrooms, they are in fact quite easy given the right conditions.

marrow of trailing habit and may be used either hot or cold.

'TURK'S CAP MARROW' So called because it is shaped exactly like a Turk's turban, the skin being coloured orange and green. It is of trailing habit, the fruits keeping well. The flesh is rich orange and of distinct flavour. The plant seems to grow better in the south: it must receive plenty of sunshine.

'WHITE CUSTARD MARROW' This is a bush marrow for summer use and is one of the few which should be allowed to mature fully before use. The marrows attain the size of a small football and are delicious served hot, the pulp removed and filled with mushrooms, chopped runner beans and little 'Atom' tomatoes.

'ZUCCHINI' An F_1 hybrid bearing dark green cylindrical fruits like the old 'Long Green Trailing' but of bushy habit. The marrows are best used when 6–8 inches long when they will be tender and of excellent flavour. It does not keep.

Mushroom
Psalliota campestris

It is quite wrong to think that mushrooms can only be grown in a heated building. With a little ingenuity they may be enjoyed throughout the year, served on toast, for filling omelettes, for stewing, pickling, for sauces, in fact with almost every meal. Like so many of these interesting vegetables, the seakale, asparagus and several more, they are quite inexpensive to grow, yet expensive to buy in the shops.

There must be few places about the home, the flat included, where there is insufficient room to grow a box of mushrooms, under the stairs or in a cupboard where they will appreciate the darkness, and the warmth of the house during winter. A garage, attic, cellar or outhouse is also ideal, especially for spring and autumn crops.

About most farms and country houses too, there are often buildings or rooms which are not being used for anything special and which might be turned to good account growing mushrooms. A loft, stable, cellar or unused outhouse are all suitable places, and as no heat may be available a summer or autumn crop should be grown, a start being made early April so that the beds would bear during summer. Garden frames, unwanted after the half hardy plants have left them in May may also be used, the lights being covered with sacks to keep out the light.

A simple method by which mushrooms may be grown between April and October if no other place is available, is to make a 3 feet wide trench in the garden, removing the soil to a depth of 12–18 inches. Select a position where there is some shade but where the ground is well drained, a sandy soil being more suitable than one of a heavy nature, which may retain too much moisture.

At the bottom of the trench place a layer of stone, crushed brick, indeed anything to prevent moisture seeping up and into the compost. Then place in the trench 9 inches of prepared compost and which should be well trodden down. This is spawned and covered with clean straw, garden lights or asbestos sheeting being placed over the top. The beds are covered with virgin or sterilised loam (cased) when the spawn has 'run', the straw being replaced and also the covers. Depending upon the way the compost has been prepared, a useful crop should result.

A more simple method is to plant pure culture spawn in a lawn or field, and to rely entirely on nature to bring forth a crop during September and October. The method is to remove the turf and top soil to a depth of 8–9 inches, filling the opening with strawy manure, inserting the spawn and replacing the turf. A dressing of common salt in July will encourage the formation of a useful crop, but this chiefly depends upon the weather, heavy picking always following a dry summer.

Mushrooms indoors may be grown in those cool, dark places so frequently to be found about a farm or country property.

The beds can be made directly on the floor, but the area may be increased if boxes stacked on top of each other are used. Any strong boxes are suitable, and if just one or two can be taken into the home when the weather becomes colder in autumn, the supply may be kept up all the year round.

Preparation of the compost The country gardener should have little trouble in obtaining horse manure from stables where the animals are bedded on straw. Wheat straw is the best, for it breaks down more readily than that of oats or barely. Very few droppings are needed with the straw, so long as it is well soaked in urine it will ferment and heat up when made into a heap. Where stable and farmyard manure is scarce, a reliable artificial compost may be made up by using wheat straw which has been saturated with water and to which an activator such as Adco M has been added to bring about fermentation. Alternatively add some poultry manure which is present on most holdings or is readily obtainable.

The heap is made up in sandwich style, first spreading out a 6 to 9 inch layer of straw on top of which should be sprinkled the activator. Then another layer of straw and this time some poultry manure, which must be quite dry. If in any way sticky it will not only be difficult to spread, but will not generate any heat besides tending to make the compost sticky and unsuitable for mushrooms. Make the heap, whether using stable or artificial manure, as high and as compact as possible and provide some protection against prevailing winds, for if the heap becomes too dry it will not heat correctly. If the heap has sufficient moisture and has been made correctly, it will be seen from the steam to be generating considerable heat after about a week. It will then be ready for turning, shaking out the straw and the materials used and adding more water if the straw has become 'burnt' with the heat. Any water needed should be added at this stage, also 56 pounds of pink gypsum to every ton of manure. This is important for it prevents the compost becoming sticky or greasy, a condition in which the spawn will not run. The advent of gypsum was one of the major introductions to successful mushroom cultivation for it eliminated 'luck'.

After another week has elapsed, the heap will be ready for shaking out again and the compost will be seen to be turning a brown colour and the straw should be shortening. It will require yet another turn at the interval of a week, when it should then be ready for making up into beds or boxes. Take care not to over-compost or it will lose heat and food for the growing spawn. The compost should by now have lost all strong smell, it should in fact carry a mushroom aroma, and when squeezed tightly, it should bind but no excess moisture must be seen. In colour it should be a rich shade of brown, in no way black or greasy, for when cold such an unsatisfactory compost would set like butter and so cut off the oxygen needed by the growing spawn.

The compost may be prepared in a cellar, in a yard or open shed. Only a small area is required for the heap is made 6 feet tall, square and compact; a ton of manure can easily be turned in an area 12 feet × 12 feet.

When making up boxes, the compost must be thoroughly pressed down with a brick or board to a depth of 9 inches. Likewise the beds made on the floor should be beaten down with a spade. This is to conserve moisture and retain the heat.

Spawning The spawn, which should have been purchased in advance, is inserted as soon as the temperature falls to 70°F. Use pure culture spawn which is sterilised and vigorous, and break up the cartons into pieces the size of a walnut, inserting them 1 inch beneath the top of the compost.

There is now available a grain spawn which may be either scattered over the surface of the bed or a dessertspoonful dropped into holes 1 inch deep. It should be used almost as soon as received and for the novice it may be safer to purchase the ordinary spawn which will keep in condition for several months. When purchasing spawn from a shop, always ask if it is reasonably fresh for old spawn will have lost its vigour.

Spawn may be obtained in three varieties or colours, pure white which should be grown indoors for market; cream, which is a vigorous all-purpose variety; and brown, which should be used for home use. This is hardy and will produce a crop under much cooler conditions than will the more temperamental white variety.

The brown variety possesses a better flavour than the white, having the true aroma of the field mushroom. It is rarely found in the shops for in the same way as the public prefer white bread to the more nutritious brown loaf, so the white mushroom is most in demand, but brown mushrooms may be grown at home.

After spawning, the boxes should be stood in any place out of cold wind and the rain, and there they should remain for 3 weeks while the spawn permeates the compost. Should the top of the compost become dry, wet paper or sacking should be laid lightly over it to wet it. Then comes the time for covering the compost with soil, 'casing' as it is called, for without this soil covering the mushrooms will not appear.

The soil should be deeply dug from a field of permanent pasture, a heavy loam being the best and to help it to retain moisture, a small quantity of peat should be mixed with it. Large stones are removed but the soil should be left fairly rough and it is then spread over the compost to a depth of 1 inch. If sterilised soil can be obtained so much the better, for there is then little chance of introducing disease spores or weed seeds.

Development of the crop Though mushrooms favour a dark, moist atmosphere, they do not like stagnant conditions which can be caused by poor ventilation. Nor must the beds or boxes be given excess water which would percolate through to the compost and kill off the spawn. Water only when the casing soil requires it, when it appears to be drying out.

After 3 weeks from the time the soil is applied the first pin-head mushrooms should appear; if the weather is cold they may take another week. To bring on the crop, a little more water may then be given. The tiny mushrooms will not reach maturity overnight, neither do they in the fields. They will take a full week to develop and may take twice as long in cold weather. The mushrooms should be twisted from the soil, or if growing from a main trunk or base, those that are mature should be broken away. Mushrooms grow in flushes, and when the beds are cleared the holes should be filled in with clean soil and all decayed stems removed. The beds should be watered and in 10 days another flush will appear. Should the weather be unduly warm, it is advisable to spray the floor and walls of the room to reduce the temperature.

If growing for sale, and mushrooms are the ideal crop for the housewife who wishes to earn an extra income at home, the mushrooms should be removed before fully open and will sell readily in quarter pound punnets. Mushrooms produced in the country would cost but little, only perhaps the activator, some spawn, and a little peat for the casing soil, which would cost only a few shillings, for straw and poultry manure may possibly be there for the asking. If only 1 pound of mushrooms were picked from every square foot which is only an average crop, then at the present price of mushrooms, a ton of compost which is sufficient for 100 square feet would yield £20–£25 worth.

But mushroom growing is like cake making, it is easy when you know how. The secret of success lies in the correct curing of the compost, and this comes only with practice. So it is advisable to begin in a small way and then when one gains in confidence, what may have commenced as a hobby may be a profitable business and a source of great interest. And of much greater importance to the epicure, there would be a far more appetising diet throughout the year.

Beds may be made up in unheated buildings, or trenches as described, during early spring; these would come into bearing early in May, continuing until almost the end of summer. Additional beds made up in July would come into bearing in early September and continue until the cold weather. Beds in a barn or cellar, where wall thickness would ensure greater warmth, would continue to crop almost until the year end.

To produce mushrooms through winter, boxes, made up in July for cropping in a cellar or barn in autumn and early winter, could be transferred to a warm place in the home late in October. Under the kitchen sink or a cupboard would suit them well and they would continue to bear until Christmas. To crop until spring, and it is generally the later winter and spring months when mushrooms are so much appreciated, fresh compost would have to be made up and boxes spawned in September. The boxes could be placed in a shed until required for taking indoors towards the year end. They would then crop until the end of spring.

Do not make the mistake of having the boxes too large to handle. It is better to use two smaller boxes, than one of such large dimensions that it will be difficult to handle. The large returnable wooden fish boxes are ideal.

When filling the boxes be sure to fill the corners, pressing down the compost with a brick or wooden block so that it does not readily dry out. Mushrooms growing in frames must be kept shielded from the sun's rays otherwise the compost will dry out too quickly and the caps of the mushrooms will crack, thus giving them an unsightly appearance.

Cleanliness Warm, moist compost and a relatively humid atmosphere will give pests and disease every chance of becoming a nuisance. No crop (unless it be the tomato) is more prone to disease, but simple precautions will enable both pest and disease attack to be kept at a minimum.

Three weeks before the boxes or tier beds are to be made up, all woodwork and the floor and walls of the barn or shed should be sterilised with a 2 per cent solution of formaldehyde. This will not only kill all diseases, but will prevent 'mushroom sickness', that strange condition which will seriously reduce a crop if grown year after year in unsterilised buildings. The fumes of formaldehyde are poisonous and so should not be used in the home. Instead, use Sterizal and as an added precaution 'burn' the woodwork of boxes, bedboards and frames with a blowlamp to kill off pests and disease.

Old mushroom bed compost is excellent to use for lightening the soil and whilst protein will have been removed, organic nitrogenous substances will have increased in value.

Pests and Diseases
BUBBLES   This is the dreaded *Mycogone perniciosa*, a disease of the soil used for covering (casing) mushroom beds. It is present in most soils and will attack the small mushrooms, turning them into the most grotesque shapes whilst they exude a brown, evil-smelling liquid. Case the beds with sterilised soil for no cure is known or with fresh soil obtained from 12 inches below the surface of pastureland. To eliminate all chance of introducing the disease, growers are now casing the beds with a mixture of peat and crushed chalk. The amateur, growing a few boxes should use sterilised soil.

DAMPING OFF   This is caused by spores of a *Fusarium,* introduced either in the casing soil or with water supplies. Casing with sterilised soil will eliminate the risk and so, too, will the use of clean water supplies. The fungus attacks the young mushrooms, causing them to turn brown and die back. Infected areas may be treated with a solution made up of 10 parts ammonium carbonate and 1 part copper sulphate, 1 ounce being dissolved in 1 gallon of water. This will usually prevent the infected area from spreading.

MUSHROOM MITE   These mites are not true insects for they have a body consisting of one complete segment only. It is white and invisible to the naked eye. They feed on the straw in the compost, severing the spawn threads and causing the pinhead mushrooms to die. Once they get a hold, they are difficult to eradicate but Gammexane dusted into the compost during its preparation will usually destroy the pest. The preparation should not be used on growing mushrooms.

PHORID FLY   By 'mushroom flies' are meant the *Phorid* and *Sciarid* flies which lay their eggs in the compost and in 6 days hatch out into shiny yellow grubs which devour the growing spawn. After 10 days they pupate and emerge as flies to lay their eggs and commence the cycle again. It is therefore important to carry out control as routine throughout the life of the crop. This is done by dusting the beds every two weeks with Black Arrow pyrethrum powder. This is safe and easy to use.

SCIARID FLY   This has a thinner body than the phorid and its larvae are larger and, as a female is capable of laying more than 300 eggs at one time, it is obvious the amount of damage to the mycelium that the grubs will do. Regular dusting with Black Arrow powder will keep the beds clear of the pests.

Mustard and cress
Sinapis alba and *Lepidium sativum*

This crop presents few difficulties and may be

grown all the year round to use in salads and in sandwiches, accompnaied by cream cheese. Mustard is properly *Sinapis alba*, though commercial growers often substitute Rape, *Brassica napus*, which is quicker to mature: Cress is *Lepidium sativum*.

Successional sowings should be made every 2–3 weeks throughout the year, during the colder months under glass, and outdoors during warmer weather, in small beds of finely sifted soil. Small boxes may be sown with seed in winter and placed in the kitchen window, to provide fresh 'green' for salads and for garnishing when it is usually scarce. In a temperature of 48°F. the cress will be ready to cut within 2–3 weeks. If mustard, with its sharper flavour is also required, sow the cress four days earlier so that both will be ready to cut together. This is done by taking sufficient in one hand as required to fill a punnet (in which it is marketed) and cutting just above the soil in a single sweep with a sharp knife.

The commercial grower will sow seed directly into 1 inch of soil placed at the bottom of a punnet. This is more labour saving whilst it remains fresher for a longer time, the housewife cutting the 'green' when required. In this way it will stand several weeks without going 'off'.

Variety
'MOSS CURLED' The best form of cress for it makes plenty of 'head' and is curled and branching, like parsley. It is darkest green with a mild but distinct flavour.

Okra
Hibiscus esculentus

This is an annual requiring a warm climate to bring it to maturity. In Britain it should be confined to sheltered gardens south of a line drawn across the centre of England. The fruit resembles a small cucumber which terminates in a sharp point, being almost daggerlike in appearance, about 1 inch across and 9 inches long. It is also known variously as 'Okro', 'Lady's Fingers' or 'Gumbo'.

The pods or fruits should be used before they become too large and, when cut up, will add their particular flavour to stews and soups, or they may be sliced and used as a vegetable.

The seed is sown in a light, sandy soil and in an open, sunny situation early in May so that when the seed germinates, the young plants will be unharmed by frost. As the plants grow up to 4 feet tall, thin the seedlings to 20 inches apart. Water copiously during hot, dry weather and feed with liquid manure when the plants come into bloom and until the end of summer.

The first pods will be ready to pick before the end of August and will continue to bear until the frosts. If kept constantly picked over, the plants will produce a long succession of pods which are tender and succulent.

Varieties
'CLEMSON SPINELESS' The dark green cucumber-like fruits are free of spines and grow 8 inches long though they will be more tender if picked when no more than 6 inches long. The plant grows 4 feet tall.
'DWARF GREEN LONGPOD' . This variety grows 2 feet tall and bears a profusion of dark green pods 6–7 inches long covered in small spines and deeply ribbed.

Onion
Allium cepa

To obtain those large globular bulbs, imported in quantity from Brittany each year, it is necessary to give the onion a long season of growth and in the colder parts of Britain this is possible only if sets are planted rather than seed. North of a line drawn from Chester to the Wash, it will be necessary to raise seedlings under glass, preferably in a warm greenhouse, otherwise in an average summer they will fail to attain maximum size and to complete their ripening.

Preparing the soil As onions may be grown in the same ground year after year, a special bed may be prepared, incorporating humus to a depth of 2 feet together with some well decayed manure. At the same time, work in 4 ounces per square yard of basic slag and 2 ounces of sulphate of potash just before the sets are planted; or give a liberal dressing of bonfire ash. The bed should be brought to a fine tilth and be allowed time to settle before planting. Certain growers famed for their mammoth onions will roll the bed before planting.

The sets are just pressed into the soil, allowing 6 inches between the bulbs and 12 inches between the rows. The best variety to grow from sets is 'Stuttgarter Riesen', approximately 300 sets weighing 1 pound. They should be firm and plump when planted and 15–20 mm. in circumference. This variety makes a large bulb which keeps well through winter, and does not 'bolt' readily in warm weather.

Growing from seed Where growing from seed (and one ounce of seed will produce sufficient plants for a 100 feet row spacing the plants 6–7 inches apart) sow in a cold frame or in boxes in a heated greenhouse containing John Innes compost. Sow mid-January when the seedlings will be ready to transplant into deep boxes containing a slightly richer compost, early in March. If raising the plants in heat, provide a temperature of 50°F. and harden the plants before they go out.

Seed may also be sown under cloches early in February or, in the warmer parts, in October and may stand unprotected over winter. An additional advantage with autumn sown onions is that they rarely suffer from onion fly attacks. Sow thinly in shallow drills and dust with Calomel before sowing.

The plants should go out into prepared beds early in April. Lift them from the boxes as they are required so as not to expose the roots to the sun or a drying wind unduly and plant so that the bulbous part is half out of the ground. Before planting, dip the roots into Calomel paste as protection against onion fly and as a further precaution, dust with Calomel four weeks later.

Whilst growing, keep the hoe moving between the rows and water copiously in dry weather. A weekly feed with dilute manure water will increase the size of the bulbs. By mid–August, watering should be withheld to enable the bulbs to finish ripening and in this they will be assisted if the tops are bent over, just above the necks, to prevent them from seeding.

Harvesting   Towards the end of September, when the soil is dry, the bulbs are lifted and laid out for eight hours on the soil to complete their drying. They are then cleaned of any loose skin and the tops removed, leaving only a small portion necessary to string them together and hang them in a dry, airy shed to be used when required. If the autumn is dry after a wet summer, the bulbs should be left as long as possible before lifting and should then be left on a stone path for fully a week to dry completely. If excess moisture remains in the bulbs, they will begin to grow again in storage or may begin to decay.

Exhibiting   Onions are amongst the most rewarding of vegetables for the exhibitor for with good culture it is possible to grow them to enormous size, often weighing 4 pounds or more and, so as not to crack the skin, they should be lifted with both hands.

Exhibitors will go to great lengths to prepare the bed, often working it 3 feet deep and incorporating some lime rubble, leaf mould, decayed manure and material from the compost heap. The soil is pulverised for several months to bring it to a fine tilth before planting. The seed is sown outdoors in autumn or in January in a warm greenhouse, the plants being grown on in small pots in prepared compost from which they are planted out in spring after hardening, without disturbing the roots. The ground should be given a liberal dressing of soot before planting for this helps it to retain the warmth of the sun and also stimulates root action in the soil whilst it is also a deterrent to onion fly. Where growing for exhibition, at least 15 inches should be allowed between the plants in the rows.

The bulbs must be harvested with care. Lift with a fork inserted into the ground well away from the bulb and after loosening, use both hands to lift the bulb from the ground. After drying, cut off the roots close to the bulb and remove any outer layers of skin which may show markings. The top is cut back to 3 inches and the remaining leaf is bent over and tied with raffia.

Pests and Diseases

DOWNY MILDEW   This attacks the plants late in their life, a white coating of fungus appearing on the leaves which, if unchecked, die back leaving the bulbs unable to develop. It is most prevalent in a wet humid season but may be controlled by dusting the plants with a mixture of lime and sulphur or by spraying with sulphide of potassium, one ounce dissolved in 2 gallons of water.

EELWORM   The pointed nematodes enter the bulbs from the soil causing large brown areas of decay which are where the female lays her eggs; upon hatching the grubs devour the tissues of the bulb. Onion seed is now protected against seed–borne eelworm infection by fumigation with methyl bromide gas.

ONION FLY   By far the most troublesome pest: the flies lay their eggs in the soil during May and June then the maggots tunnel into the bulbs causing the leaves to turn yellow and making the bulbs useless for any purpose. Dusting the rows with Calomel before sowing and dipping the roots of young plants into Calomel solution before planting will prevent an attack.

SMUT   This attacks seedlings at soil level and is so destructive that the Ministry of Agriculture has classified it as a 'notifiable' disease. Black spots appear on the bulb scales and leaves and cause the plants to die back: the spores can remain active in the soil for 20 years or more. Immersing the seed in formalin (1 pint to 16 gallons of water) for an hour before planting will ensure freedom. Formalin is a poison and must be used with care.

WHITE ROT   This fungus appears at the base of the bulb as fluffy white mycelium. Later black sclerotia develop on it, which detach themselves and remain in the soil for years. The sclerotia may be present in untreated seed samples so that specialist seedsmen treat their seed with Calomel before packeting. Five ounces of Calomel to 1 pound of seed is considered satisfactory.

Varieties

'AILSA CRAIG'   The best all-purpose onion for it makes a large bulb of deep golden-yellow and is ideal for exhibition. It is an excellent keeper.

'BEDFORSHIRE CHAMPION'   An old favourite which still holds its own in any company, the large globular bulbs having a light brown skin and firmness of flesh.

'RELIANCE'   A flat onion of great keeping qualities, it makes a large firm bulb of mildest flavour and does well in all soils. It gives best results from an autumn sowing.

'SHOWMASTER'   Raised by Dobies of Chester, this is the outstanding exhibitor's onion, under good cultivation producing globe-shaped bulbs up to 2 pounds in weight.

Onion, Japanese
Allium fistulosum

known as the Japanese Bunch-onion because the plants form clusters of shallot-size bulbs which are lifted in autumn and dried for winter use. The plants require a rich soil brought to a fine tilth and an open, sunny situation to ripen. The bulbs are merely pressed into the surface at intervals of 10 inches and will benefit from an occasional watering with dilute liquid manure until they begin to ripen. The leaves and stalks may be used in salads, the bulbs in stews. It is highly resistant to pest and disease.

Varieties
'IWATSUKI GREEN' A bunching onion with leaves possessing excellent eating qualities whilst it grows in clusters of 8–9 bulbs.
'KUJO GREEN' This forms clusters of 6 bulbs with slender leaves and stems 2 feet tall which are crisp and tender when used in salads. The stems grow white for about the first 6 inches.

Onion, pickling
Allium ascalonicum

These small onions are grown especially for pickling, being white with a mildness of flavour which gives them a special attraction when used with cold meats. 'Paris Silver-skinned' is the best variety to grow, the seed being sown in April in shallow drills made 10 inches apart. Sow into clean ground and into soil brought to a fine tilth. It should have been manured for a previous crop. Dust the drills with Calomel before sowing and keep the ground aerated by constant use of the hoe between the rows. Thinning is not necessary and as the onions should not grow larger than the size of marbles, lift at the end of August and dry in an airy room before pickling.

Onion, potato
Allium ascalonicum

At one time this valuable onion, also known as the 'Multiplier onion', was to be found growing in every cottage garden in Southern England. As it is planted in January and lifted late in July or early August, it is best confined to warm gardens, preferably of the south and west. The onions grow to the size of golf balls and form, like potatoes, beneath the surface of the soil. They are lifted in the same way as potatoes and are the most pleasantly flavoured of all onions, being sweet and succulent with the mild chive flavour.

They require a rich friable soil which is well drained for the plants occupy the ground during the time of heavy rains. Plant 12 inches apart, merely pressing the sets into the soil surface with the tops exposed. Early in spring, hoe between the plants and during May and June, feed with liquid manure. At this time, it may be necessary to water copiously otherwise the bulbs will fail to swell.

The ball-like onions grow just below the soil surface and, to assist with their ripening, early in July carefully scrape away the soil with the hands, so that they may receive the maximum amount of sunshine. They are lifted early in August when the soil is dry and so that it may be readily shaken from them. The bulbs are then detached and laid out on the greenhouse bench or in an airy room to dry when they are placed in boxes for use when required whilst the best are saved for replanting.

The bulbs should be treated almost like any other bulbs such as tulips or daffodils, planting them in January to allow them 6 weeks to form their roots before the spring sunshine stimulates them into active growth.

Onion, tree
Allium cebe

Also known as the Egyptian onion or the Catawissa onion, this is a most valuable plant which could be grown as a substitute for all other onions where space is limited. It may be pickled or dried and used in stews; chopped in salads or used in sandwiches, and has many other uses whilst it is hardy and easy to grow.

The plants provide clusters of 5–6 small bulblets, about the size of small shallots, which form at the top of the stems. They may be used as required or left to ripen, to be stored and used over winter. They may be grown against a trellis fixed to a wall or may be planted in beds where the stems are allowed to fall over when ripe, the bulblets taking root and forming a jungle of onions. Or they may be increased by planting the ripe bulblets as for shallots, but to get them away to a good start, it is advisable to plant the whole cluster rather than to split them up.

Plant in September, in a well drained soil containing plenty of humus and some decayed manure for, like all onions, these are gross feeders. They will quickly establish themselves and in spring will grow tall, forming their clusters of bulblets during summer. They should be given a sunny situation and, as they will grow up to 3 feet tall, where not growing against a trellis, they should be staked to enable them to ripen.

Onion, Welsh
Allium fistulosum

A native of Siberia, this has been grown in Wales since an early date for it is extremely hardy. It is grown like the chive, as an edging plant for flower beds. It is perennial and is used in its entirety, being like a small leek with a thick blanched stem but with the tubular leaf of the onion. It grows 12 inches tall and may be used in salads or to flavour stews. The plants are lifted and divided every 2 or 3 years, several offsets being replanted 6 inches apart to grow on to form clumps in 2 years' time.

Plants may be raised from seed sown in autumn or early spring in shallow drills made 9 inches apart or as an edging. They will be ready to use the following summer, the largest being pulled first as required.

Onions, spring

No summer salad is complete without its spring onions which are raised from seed sown in shallow drills in October and again in early spring. Those from an autumn sowing will be ready to pull early in April; those from a spring sowing being ready from June onwards.

It is important to keep the ground free from weeds so allow 10 inches between the rows to allow for hoeing. Dust the rows with Calomel before sowing and when the seedlings appear, give a dressing of weathered soot between the rows to absorb the winter sunlight and warm the soil. Early in the year, give a light sprinkling between the rows of nitrate of soda, preferably during wet weather. This will encourage the plants to make some size.

As they begin to swell at the base, lift and use the largest plants first.

Varieties
'WHITE LISBON'   Most commonly used for pulling 'green' in spring owing to its hardiness and mild flavour.
'WHITE SPANISH'   A bunching onion of mild and distinctive flavour. It is also suitable for autumn sowing.

Orache
Atriplex hortensis

Also known as Mountain Spinach, this is a hardy annual with arrow-shaped leaves which may be cooked and used like ordinary spinach.

It requires rich, well manured soil containing plenty of humus and the seeds are sown in spring where they are to grow. A sowing may be made every 4–5 weeks until the beginning of September to maintain a supply. Sow 1 inch deep and thin to 15 inches apart and to prevent the plants running to seed, pinch out the flower spikes as soon as they appear. This will encourage the plants to grow bushy and make leaf. Water copiously during dry, hot weather and remove the leaves before they become old and coarse.

Variety
'GIANT RED'   This is the most succulent form, the leaves being large but in no way coarse. The

crimson-red colouring disappears in cooking.

Parsnip
Pastinaca sativa

A British native, the whole plant including the root emits an unusual aromatic smell. It has been appreciated by epicures of good food since earliest times. It is somewhat neglected by modern gardeners for it requires a long season to mature and a deeply worked soil when it is capable of producing a root 3 feet in length or even longer.

It should be given a soil not lacking in lime and one which has been manured for a previous crop, though humus materials may be dug into a depth of 2–3 feet. The parsnip requires a light friable soil and, where strawy manure or old mushroom bed compost has been used for a previous crop, so much the better. All large stones should be removed before sowing as it is necessary for the long roots to descend straight down into the ground.

Where growing for exhibition, parsnips are grown by the bore-hole system. After preparing the soil to a depth of 2 feet and allowing the seed bed to consolidate, holes are made at intervals of 12 inches in rows 18 inches apart. Each hole is made about 1 inch in diameter and 18 inches deep and is filled up with a mixture of finely sifted soil, peat, wood ash and anything which will make the compost friable. This is lightly pressed into the hole with a wooden dibber until it reaches the bottom and the hole is gradually filled in and marked by a stake. Two seeds are sown in March at the top of each, just covering them with soil. The weakest seedling is removed when sufficiently large.

To grow for kitchen use, sow in drills 18 inches apart and thin the seedlings first to 5 inches then to 10 inches apart in the rows. It should be said that only fresh seed should be sown. Even if two years old, parsnip seed will fail to germinate. If any seed is left over from a sowing, it should be thrown away. Even fresh seed will germinate irregularly and it should not be sown too thinly.

Feeding with liquid manure once a fortnight from the end of June will help to form those large succulent roots which are the envy of all who see them on the show bench.

The roots will be ready to lift early in November and care is needed so that the tapering roots are not damaged. They may be stored in boxes of sand or left in the ground until required. If baked, the roots will be floury with a chestnut-like flavour and will be greatly superior to those which are boiled. Like turnips, parsnips are improved with frosting.

Exhibiting   To have the roots ready in time for the late autumn shows, it is necessary to sow early in March and to keep the plants growing with copious waterings in dry weather and with a fortnightly feed of liquid manure. For exhibition, allow the roots to remain in the ground until the previous

83

Parsnip

day and, when lifting, insert the fork well into the soil and gently prise with one hand whilst pulling the parsnip with the other, twisting the root at the same time.

Before lifting, soak the soil thoroughly if dry. Remove the leaves to about 2 inches of the top and carefully lay the roots on sheets of brown paper and wipe them clean with a damp sponge. They are then placed in long boxes such as those used for sending roses and other long-stemmed flowers to market.

Pests and Diseases

CANKER   It is the only serious disease to trouble the parsnip and may cause damage to half the plants from a sowing. An outbreak may occur if growing in freshly manured soil or in a soil lacking in lime. It begins at the crown, a small part of which turns brown, then large cracks form horizontally around the root which takes on a scabby appearance. There is no known cure but an outbreak may be prevented by correct cultivation whilst there are a number of resistant varieties.

CARROT FLY   This pest, which also attacks turnips and swedes, may trouble parsnips, though only rarely. It lays its eggs in the soil and the yellow larvae tunnel into the roots causing the foliage to turn yellow and making the roots unfit for any purpose. To prevent an attack, dust the seed with Lindex before sowing and dust the rows again, about mid-June as the grubs may prove difficult to eradicate.

Varieties

'AVONRESISTER'   This has a high resistance to canker and should be grown in preference to others where this disease has been experienced. The roots are small but uniform in size so that they need be thinned to only 4 inches apart.

'EXHIBITION LONG-ROOTED'   The root is long and tapering, the flesh milky white whilst the skin is thin and smooth.

'HOLLOW CROWN'   This variety is hollow at the crown and is one of the most handsome varieties, the roots being long and tapering and of excellent size with a clear bright skin.

'RYDER'S INTERMEDIATE'   Valuable where the soil is shallow for the roots are thick and stumpy and in no way coarse whilst the flavour is excellent.

'THE STUDENT'   An intermediate variety of medium length with uniform roots of outstanding flavour.

Peas
Pisum sativum

Peas have been valued as a staple diet since the time of early man for dried peas will last all winter and were used with lentils to make pottage. The garden pea first came to be cultivated for its enjoyment as a fresh vegetable during Tudor times though not until Louis XIV almost died of a surfeit of them did the pea become to be more widely cultivated. Though neglected by modern gardeners, the Sugar Pea was described in Gerard's 'Herbal' and Parkinson listed nine kinds, including the Runcival pea, for centuries the standby of the cottage gardener, though he dismisses its cultivation in but a few lines. Today, the pea has an all-year popularity and when not in season, the canned and frozen product is in great demand.

By planting early, mid-season and late maturing varieties, it is possible to have a succession of crops from the end of May until early autumn. Those gardening in the south may make the first sowing in autumn and there will usually be no need to protect the plants as there is in northern gardens where this is usually done by covering them with barn-type cloches. These are placed over the plants early in December but should be removed whenever the weather is mild. The round-seeded varieties should be used for winter planting for they do not hold moisture as do the wrinkle-seeded varieties, the first of which were raised early in the 19th century by Andrew Knight, a squire of Herefordshire who was one of the first men to raise plants by cross-fertilisation. The marrow fat peas are wrinkled because some of the starch content has been converted into sugar, hence their superiority in flavour and sweetness.

The first outdoor sowing unprotected in the north is made towards the end of March but, should the weather remain cold, it is better to delay the sowing for ten days: main crop and later maturing varieties should then be sown at fortnightly intervals until the end of May. Early in June, sow a quick maturing early pea to mature early in autumn. For successful cropping sow:

Variety	Height	Sowing time	Maturing
Histon Mini	15 inches	November	end May
Early Onward	2 feet	mid-March	mid-June
Kelvedon Monarch	3 feet	end March	end June
Onward	2 feet	early April	mid-July
Histon Maincrop	3 feet	late April	early August
★Kelvedon Wonder	2 feet	May-June	September

★This variety may also be sown in March to mature early.

Sowing The pea enjoys a soil which has been well manured for a previous crop but to grow well, it requires a soil provided with liberal quantities of lime. The finest fertiliser for peas is sewage manure which has been collected over lime, a process which is being gradually discontinued by local authorities. If this is unobtainable, give the ground a liberal dressing of hydrated lime during winter.

It is a moisture retentive soil rather than one rich in nitrogen that the pea requires. An excess of nitrogen will result in an abundance of foliage and large pods containing only small peas. To provide humus, used hops are valuable as is anything from the compost heap whilst at planting time, to ensure early maturing and well filled pods, rake in a 2 ounce per square yard dressing of sulphate of potash and 1 ounce of superphosphate. A light loam, containing plenty of humus suits the pea best and a well drained soil is essential for autumn planting. A deeply worked soil is also vital for a heavy crop for peas are deep-rooting plants.

A November sowing may be made near a row of broad beans with winter lettuce between the rows. To sow, take out a shallow trench 1–2 inches deep and to the width of a spade. The seeds are planted separately, spacing them 2 inches apart to allow the plants room to develop. In this way, a half-pint of seed (peas are sold by the pint) will sow a 10 yard row. Before filling in the shallow trench, sprinkle peat over the seed and put the covering soil through a sieve to remove any stones which might interfere with plant growth.

With winter sown seed especially it is advisable to protect the peas from mice by shaking up the seed-peas in a tin containing red lead and paraffin. Wash the hands and destroy the tin after planting to prevent it from coming into contact with children or animals. To protect the peas from pigeons cover the rows with wire netting pea guards.

To assist with germination keep the soil moist and when the plants appear above ground, place twigs on either side of the row to enable the tendrils to take hold early in their growth. Dwarf peas will require only small twiggy sticks but the taller varieties need supporting by tall stakes

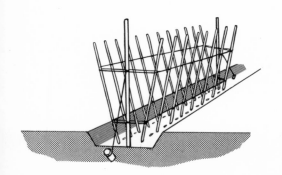

pressed well into the ground: these should be as high as the plants will grow.

General cultivation Where pea sticks are difficult to obtain, the rows may be surrounded with netting, held in place by canes or stakes. The plants will pull themselves up the netting and will be prevented from falling onto nearby plants as so often happens when sticks are used. Long lasting green netting made from polypropylene fibre film is satisfactory. After use, the pea haulm should be pulled away and the netting folded and stored in a dry, airy room.

If the soil tends to be heavy, or where gardening in the more exposed parts, peas may be sown in a greenhouse or frame in February and the plants set out early in spring when the soil is friable. So that there is a minimum of root disturbance, sow the peas separately in mini-size Root-o-Pots, made from sphagnum peat and wood fibre. These are placed in seed trays and the pots filled with John Innes compost after sowing. The plants are set out in their pots 3 inches apart into prepared ground.

The peas will be ready to harvest when the pods are well filled and firm when pressed, but they should not be left until they become hard for they will then have lost both flavour and sweetness. The pods are removed by cutting them from the haulms so as not to pull the plants from the ground. Those lower down the plants are removed first and will allow those at the top to mature later.

Exhibiting Maturing throughout summer and autumn, and forming a pleasing exhibit when well grown and tastefully arranged, peas are a most desirable crop for the exhibitor. For the very finest pods, grow peas in the cordon manner, using cane support or plant in a single row and support with netting. They may be sown directly into the ground or raised under cloches or in a frame by sowing in peat 'pots'. As for cordon sweet peas, allow the plants to produce only a single main stem, all side growths being pinched out. To encourage the formation of large well-filled pods, stop the plants at the sixth flower and from then on, feed once a week with dilute manure water whilst moisture may be retained in the soil by giving the plants a mulch with strawy manure. During warm weather, they will appreciate a daily syringe with cold water.

Pests and Diseases
FUSARIUM WILT The most troublesome of pea diseases, the fungus attacking the roots causing the plants to turn yellow and die back. Good cultivation and quick germination of the seed will usually ward off an attack but on land where an outbreak has been known, a resistant variety such as 'Vitalis' or 'Recette' should be grown.
LEAF SPOT A seed fungus which attacks the leaves, stems and pods causing them to be covered with small brown spots. The pods may fall off before reaching maturity. The disease may be more

troublesome in a soil deficient in potash whilst an attack may be prevented from spreading by spraying the foliage with weak Bordeaux Mixture as soon as noticed.

PEA APHIS   This attacks most of the legumes and is a 'green fly' which devours the leaf tissues causing both leaves and pods to turn yellow. Dusting with Lindex will prevent an attack or dust with Gamma-BHC before the pods begin to form.

PEA MOTH   These moths are most troublesome during June and July when they lay their eggs on the flowers. The white larvae eat their way into the pods, devouring the peas and where not kept in check, may consume large plantations. They are eradicated by treating the soil with Aldrin dust before planting and by spraying the plants with Sybol at fortnightly intervals from flowering time and until the first pods have formed.

PRE-EMERGENCE DAMPING OFF   In a cold year, the seed may occupy the ground several weeks before germinating and may entirely decay before germination takes place. Treating the peas with Orthocide (including 65 per cent Captan) before sowing will prevent the trouble.

THRIP   This pest hibernates in the soil and on pea sticks so the sticks should not be used for a second year. The small steely-black insects feed on the leaves, causing mottling and eventually the leaves turn brown. Dusting the plants with Lindex will give control.

Varieties   To sow October or March:

'FELTHAM FIRST'   Round-seeded, this variety grows 18 inches tall and bears well filled pods of excellent flavour.

'HISTON MINI'   Raised by Unwins of Histon, this is a round-seeded variety growing 12–15 inches tall and is suitable for growing under barn cloches. It is a dwarf counterpart of 'Forward', bearing heavily with well filled pods of outstanding flavour.

'METEOR'   A round-seeded variety of great hardiness and heavy cropping qualities.

'RADIO'   Round-seeded, this variety grows 18 inches tall and comes quickly into bearing, the plants being loaded with well filled dark green pods 2–3 inches long.

For spring sowing and early to mature:

'BLUE BANTAM'   Raised by Burpee & Co, this variety grows 18 inches tall, the large dark green pointed pods growing 4 inches long and containing 8 or 9 peas of excellent flavour and ideal for freezing.

'EARLY ONWARD'   A shorter version of the celebrated 'Onward', bearing blunt-nosed well filled pods of superb flavour.

'KELVEDON MONARCH'   This follows 'Early Onward' and grows 2–3 feet tall, its blunt-ended pods appearing in pairs and filled with 8 or 9 deep green peas which are excellent for freezing.

'KELVEDON WONDER'   This grows 18 inches tall and is quick to mature, the dark green pointed pods being well filled with sweet, mild flavoured peas.

For later sowing to mature later:

'ALDERMAN'   Growing 5 feet tall, this remains one of the outstanding late maturing peas, the pods being 4 to 5 inches long, filled with 8–9 large peas of sweet and delicate flavour.

'GREEN SHAFT'   Raised by Hurst's of Kelvedon in 1971, this is possibly the finest of all main crop peas. It grows 28 inches tall, is resistant to *Fusarium Wilt* and bears pods 4–5 inches long containing 9–10 seeds in each. An exhibitor's variety of outstanding flavour.

'HISTON KINGSIZE'   A late main crop pea for the exhibitor, growing 4 feet tall and bearing an immense crop of 4 inch long pods each containing 8–9 large seeds.

'HISTON MAINCROP'   This grows 2–3 feet tall and bears, in pairs, large deep green pods well filled with peas of delicious flavour.

'ONWARD'   One of the most popular peas ever introduced, a mid-season variety growing 2 feet tall and bearing, in pairs, dark green blunt-nosed pods filled with 8 or 9 large peas of excellent flavour.

'RECETTE'   The introduction of this variety marks a notable advance in pea breeding for its large pointed pods are borne in three's (it being the first triple-podded pea) which makes for larger crops and easier gathering. Resistant to Fusarium Wilt, the pods are ready within 12 weeks of sowing and are filled with 8 or 9 rich green peas of excellent flavour.

'VITALIS'   Highly resistant to Fusarium Wilt, this grows 3 feet tall, bearing its dark green well filled pods in pairs.

Peas with a difference

'CARLIN PEA'   A tall growing pea grown for winter and spring cropping. The dark green peas are harvested and dried in August for use during winter. The seeds are soaked for twenty-four hours and are covered with brown sugar and slowly simmered.

Rarely troubled by pest or disease, the seed is sown early in spring and the plants will eventually reach a height of 6–7 feet. During August, they will be heavy with multitudes of short pods which should be left hanging until the peas are fully ripe when the plants are pulled up and the pods 'shelled' The peas should be dried in a sunny room and stored for winter use.

'MANGE TOUT'   This is a tall-growing variety of the Sugar pea reaching 5 feet and almost as much in width so it must be allowed plenty of room. The pods should be removed a few minutes before they are to be cooked, otherwise they become tough and stringy: the pods should be sliced and eaten with the peas as for the Sugar pea.

'PETIT POIS'   The true French pea of outstanding flavour which should be sown throughout spring and early summer at regular intervals. Seed is sown 4 inches apart and requires copious amounts of moisture. The pods grow 2–3 inches long and if gathered just before required, steamed in their pods and 'shelled' afterwards, their full flavour will be retained. Serve piping hot with melted butter.

Peppers
Capsicum spp.

Peppers are of two groups, the sweet and the hot, the former being *Capsicum annum*, the latter *C. baccatum*, also known as the chillie or Bird Pepper. Both are suffciently hardy to grow in the open in the milder parts of Britain. In the colder parts, they are best grown in the greenhouse or frames. The sweet-fleshed peppers grow large, like rectangular-lobed tomatoes; they may be sliced for use in salads or cut into halves and (after removing the seeds) baked and served with meat. Again, like the tomato, they are green and change to bright red only when fully ripe, though one variety, 'Oshkosh', is yellow. The F_1 hybrid peppers are hardier and more vigorous and may be grown outdoors where others would crop with difficulty. The round Cherry and long Cayenne peppers are less hardy.

Sowing Seed is sown early in March in small pots containing John Innes compost in a temperature of 60°F. Or it may be sown in boxes and the seedlings transplanted to small pots when large enough to handle. Grow on in a similar temperature, syringing the plants frequently to prevent an outbreak of red spider and, about May 1st, move to larger pots containing a compost made up of equal parts of fibrous loam, decayed manure and coarse sand. About June 1st, plant out after hardening into a sheltered sunny border and into a soil containing material from the compost heap or some decayed strawy manure. Allow 18 inches between the plants. If growing under glass, discontinue artificial heat in early May and, towards the month end, move to larger pots containing a compost similar to that recommended for the earlier potting. Give the plants a daily syringe and never allow the compost to dry out. Weekly applications of dilute liquid manure will enhance the quality of the fruits.

To guard against Blossom-end Rot which is caused by physiological disturbance and allows the fruit to become infected by bacteria, never expose the plants to droughts where growing under glass, especially when the fruit has set.

Exhibiting Well grown capsicums make an interesting and exotic display. Careful feeding and watering is necessary for the fruits to reach exhibition size. When removing from the plants handle carefully for the skins bruise easily and wrap each in tissue paper before taking to the show. The fruits should be fresh, plump and brightly coloured. They should have about half inch of stem attached.

Pests and Diseases
FRUIT SPOT This is caused by the fungus *Colleto-trichum nigrum*, spots appearing on the fruits as red depressions. Control by removing infected fruit and spraying with weak Bordeaux Mixture. The trouble may be eliminated by soaking the seed in cold water for 12 hours, then draining before immersing the seed for 5 minutes in copper sulphate solution (quarter ounce to 1 pint of water), drying off and sowing without delay.
GREY MOULD It is *Botrytis cinera* which attacks the stems and leaves, also the fruits causing the appearance of large grey spots. Spraying the plants before coming into bloom with Shirlan AG will give control.
RED SPIDER This is the most troublesome pest for plants growing under glass and is most prevalent where conditions are too dry. Frequent syringing of the plants as for tomatoes and cucumbers will usually prevent an outbreak but where growing commercially, fumigation with an azobenzene smoke will safeguard the plants; this is repeated after 14 days, before the first fruits set.

Varieties
'CANAPE' (Sweet) An F_1 hybrid cross between a Japanese mosaic-resistant line and an American variety. It is early to mature and shows typical hybrid vigour through all stages of its growth. The plants grow 30 inches tall with dark green leaves and it crops heavily. The fruits are about 2 inches square, 3-lobed, with sweet flesh and quick-maturing: it is highly recommended for short-season gardens.
'EARLY BOUNTIFUL' An F_1 hybrid, raised by Sakata & Co of Japan, this received an Award of Merit from the R.H.S. It makes a much-branched plant 18 inches high with dark green foliage and bears fruits 3–4 inches long. It matures quickly and is a prolific cropper.
'FORDHOOK' A heavy cropper, the fruits being almost square, measuring 3–4 inches deep and the same across, with 4 lobes and smooth skin. The walls are thin, the flesh tender and crisp.
'OSHKOSH' The skin turns to bright canary yellow when ripe whilst the flavour is different from that of other peppers, being sweet and mild. The fruits measure 4 inches long and are about 3 inches across the top.
'RUBY KING' The fruits are large, often 6 inches long and 3 inches across the top with walls of medium thickness, the flesh being firm and sweet.
'TASTY HYBRID' A hybrid variety which bears large crops of elongated fruits which have thin walls. They may be eaten raw like an apple and have a similar crisp, tangy flavour. It makes a large spreading plant.

Varieties
'HUNGARIAN WAX' The fruits resemble carrots in size, shape and colour, growing 8 inches long with a waxy orange skin.

Pokeweed 'RED CAYENNE'   Of pencil thickness and growing 6 inches long, being curled and twisted and hot to the taste.

'TABASCO'   Slow to mature, this variety requires warm greenhouse culture. The small upright peppers turn to orange-scarlet and are hot and bitter.

Pokeweed
Phytolacca edulis

Introduced into Britain from its native North America early in the 17th century when it was grown as a border plant, it was the late André Simon who first mentioned its culinary virtues. Though its roots are poisonous, the young shoots of early summer are delicious when removed about 10 inches high and boiled until tender. To remove any acidity, first boil for 10 minutes, then pour away the water and simmer in fresh water until tender. Serve with butter or with oil and vinegar and the flavour will greatly resemble that of asparagus.

The pokeweed is a perennial which will attain a height of 4–6 feet in a moist friable soil so that it is necessary to allow 3 feet between the plants. Plants are readily raised from seed sown in shallow drills in April. By the end of summer, they will be large enough to move to their permanent quarters and will become established before winter.

Potato
Solanum tuberosum

A native of South America, the tubers are believed to have first reached Europe from Peru. Today, the potato is the staple diet in many countries round the world but nowhere does it grow better than in the cool, moist climate of Britain where more than ten million tons are produced each year.

Apart from its food value, the potato possesses another important quality. That is its ability to crop well in 'dirty' land provided it is well manured. This is land which has become infested with perennial weeds which are often difficult to eradicate. Due to the process of lifting and general cultivations, the soil is thoroughly cleaned and after manuring, it will be in perfect condition for the planting of other vegetables the following year. Again, land of a peaty nature, often low lying and which would grow few other crops apart from strawberries will, if well manured, grow good potatoes which prefer an acid soil. For this reason, soil well limed or of a calcareous nature will produce a crop liable to scab and one much reduced in weight.

A heavy soil, which in a summer of high rainfall will remain wet and cold, may cause the tubers to decay from fungoid diseases so that a clay soil should be brought into condition by incorporating quantities of garden compost or decayed strawy manure. Peat, leaf mould and wood bark are also valuable to lighten the soil and will also help to retain moisture

if dug into a light, sandy soil.

The ground should be made ready during the early winter months, leaving the top soil in a rough condition, to be pulverised by frost and wind during winter.

Starting the tubers   The yield of a crop will be much increased if the tubers are sprouted before planting whilst this will ensure the earliest possible crop depending upon soil and situation. With early potatoes, a crop at least 3 weeks earlier than with unsprouted tubers may be expected, whilst with the maincrop a 20 per cent heavier crop may be obtained, due to the longer growing period. The tubers should be clean and even in size.

A frost-proof room is essential for the sprouting but first obtain the tubers or 'seed potatoes', as tubers produced for replanting and grown on maiden land are called, from a reliable grower. They should be 'certified' as having been grown in Scotland or Ireland or on one of the islands situated in the more remote parts of northern Britain. Potatoes grown for seed on high ground in the north of England will be almost as good, being clean and possessing exceptional cropping vigour.

A method of sprouting is to place the tubers, 'rose' end upwards close together but not quite touching, in peat 1 inch deep in a shallow wooden box. The tubers should not be cut. The 'rose' end is usually the wide end containing the greatest number of eyes. Place the boxes in a light airy room but not in sunlight whilst frost must be excluded. The Fenland growers stack the boxes in specially constructed sprouting houses.

When to begin the sprouting will depend upon planting time. The earliest plantings are made in Cornwall and Pembrokeshire where spring frosts are almost unknown and where early potatoes are planted in February. They are put down for sprouting about Christmas time. In other parts of south-west England and Scotland, the early crop is planted in March; elsewhere, mid-April is a suitable time and as the earlies are more tender, it is usual to plant 'late' potatoes (the maincrop) early, and early potatoes late'. Sprouting should commence about 6 weeks prior to planting time but this will depend upon where the sprouting is to take place and the amount of warmth given. Short sturdy sprouts are required, not more than 1 inch long, otherwise they will break off when planted. Where there are more than two sprouts, the two strongest are retained and all others rubbed out. Do not plant too early, wait until the soil is in a friable condition and has begun to warm. This may not be until early May in the north especially if the soil is heavy.

For a heavy crop, take out a trench to a depth of 9 inches and make the trenches 2 feet apart to allow for 'earthing'. At the bottom place 3 inches of decayed manure or material from the compost heap and over this, 3 inches of peat. Into the peat, the tubers are carefully pressed 2 feet apart, the sprouts (or eyes if not sprouted) uppermost and about 4 inches below the top of the trench. Before covering them with soil, place more peat around the tubers or use soil which has been passed through a fine riddle.

To the soil to be used to fill up the trench, give a 2 ounce per square yard dressing of superphosphate of lime and sulphate of potash mixed together. This will increase the yield, encourage earlier maturity and help the plants to resist disease. The mixture should be in the proportion of 2 parts superphosphate to 1 part potash. Nitrogenous fertilisers should not be used for they tend to make for excessive top growth and a 'soft' tuber, liable to attack by disease whilst they become dark after cooking.

On low-lying land of a heavy nature, the tubers should be planted on ridges, in V-fashion. At the top of the ridge a drill 6 inches deep is made and lined with peat. Into this the tubers are pressed and the drill filled in with finely riddled soil containing the superphosphate and potash. Never plant potatoes too close together or the haulm (the leaves and stems) will grow weak and be prone to disease. Weak haulm will mean a greatly reduced crop.

It is important to plant potatoes in an open, sunny position so that the plants may obtain the maximum of sunshine. Make the rows from north to south, to allow both sides of the rows to receive the same amount of sunlight. If possible, early potatoes should be given a southerly slope and as light a soil as possible: this will ensure that maturity will be two weeks earlier than where growing in a less favourable situation.

For an early crop in the more exposed gardens, an early variety may be planted in a frame over a mild hot bed. A 6-inch depth of compost is placed in the frame and on top is placed a 6-inch depth of riddled soil into which the tubers are planted with a trowel, spacing them 9 inches apart and just covering them with soil. Water in and cover with lights. Should there be frost about, cover the lights with sacking at night and remove by day. If the tubers are planted about mid-March, they will yield a useful crop of 'new' potatoes at the end of May. If the haulm is earthed up with a peat and soil mixture this will help to prevent loss of moisture about the tubers as the days become warmer.

As the foliage appears above the soil, it should be earthed up about 3 inches and again a month later to a similar depth. This will prevent the foliage from being damaged during cultivations. At the same time and as a precaution against 'Blight', spray the foliage with Bordeaux Mixture.

Harvesting A reliable indication as to when the crop is ready to lift is when the foliage begins to die down, though for show or where the crop is required to eat at home, lifting of the early varieties may commence in June, and the maincrop towards the end of August. If earlies, second earlies and maincrop varieties have been planted, there will be tubers to harvest from June until October when the winter supply will be available from storage.

Lift the tubers with a fork, taking care to place it well away from the plant for the tubers spread out and are easily damaged by careless lifting. Where lifting for exhibition, it is better to do so with the hands, selecting a day when the soil is dry and friable. Scrape away the soil and lift the tubers one at a time placing them, after shaking away the soil, into a bucket lined with a clean sack which is then used to cover the tubers to exclude light. Potatoes lifted early for use or for exhibition should be kept under the stairs or in a cellar, away from light otherwise they will turn green.

'New' potatoes may be enjoyed all the year round if a quantity are placed in a metal biscuit tin filled with dry peat and buried 12 inches deep in the garden, a stone marking the position.

After lifting, burn the haulm so as not to perpetuate disease which would contaminate the garden compost heap.

Exhibiting The potato is one of the most interesting of all vegetables on the show bench for it is obtainable in many sizes, shapes and colours and never ceases to entertain. The tubers are lifted about mid-August whilst the soil is still friable and readily falls from them. They should not be washed but on show day may be wiped with a damp cloth, taking care not to damage the skin. The tubers must be dry when placed in tissue paper and packed in cotton wool in a box or basket. They should have been selected for uniformity, each being free from marks or slug damage and showing no traces of 'greening'. Usually six tubers of a single variety are arranged around a dish. They must be neither too large nor too small and should have few eyes which should be shallow. 4 points are awarded for condition; 4 for size; 4 for shape; 4 for eyes; and 4 for uniformity.

Four different types or classes are provided for

(a) Kidney-shaped—white
(b) Kidney-shaped—coloured
(c) White rounds
(d) Coloured rounds

Outstanding exhibition varieties are 'Craig's Royal' (d); 'Pentland Cream' (b); 'Arran Comrade' (d); 'Catriona' (b); 'Dr. McIntosh' (b); 'The Bishop' (a); 'Angus Beauty' (b); 'Dunbar Standard' (a); 'Arran Victory' (d).

Pests and Diseases

BLACK LEG Bacterial rot of potato tubers may be troublesome in a wet season. The disease starts at the end of a tuber causing slimy areas and when cut, emits an unpleasant smell. Clean seed will do much to prevent an outbreak whilst it is preferable to plant whole tubers rather than cut portions containing an eye.

BLIGHT Dangerous if it takes hold but is easily prevented by spraying the foliage in early July and again a month later with Bordeaux Mixture. The Blight attacks the leaves as brown spots; later the whole plant turns brown whilst the tubers are also damaged, sunken areas appearing on the surface.

COLORADO BEETLE   Rare in Britain, it is so destructive to potatoes that it is a 'notifiable' pest. It has orange and black stiped wings and when fully grown measures half an inch long. It winters in the soil and lay its orange eggs on the plants. The grubs are also orange and where in numbers will quickly wipe out a plantation. As a precaution, treat the soil with Aldrin dust before planting.

EELWORM   This pest attacks the tubers causing them to become a slimy mass whilst the foliage turns yellow and dies back. There is no known cure and badly infested land should be rested from potatoes for four years. Where they have caused only limited trouble, treat the soil with Jeyes Fluid at a strength of 2 tablespoons to 1 gallon of water a month before planting.

LEAF SCORCH   Due to potash deficiency, the leaves curling at the margins. Later, bronze and yellow blotches appear. A light application of sulphate of potash at planting time will prevent an outbreak.

SCAB   This attacks the tubers in the form of rough, scab-like spots and, where the infestation is severe, the scabs may cover the whole surface. It is prevalent only on land of a calcareous nature or where heavily limed for a previous crop. Green manuring before planting potatoes, by sowing and digging in rape when 2 inches high will do much to prevent an outbreak.

WART DISEASE   A 'notifiable' disease and on infected land only wart-immune varieties such as 'Arran Pilot' (early) and 'Dr. McIntosh' (maincrop) should be grown. It first attacks the stems and lower leaves but it is usually found only on the tubers which upon lifting may have the appearance of cauliflower-like structures. Many will break off in the soil where they remain to contaminate the following potato crop. Clean seed will go far in contributing to immunity.

Varieties

FIRST EARLY: 'ARRAN PILOT'   One of the earliest to mature, it crops heavily, its white kidney-shaped tubers having outstanding flavour.

'DI VERNON'   This bears a handsome kidney-shaped tuber, being creamy white shaded mauve and is a heavy cropper. A waxy-fleshed potato with a slight earthy flavour.

'ECLIPSE'   May be classed as a late early but bears a heavy crop, the small white kidney-shaped tubers cooking well.

'EPICURE'   Very early, it stands cold weather better than any other early potato and is a round white of delicious flavour.

'HOME GUARD'   A round white with shallow eyes and cropping heavily, the tubers growing uniform in size making it ideal for exhibition.

'ULSTER CHIEFTAIN'   This one favours a warm climate to crop to advantage, bearing heavily whilst the round white tubers cook to a floury texture.

SECOND EARLY: 'CATRIONA'   A handsome exhibition variety which crops heavily on poor land. Introduced by Archibald Finlay early in the century, it is of flat kidney shape, of pale cream colouring with shallow purple eyes. It is susceptible to dry rot if not stored carefully.

'CRAIG'S ROYAL'   A kidney potato with a soft pale creamy-pink skin with darker pink around the shallow eyes. It bears a heavy crop and is good for exhibition.

'DUNBAR ROVER'   Immune to Wart Disease, this is a reliable cropper for a light soil, the oval-shaped tubers being pure white, delicious when baked in their skins.

'SUTTON'S OLYMPIC'   Though early to mature, this will keep through winter, whilst it crops heavily in all parts of Britain, the tubers being round and pink skinned.

'ULSTER ENSIGN'   Raised by Mr. John Clarke in recent years this is a tremendous cropper though it keeps badly. It is of rounded kidney shape with a cream skin and pink eyes.

MAINCROP: 'ARRAN COMRADE'   A round potato, raised by Mr. Donald MacKelvie on his Isle of Arran croft, is late to mature. The tuber is white with faint netting and makes delicious eating when baked.

'ARRAN VICTORY'   A round purple variety now grown in Ireland to the exclusion of most others, being outstanding both in flavour and in its cropping powers.

'DR. McINTOSH'   Producing a larger number of uniform tubers per plant than any other variety, this requires a long season to mature. The long white kidney-shaped tubers have shallow eyes and are borne in abundance.

'DUNBAR STANDARD'   A white kidney with shallow eyes of excellent flavour though tends to break up when cooked. The upright foliage makes earthing easy.

'KING EDWARD VII'   Raised in Northumberland, this pink skinned kidney-shaped variety is without a peer for baking whilst it has excellent keeping qualities.

'PENTLAND CROWN'   Raised in Scotland, it is a round variety with a cream skin and handsome rust markings. It crops heavily in all soils.

'STORMONT DAWN'   A heavy cropper, 13 hundredweight having been gathered from 56 pounds of seed whilst it keeps almost 12 months. It has 'Golden Wonder' for a parent and has the same nutty flavour.

'THE BISHOP'   Of handsome appearance and with a distinctive flavour, this is the Cox's Orange of the potato world, being a shy cropper unless grown well. The long kidney-shaped tubers are pure white and almost free of eyes.

Radish
Raphanus sativus

Every salad is enhanced by the appearance of sparkling red radishes, but it was as hors d'oeuvre that they were first used in Tudor times, 'as a stimulant before meat, giving an appetite thereunto'. The ancient Egyptians grew the radish, and it was appreciated by the Romans long before the conquest of Britain and they may have brought it to these shores. To the Saxons, it was known as the 'raedic'. During Shakespeare's time we are told that 'gardeners used great fences of reeds tied together, which seemeth to be like a mat upright, to defend them (radishes) from cold winds and to bring them forward the earlier'.

The radish still receives attention from the market gardener, an early crop being sown over a mild hot bed in a frame early in March and at regular intervals from the month end outdoors in prepared beds.

Radishes require growing quickly otherwise they will grow hard and woody and, to have them sweet and succulent, the turnip-rooted varieties should be no larger than a shilling, those of tapering form no longer than the thickness of one's little finger. Used in this manner, they will be juicy and nut-like. If grown slowly or left too long in the seed bed, radishes will be bitter and stringy.

General cultivation The seed bed should contain plenty of humus to retain summer moisture and old mushroom bed compost is ideal or work into the soil a mixture of peat and decayed farmyard manure. Early in March, bring the seed bed to a fine tilth and when the soil is friable, sow thinly and preferably broadcast, raking the seed into the top inch of soil.

During dry weather, keep the ground moist and the radishes will be ready to use within a month of their sowing. To maintain a succession of succulent, mild roots, make a sowing once a month until early September and, for winter use, sow in July the 'China Rose' and 'Winter Black' radishes which were popular in Tudor times. 'The Black radishes are most used in winter,' wrote Parkinson 'and must be sown after mid-summer; if sown earlier they would run up to seed'.

Winter radishes are sown in drills 9 inches apart, the Black being thinned to 6 inches in the rows for they grow as large as a turnip. Keep the soil moist during summer and give an occasional watering with liquid manure. The roots are lifted early in November and are stored in sand until required.

Exhibiting On the show bench, radishes are built up in cone fashion with the roots facing to the front, those of contrasting red and white presenting a most attractive appearance. Pull the roots as near to show time as practical, brush away the soil and place in a colander, syringing them to maintain their freshness.

Pests and Diseases

CLUB ROOT The swelling of the tap root may be due to this common disease of brassicas and may be prevented by treating the seed, or the soil, with Calomel dust before sowing.

RADISH FLY The pest lays its eggs in the soil, the larvae attacking the roots. Dusting the ground with Lindex before sowing will prevent an attack but Lindex must not come into contact with potatoes.

TURNIP FLY This, is a troublesome foe but may be kept away by dusting the ground and the plants with derris, shortly after the seed has germinated and repeating the treatment a fortnight later.

WHITE BLISTER This usually attacks horseradish in the form of white pustules which appear on the leaves, the spores surviving in the soil for several years. Spraying with weak Bordeaux Mixture will give control.

Varieties

'BURPEE'S WHITE' The finest white globular radish, the flesh being crisp and sweet without any trace of bitterness. Best eaten when no more than 1 inch in diameter.

'FRENCH BREAKFAST' An intermediate variety, the elongated roots being bright red tipped with white. The market growers favourite as it makes a striking bunch.

'ICICLE' The long tapering root of this variety is like a white transparent icicle and remains crisp, cold and juicy longer than any other variety.

'INCA' A new radish which forms a cherry-like globe and which reveals a crisp white flesh when of large size. Sliced, it makes for delicious eating.

'SAXA' Ideal for early forcing, it matures rapidly and makes a round brilliant scarlet root with crisp white flesh.

'SCARLET GLOBE' The brilliant crimson roots are like large cherries and have white flesh of delicate flavour.

'SPARKLER' A rapidly maturing globular variety with white sweet flesh and a scarlet skin, white at the base.

For winter:

'CHINA ROSE' In appearance, this is tubular, like a large 'French Breakfast', thickening towards the base. The colour is bright rosy-red with the flesh white and crisp. It is delicious sliced and used with Lamb's Lettuce and cream cheese in a brown bread sandwich or used to add colour to a winter salad.

'WHITE CHINESE' The sweetest of all winter radishes, the pure white roots growing 6 inches long with a diameter of 2–3 inches. The flesh remains crisp and juicy all winter.

'WINTER BLACK' This is illustrated in Parkinson's 'Paradisus' (1629) which shows it as a large round root like a small turnip covered in a jet black skin. The flesh is white and succulent and has a distinct nutty taste. It may be sliced or grated for use in a winter salad.

Rampion
Campanula rapunculus

A native British plant, also known as the Rampion Bellflower, this is often found on shady banks, usually near houses. It has a thick fleshy root, like a radish which exude a milky juice. In early times it was cut up and used in salads. It is a pretty un-branched perenial, bearing small violet-coloured bell-shaped flowers and, like horseradish, once established in the garden it tends to take over, proving difficult to keep under control.

Rhubarb
Rheum rhaponticum

Though the edible part of this plant is often referred to as a fruit, it is of course a vegetable, and is grown in the vegetable garden. Owing to its ability to produce a large quantity of fruit over a long period and from a limited space, no garden should be without a few roots, several of which may be lifted and forced in a cellar or greenhouse to provide an early crop, or for a later supply, the roots may be covered where they grow, to be followed by fruit for early summer use from natural-ly grown roots.

The value of rhubarb is in its earliness to bear the familiar long red succulent sticks which may be used for stewing and for making tarts and flans, at a time when its fruity flavour is most appreciated and when it has little competition. Later, when the summer fruits begin to ripen, there is little demand for rhubarb for by then, the bright crimson sticks will have lost their early quality. With a little care, it is possible to have a supply of sticks from early Janauary until early June when the more choice soft fruits begin to mature.

Soil preparation Rhubarb requires a heavy soil, lightened with humus to produce the best sticks. Its commercial culture is concentrated in the heavy clay soils of central Yorkshire which receive liberal dressings of shoddy from the nearby woollen mills and by 'clinker' from the local coal mines. To en-courage a heavy crop of large succulent sticks, the land must be deeply cultivated and enriched with organic manures which will slowly release their supply of nitrogen. Besides shoddy, farmyard or artificially composted manure is suitable and should be applied liberally for it is necessary to build up a strong root if it is to be used for forcing the follow-ing year. Old mushroom bed compost is also suitable whilst the plants will respond to a 4 ounces per square yard dressing of bone meal when the ground is prepared or, if the soil is unduly heavy, substitute basic slag, used at the same rate. Rhubarb will also benefit from a light dressing with hydrated lime applied to the soil around the plants each autumn.

Early varieties which are to be forced in the spring will respond to a dressing of 2 ounces per square yard of nitrate of soda given early in the year before the plants are covered, and again when they start into growth. Plant the roots 3 feet apart for in several years they will form large clumps of a dozen 'eyes' or more. November is the best time to plant and each offset should contain a bud and piece of root. Plant with the soil just covering the bud and tread firmly around.

No sticks should be removed in the first season and only one or two in the second year. If it is required that the plants should then be forced, then no pulling at all should be done in their second year. During summer, give a heavy mulch of decayed manure so as to build up a sturdy crown. This may be covered with a barrel or tub, or it may be lifted and forced in gentle heat in a greenhouse or cellar.

Forcing To obtain the earliest sticks, the roots are lifted in December after being cleared of foliage and left for several weeks, exposed to frost and wind. This will bring them into such a condition that when placed in gentle heat, they will be quickly stimulated into growth.

One method of forcing is to prepare a hot bed by the artificial composting of straw with an activator such as Adco 'M', adding to it a quantity of poultry manure or horse droppings to encourage it to generate additional heat. The compost is prepared early in the year and should be ready to place in a cellar or shed by the end of January. It is spread out on the floor or in deep boxes to a depth of 6 inches and over it is placed several inches of soil. Into the top soil the roots are planted with peat packed between them. The roots should almost touch each other. They are given a thorough soaking and light is excluded to encourage the sticks to grow long and straight. When 18–20 inches long, the sticks are removed by pulling them from the roots. Rhubarb should not be cut. It will take about a month before the first sticks are ready and the roots will continue to bear for about 6 weeks. Afterwards, they are planted out again, into a well nourished soil and should not be pulled again for 2 years.

To force the roots in the open, where the plants grow, cover with hot-bed manure and place over them a barrel or tub to exclude light. After pulling the sticks, remove the covering and do no more pulling until the following year when different roots should be forced. By alternating the roots to be forced, the plants will have time to recover and the quality will be maintained.

Rhubarb may also be forced in pits or deep frames covered with lights over which sacking is placed to exclude light. If the roots are planted over a hot-bed, the sticks will be ready several weeks earlier.

Propagation Rhubarb is increased either by divi-sion of the crowns or from seed, though named varieties can only be increased by division, the

Top Sowing small seeds. (1) Small seeds need to be planted shallowly, and the simplest way of drawing a suitably shallow drill is to do it with a wooden plant label, following a tightly stretched line. The soil must first be worked to a fine tilth.

Bottom Sowing small seeds. (2) To sow the seeds evenly they should be placed on a crisply folded piece of paper and the paper gently tapped with a finger as it is moved along the drill. Small seeds should only just be covered with soil.

Top Sweet Corn 'Stowell's Evergreen Hybrid'. One of the new hybrid strains specially bred and selected to mature in the short, cool summers of north-western Europe. It needs a sunny, sheltered site in light, rich soil to fully ripen in cobs.

An amateur's prize-winning exhibit. As much care has been taken over the preparation of the vegetables in the exhibit as over the growing of the vegetables themselves. No amount of dressing will make poorly grown vegetables look good.

Japanese Flowering Cabbages. These ornamental cabbages put an end to the old-fashioned idea that vegetables are not decorative. Although edible, they are usually grown in the flower border, and the foliage is much used in floral decoration.
Courtesy of W. J. Unwin Ltd.

Vegetable marrow 'Bush Green'. One of the best marrows
to grow in a small garden, forming a compact, bushy
plant and producing a heavy crop of evenly shaped, dark
green fruits with pale green stripes—marrows of classic
shape and delicate flavour.
Courtesy of W. J. Unwin Ltd.

clumps being lifted in November and cut into several pieces, each containing a bud or eye. A 3-year root may be divided into six or more pieces which are re-planted 3 feet apart into freshly prepared ground. The divisions are made with a sharp spade or knife and should have the cut portion dusted with lime before planting. It is important that the eyes are not damaged for this would prevent the plant from growing, though eyes will survive with virtually no root attached.

Raising plants from seed is an inexpensive way of obtaining a stock though they will take 18 months longer to come into bearing. The seed must be fresh: it will then germinate quickly and evenly. Sow in March, in a frame or in shallow drills which are then covered with cloches. Provided the seedlings are kept moist, they will be ready to transplant by early July when they are planted in beds 12 inches apart. The following year, alternate plants are lifted and may be re-planted 2 feet apart into clean ground. No sticks should be pulled for at least 18 months.

Those gardening in the most favourable areas may sow in September, thus saving almost a year in crop production.

It should be said that when pulling has finished in summer, those plants bearing seed stems should have them removed as soon as they form so that the plant may concentrate its energies in building up a strong crown rather than in seed production. At this time, the plants will also benefit from an occasional application of dilute manure water.

Exhibiting   The sticks should be pulled as near to show time as possible to retain their freshness. The leaves are trimmed to within about 3 inches of the top whilst the sticks should be long, straight and of good colour.

Rhubarb suffers neither from pests nor diseases.

Varieties
EARLY: 'EARLY SUPERB'   A modern variety which matures before 'Royal Albert' and forces well either indoors or in the open ground.
'HAWKE'S CHAMPAGNE'   Very early, this bears long well coloured stems and forces excellently.
'PARAGON'   This is best forced outdoors where, in a heavy soil, it bears large bright scarlet sticks which when cooked have a brisk flavour.
'ROYAL ALBERT'   One of the best early rhubarbs for outside forcing, being hardy and producing a large stem of bright scarlet.
'TIMPERLEY EARLY'   An early variety which forces well under all conditions, the stout stems being of deepest crimson.
SECOND EARLY: 'CANADA RED'   A Canadian rhubarb which is excellent for cool forcing, the large crimson sticks being produced over a long period.
'DAWE'S CHALLENGE'   Raised in Norfolk, this is almost a mid-season variety and is unrivalled under all conditions of soil and climate.
'STOTT'S MONARCH'   A strong grower, the stems

mature green and have a delicious pine flavour when cooked.
LATE: 'DAWE'S CHAMPION'   This matures after 'Challenge' and just before the later varieties such as 'Myatt's Victoria'. A heavy bearer, the large sticks are the reddest of all.
'GLASKIN'S PERPETUAL'   A continuous cropper with large thick green stems, shaded red and of outstanding flavour.
'MYATT'S VICTORIA'   The latest to mature and the most popular for open ground pulling. A heavy cropper, it makes a strong red stem, the favourite of the canners.
'THE SUTTON'   Late and probably the best garden rhubarb for it does not seed and bears over a long period. It also forces well and makes a large thick stem of brilliant crimson.

Salsify
Tragopogon porrifolius

A native of most European countries but not of the British Isles, this is known as the 'Vegetable Oyster' because of its unique and delicate flavour.

Like most vegetables which form a long tap root, it should not be grown on newly manured ground otherwise its roots will grow forked. It requires a rich friable soil, manured for a previous crop and the seed is sown in shallow drills made 12 inches apart. Sow early in April, thinning the seedlings to 8 inches apart. Keep the hoe moving between the rows and water copiously during dry weather. It requires a long growing season.

The roots will be ready to use early November when they may be lifted and stored in boxes of sand or, in those gardens enjoying a mild winter climate, they may be left in the ground and used when required. When grown for sale, the roots are tied in bundles of twelve.

To retain the flavour, scrape the roots before cooking. This should be done just before it is intended to use them, placing them in a bowl of water, to which lemon juice has been added, to preserve the whiteness. Boil whole until tender and serve with white sauce. The roots should never be peeled or they will 'bleed' and lose flavour.

Salsify is troubled neither by pest nor disease.
Variety
'SANDWICH ISLAND MAMMOTH'   The roots grow large and when scraped have creamy white flesh with the delicious taste of oysters. They grow 8–9 inches long and are 1 inch in diameter, tapering slightly from the shoulder to the end.

Savoy
Brassica oleracea bullata sabauda

The largest heading cabbages and the hardiest of all, being at their best in the new year after being subjected to frost, which makes them crisp and tender. Their crinkled and deeply veined leaves enable winter rains to drain away quickly so that the hearts never become wet and soggy. Their curled leaves are similar to those of kale when cooked.

Savoys require a long growing season and a well manured soil. Sow early in April, in shallow drills and plant out in May 2 feet apart. The plants will occupy the ground until the following spring and require a soil containing plenty of humus and nitrogenous manure. Composted strawy manure or shoddy suits this plant well and the ground should have been well limed in winter. If not, rake in 4 ounces per square yard of nitro-chalk before planting.

Varieties

'ASMER SHORTIE' This makes a dwarf, compact plant of dark green crinkled leaves and hearts quickly and uniformly.

'IRISH GIANT' A late maturing drumhead, making a large succulent heart with heavily curled outer leaves.

'OMEGA' The latest to mature, forming a large bluegreen head which stands well and is extremely hardy. May be cut as late as April.

'SAVOY KING' A Sakata hybrid bearing large flat heads, uniform in size and weighing 4 pounds each. The heads begin to heart at an early age so that they may be used over a long period. It also resists heat better than any other savoy and will crinkle well even in a warm climate.

'TOM THUMB' The best for a small garden for it makes a miniature head which is sweet and succulent and of darkest green. As it matures quickly, two sowings should be made, one in April to heart before Christmas, another a month later to mature in the new year.

Scolymus
Scolymus hispanica

Known as the Spanish thistle or Spanish oyster, the white stalks are eaten in parts of Spain and have much of the flavour of cardoons. But it is the roots which are mostly prized, having a taste like that of salsify to which it requires similar culture.

Sow early April, in a light soil manured for a previous crop. Make the rows 18 inches apart and thin out to 15 inches between the plants. Water during dry weather and feed occasionally with dilute liquid manure which will improve the texture of the stems and roots.

The plants may be lifted in November or the roots allowed to remain in the ground until ready to use which is preferable as, like salsify, they shrivel and lose flavour when lifted.

Scorzonera
Scorzonera hispanica

Known to the Spaniards as Viper's Grass, this is a native of the Iberian Peninsula and was originally grown as a medicinal herb for curing snake bite and to relieve indigestion. It was for this purpose that Louis XIV ordered the plant to be grown in large quantities in his Royal Gardens.

It has a flavour similar to that of salsify and like that plant, it will 'bleed' and entirely lose its flavour if carelessly lifted or if cut before it is cooked. In this era of kitchen cleanliness, its black skin has given it an undeserved unpopularity. During Elizabethan days, the roots were candied like eringoes.

A perennial, it forms a long fleshy tap root whilst its lance-shaped leaves may be used in salads. Seed is sown in a light, rich soil which has been manured for a previous crop. Sow in April in shallow drills 12 inches apart and thin out the seedlings to 8 inches. Keep the hoe moving between the rows and water copiously during dry weather.

The plants will be ready to lift in November but may be left in the ground until required. In this way, the roots will not shrivel whilst their full flavour will be retained.

Seakale
Crambe maritima

A native maritime plant which Gerard tells of finding on the seashore on several parts of the Essex coast and which one well known writer describes as being 'easy to grow, simple and inexpensive to force, free from pests and diseases, wholesome to consume'.

Like celery it enjoys a deep, rich, well worked soil, preferably of a sandy nature and again like that plant, the sturdier the stems, the more tender will they be so it should be grown as well as possible. Being a maritime plant, it requires salt in its diet; this is generally given in the form of Kainit at a rate of 2 ounces per square yard and worked into the soil as the beds are prepared in autumn. At planting time 2 ounces per square yard of superphosphate should be raked into the soil.

General cultivation Taking almost two years to mature from seed, seakale is usally grown from thongs which are sent out early in March by specialist growers and which will have been removed from the main root before it is forced. They come in bundles, the top of each thong being cut level, the bottom slanting, so that the bundles can be made up with each thong in the same direction. Having once formed a bed, it should not be necessary to have to purchase more thongs.

The bed is made 5 feet wide to allow for weeding and lifting without having to tread it. A slightly raised bed will prevent excess moisture remaining about the roots during periods of heavy rain.

Work into the soil plenty of decayed manure and as much humus as obtainable for though seakale enjoys a light, sandy soil it requires humus to maintain summer moisture. Where readily obtainable, seaweed, well chopped, is an excellent manure for this plant.

Towards the end of March the thongs are planted with the level end at the top and about 1 inch below soil level. Plant in rows 16 inches apart and allow a similar distance between each thong. Throughout summer, keep the hoe moving between the plants but a thick mulch of peat and decayed manure between the rows when the plants are making growth, will suppress weeds and conserve moisture in the soil.

By mid-October, the foliage will begin to die down and should be removed whilst, nearer to the month end, the roots are lifted, trimmed and stored in damp sand in a shed or cellar to be used for forcing when required, after removing and replanting the side shoots for next year's crop.

Forcing the roots Provided complete darkness can be given, the roots may be forced almost anywhere, in deep boxes in a cellar or cupboard or in the open if indoor space cannot be found. A 'pit' may be constructed against an outside wall and on three sides, corrugated sheets are let into the ground to a depth of 6 inches, held in place by strong stakes. A small hot bed is then made up, using manure and decayed leaves, to a depth of 12 inches and over this is placed 6 inches of finely sifted soil. Into this the roots are planted 4 inches apart, with the crowns level with the top of the soil.

Water them in and cover the bed with straw to a depth of 6 inches. Then across the straw, fasten sacking or additional sheeting to exclude light.

If a shed, cellar or outhouse is available, make up a forcing bed there for conditions will be darker, warmer and better in every respect. Loose bricks or planks could be placed around the hot-bed to hold it together and maintain warmth.

Harvesting The shoots will be ready when 7–8 inches long which will take 4–5 weeks depending upon available warmth. During the mid-winter months, it will be necessary to provide a temperature of 50°F. if succulent shoots are to be obtained in a reasonable time but too high a temperature will result in tough, soft roots which have lost their crispness.

When ready, cut off the heads just below soil level: however they should not be removed until required, and maybe used in a winter salad or to steam until tender. It should not be over-cooked, otherwise it will become tough and stringy.

After removing the heads, destroy the roots and begin again in spring.

Variety
'LILY WHITE' This is the best form, producing long, tender shoots of most agreeable flavour.

Shallot
Allium ascalonicum

The name of this vegetable is supposed to be a corruption of Ascalon where, in 1192, Richard I defeated the armies of Saladin and it is probable that he brought back this small onion to England. They could have been a valuable complement to the winter diet of mediaeval times; now they are grown chiefly for pickling, to use with cold meats and no vegetable is more easily managed.

Shallots require a light soil containing humus, preferably in the form of decayed manure or old mushroom bed compost. Bring the soil to a fine tilth and, before planting which should be early in March, rake in 2 ounces per square yard of sulphate of potash and roll or tread to ensure a firm bed.

Plant when the soil is in a suitable condition, merely pressing the sets (as the small bulbs are called) into the surface, in no way covering them. Set them 10 inches apart and keep the soil moist. Feeding with dilute liquid manure will help to build up a large crop and enhance the quality of the bulbs.

Harvesting Towards the end of August, bend over the necks to encourage the bulbs to ripen, when towards the end of September, the clusters of small bulbs are lifted and dried. They should be pickled within a month of drying if their full flavour is to be preserved.

It is always preferable to plant sets rather than to raise seedlings which are often wiped out by onion fly whilst seedlings rarely have time to reach full maturity in an ordinary British summer.

The finest variety is Dutch Yellow, the offsets being harvested in Holland where they have a longer ripening season and are stored under ideal conditions.

Skirret
Sium sisarum

The Scots know this vegetable as Crummocks, and in Tudor times it was widely grown for its roots which Parkinson said were the most delicious of all root vegetables. When the plants are lifted, the roots are to be seen growing from around the base of the stem, like thin parsnips 4–5 inches long and they have a pleasing aromatic smell and taste. They should be removed separately from the base of the stem and, after lightly scrubbing, stewed and served with butter or white sauce.

In the old days cottage gardeners would increase their stock by lifting and dividing the roots in spring each year, tearing apart the crowns and the roots attached to them, and re-planting 12 inches apart and 3 inches deep, in soil in good heart after manuring for a previous crop. This is still the best method, but alternatively plants may be raised from seed sown in drills made 12 inches apart and thinning them to 10 inches in the rows. Keep well watered and feed occasionally with dilute manure water. The roots will be ready to lift early in October.

Sorrel
Rumex acetosa

This is a common plant of meadowlands, with dainty spikes of reddish-brown and arrow-shaped leaves. It is a perennial and requires a rich soil and an open, sunny situation. The roots may be lifted and divided in spring or plants are readily raised from seed sown in April. Transplant the seedlings to 12 inches apart and water well during dry weather.

The French Sorrel, *Rumex scutata* has larger leaves, paler in colour and less acid in flavour than those of the common sorrel. The leaves of both may be used to make a tasty 'green' sauce to serve with fish. Used with water cress or parsley and an onion, they are first chopped and placed in a saucepan without water over a gentle flame. A tablespoonful of olive oil is added and a few drops of vinegar and the whole stirred to a paste of a cream-like consistency. It is then ready to use, hot or cold.

Fresh sorrel leaves add piquancy to a salad, those of the French sorrel being less acrid to the taste. They also add their distinctive flavour to an omelette. Tasty though sorrel leaves are, beware of eating them to excess: they contain acetic acid which is not too good for the system in large quantities, though harmless in small quantities.

Soya bean
Glycine max

The Soya Bean or Soybean requires a warm, moist climate to grow well and makes an erect bushy plant which, at the end of summer bears a heavy crop of short pods each containing 2–3 oval beans, bright green in colour which should be allowed to hang until fully mature. They are then removed and dried in an airy room before being 'shelled' when the beans will have turned yellowish-green. Useful for canning and quick freezing, they are cooked and used in the same way as butter beans and are both tasty and nourishing.

Plant 15 inches apart in April, where hard frosts are not expected, and in a well manured soil. Keep the plants hoed and well supplied with moisture until the seeds have filled the pods when they may be partially dried off. They are harvested about mid-September or, if required for use fresh, are picked as soon as the pods begin to swell and are cooked like broad beans.

The best variety for the English climate is 'Kanrich', the beans being ready to use fresh by early August.

Spinach
Spinacea oleracea

This plant is not a universal favourite, nor is it very successful in the garden, for summer spinach readily runs to seed, whilst plants of winter spinach may decay in excessively damp weather, but the plant has health giving qualities and many appreciate its unique 'earthy' flavour.

Summer spinach is best grown from a succession of sowings made from the end of March and every three weeks until late in July. To prevent the plants running to seed, select a position of partial shade and provide a humus laden soil. The plants require a rich diet and should be grown as cool as possible.

As what is wanted is that the plants should produce an abundance of leaf, dig into the soil some nitrogenous manure augmented by a $\frac{1}{2}$ ounce per square yard dressing of nitrate of soda to be given as soon as the plants begin to grow.

Sowing Sow the seed in shallow drills made 12 inches apart and thin the plants to 9 inches in the rows. It is the round leaf varieties that are sown for summer use, the leaves being gathered when young and tender. As soon as the plants run to seed, grub them up. Copious amounts of moisture in summer will delay the plants from seeding and an occasional watering with dilute liquid manure will improve the quality and extend the season.

Hoeing between the rows will keep the soil aerated and suppress weeds. It should be said that winter spinach should not be too heavily cut or the plants may be harmed by frost.

Spinach should never be boiled in water but, after chopping, should be cooked in its own moisture. It should be steamed for about half an hour and served with butter.

Disease
DOWNY MILDEW This disease is recognised by the pale yellow spots on the upper surface of the leaves and the blue-grey mildew which forms on the underside. The fungus may winter in the soil so rotational cropping is desirable. Dust the plants with flowers of sulphur if an outbreak is noticed but the best way to prevent an attack is to soak spinach seed in 1 per cent copper sulphate solution for 2 hours and then to dry off before sowing.

Varieties
SUMMER: 'CLEANLEAF' Of recent introduction, its smooth dark green leaves are rounded at the ends and held well above the soil on a long stalk so that

washing is not necessary.

'MONSTROUS VIROFLAY' Strangely named yet it is one of the best for summer use, making a large plant with an abundance of smooth round leaves.

'SUPERB' A new variety of good leaf quality and highly resistant to downy mildew, the most troublesome of spinach diseases. The medium green leaves are held well above the soil.

'TAMPALA' This variety is of American origin and is ready to pick within 8 weeks of sowing. The plants may be used entire in a salad or the young leaves may be cooked like spinach. It holds its green colour well when frozen whilst the stems may be cooked and used like asparagus.

'VICTORIA LONG-STANDING' This variety is slow to run to seed in dry weather and bears an abundance of large thick dark green leaves over several weeks.

WINTER: 'BLOOMSDALE LONG-STANDING' Hardy long-standing for winter use, the dark green leaves being large, extensively crinkled and held well above the soil, remaining in rosette form for several weeks.

'GIANT WINTER' A vigorous round-leaf variety, hardy and productive all the year through.

'HOLLANDIA' A most attractive plant in the garden for its long dark green leaves are arrow-shaped and are rarely troubled by adverse weather.

'NEW ZEALAND' (*Tetragonia expansa*) Botanically unrelated to the spinach, this is quite distinct in its habit, forming a low spreading plant and producing an abundance of thick fleshy leaves. It is untroubled by warm, dry weather whilst the leaves and young stem tips may be picked throughout summer and autumn and well into winter.

Spinach beet
Beta vulgaris

Also known as Perpetual Spinach, this grows well in ordinary soil and presents no difficulty in its culture. Seed is sown in spring in drills made 15 inches apart and the plants are thinned to 8 inches in the rows. Hoeing between the rows and regular watering in dry weather is all the attention it requires.

Plants will produce an abundance of leaf throughout the year except during severe frosts. Even if not required the leaves should be picked over continually for they become coarse and tough if left too long on the plants, whilst leaving them on reduces the supply of young leaves. Cook the leaves as for spinach.

Sugar Pea
Pisum sativum

This resembles a bean in the shape of its pod which is sliced and cooked in the same way. It has something of the tenderness of the French bean and the flavour and sweetness of fresh green peas. It should be gathered as soon as the peas can be seen through the pod, but before they begin to swell. The pods should be stringless and succulent and free of fibre when sliced.

Sugar peas require a warmer climate than ordinary peas so that they can mature quickly for, if the pods hang on the plants for any length of time they became tough and flavourless. The pods may be steamed whole or sliced.

Sowing Seeds are sown in April, planting them individually in trenches made 6 inches wide and spacing out the peas to 2 inches apart. Ordinary soil, manured for a previous crop will suit them well but some moisture-retaining humus should be dug in before planting and give a liberal dressing of lime.

As the plants make growth, insert a few twigs amongst them for the young tendrils to hold on to and later, place some pea sticks or laths about the rows. The vines will grow 2 feet high for the dwarf types and 4 feet high for the more vigorous kinds.

Keep the plants well watered during dry weather and, when about 12 inches high, begin watering once each week with dilute liquid manure. This will ensure tender, succulent pods which will be ready towards the end of July. They should be removed when 3 inches long.

Varieties

'BURPEE'S SWEETPOD' This variety is highly resistant to Fusarium Wilt and grows 4 feet tall, cropping heavily in all soils, the pods reaching 4 inches long before the peas begin to swell.

'DWARF GREY' This variety grows only 2 feet tall but is extremely prolific, the grey-green pods being sweet and tender and slightly curved. They are ready to gather when 3 inches long.

Swede
Brassica napus var. *naprobrassica*

In the United States this is considered to have a better flavour than the turnips. In Britain it is known as swede and is distinguished from the turnip by deep yellow flesh. A valuable crop in the 4-course rotation of farmlands, rutabagas (swedes) are equally valuable in the home vegetable garden for they are hardier than turnips. They may be left in the ground during winter and lifted when required. They are delicious boiled and mashed with butter and served with meats.

Sowing Seed is sown early in May, in drills made 18 inches apart, the seedlings thinned to 9 inches in the rows for they grow larger than turnips. Thinning should be done as soon as the seedlings are large enough to handle. Water copiously during dry weather for this is a plant that will make ample growth and remain free from stringiness only if supplies of moisture are available.

The roots may be used when of tennis ball size when they are especially sweet and succulent. They will reach maturity by mid-October and may be lifted and stored in a cellar or shed and covered with straw, or they may be lifted whenever required. The flavour will be improved after being subjected to hard frost.

They suffer from the same pests and diseases as turnips.

Variety

'PURPLE-top YELLOW' The finest variety, the globe-shaped roots are coloured purple at the top whilst the sweet, closely grained flesh cooks to deepest orange.

Sweet Corn
Zea mays

Maize, Indian Corn or Corn-on-the-Cob as it is variously called first achieved popularity in Britain with the arrival of the American armies during the Second World War. The old strains, however, were unsuited to the climate and not until the hybridisers were able to develop several varieties which would mature in the short summer of northern Europe, did sweet corn become a satisfactory crop. Even so, it requires a long, warm summer to grow well.

Sowing As it is necessary to allow the plants as long a season as possible, seed is sown in a warm greenhouse early in March or over a hot-bed in a frame. Sow one seed to a small pot containing John Innes Seed Compost or sow in peat pots which are plunged into the hot-bed. The frame should be closed to retain the maximum of heat. The minimum of root disturbance is desirable for the plants should at no time suffer any check.

If cloches are available, plants may be set out about mid-May, otherwise early June is a suitable time. The main cause of failure is cold winds, so protection should be given by placing the cloches on their ends around the plants or by erecting polythene lights around the beds or on the side of the prevailing wind. If the plants can be started under cloches they will mature a month earlier than if not protected and, in a dull summer, it will make all the difference as to whether the cobs ripen or not.

Select a sunny situation and provide the plants with a rich soil. A light well drained soil containing plenty of humus is required. Sweet corn thrives on wool shoddy whilst used hops are of value. Decayed strawy manure is also suitable. The soil must be in good heart and not lacking in lime.

Pollination will play a part in determining planting distances, 15 inches between each plant proving suitable. Water well in and never allow the plants to lack moisture throughout summer or the cobs will fail to swell and will be tough and unpalatable. A weekly application of dilute manure water will assist the cobs to grow sweet and suc-

culent whilst about mid-July, the plants will benefit from a mulch of decayed strawy manure.

Pollination Nature has no more wonderful way of pollinating. The plants produce the male flowers at the top of the tassel-like inflorescence whilst the female flowers, which produce the cob, develop from the leaf joints at the bottom of the plant, the silky tassels catching the pollen grains as they fall from the male flowers.

Though the plants should not be unduly cramped when set out, the closer they are planted, the better will be their pollination, so plant about 15 inches apart and allow the same distance from row to row. Preferably, plant in blocks or beds of four rows with a path down each side from which cultivations and picking may be done.

Harvesting Where the plants have been grown in the open unprotected, the cobs will be ready towards the end of August but in a summer lacking in sunshine, a warm autumn may be necessary to ripen them. By then the stems will have grown 6–7 feet tall and, to prevent them from breaking, it will be necessary to provide support by looping round them strong twine taken from one end of the row to the other. Or insert a tall cane to each stem.

The cobs are harvested as soon as fully ripe when the seeds are firm and juicy yet have not become hard. They are at their best eaten as soon as possible after removing. Take off the husks at once and, if it is necessary to keep them for a few days, place in a plastic bag in a cool room. To prepare, boil for 15–20 minutes, no longer and serve with white sauce or melted butter.

Exhibiting To display them, the cobs should have part of the husk removed but the silky threads at the end should be left intact. The rows of seeds should be well developed along the rows and this will occur only if correct pollination has taken place. The seed should be well developed but must not be hard. It must be of a uniform colour, either yellow or white, whilst the cob should be fresh and cylindrical.

Diseases

DAMPING OFF Should adverse weather cause delay in germination, there may be pre-emergence damping off of the seed and, to prevent this, seedsmen will, for small extra cost, dress the seed with Orthocide dust (continaing 65 per cent Captan).

Varieties

'GOLDEN BANTAM' This variety grows 5 feet tall and bears a profusion of cobs of outstanding quality. They grow 6 inches long with 8 rows of kernels which are sweet and tender and which mature quickly.

'FIRST OF ALL' An F_1 hybrid of outstanding quality. The earliest variety to mature, producing fine, medium-sized cobs ideal for table or exhibition.

'GOLDEN CROSS' A hybrid of remarkable uniformity, excellent for canning and deep freezing. The long, straight cobs have 12–14 rows of golden yellow kernels which are sweet and juicy.

'HONEYCROSS' A high-yielding hybrid of top quality cobs which measures 9 inches long, filled with 16 or more rows of bright yellow kernals of outstanding flavour.

'HURST'S HONEYDEW' Early and of outstanding vigour, this is a hybrid variety bearing pale yellow kernels which are sweet and tender. The cobs grow 8 inches long with the kernels well protected by the tight outer sheaths.

'SNOW CROSS' The earliest and best of the white varieties, the cobs, which taper to a point, measure 8–9 inches in length and with 12–14 rows of clear white kernels of outstanding flavour.

'WHITE MIDGET' The most compact, growing only 3 feet tall and bearing cobs 5–6 inches long with 12–14 rows of delicately flavoured kernels of purest white.

Sweet Potato
Ipomoea batatas

It is the root of this plant that was the first 'potato' used as a vegetable in England. 'Let the sky rain potatoes' said Falstaff, and this was the potato he meant. The tuberous roots require a long, warm summer for them to swell and multiply and their culture should be confined to the warmer parts.

The roots resemble dahlias and should be given a sunny situation and a friable soil enriched with some well decayed manure. Old mushroom bed compost is ideal.

Plant in April 6 inches deep and 15 inches apart and keep the plants well supplied with moisture when the weather is dry. An occasional watering with dilute liquid manure will increase the size of the roots.

Lift in early October before the frosts and store in boxes of sand in a frost free room until required.

Swiss Chard
Beta cicla

This variety is of the beet family and is known as Seakale Beet, and its top growth may be used in the same way as spinach. The long ribbed stems of the 'Ruby Chard' are identical in colour to rhubarb stems which they resemble in appearance, whilst the curled leaves formed at the top may be cooked and served as spinach. They possess a sweeter, less earthy flavour and are rich in vitamin content.

Swiss Chard grows well in a soil which has been manured for a previous crop. It requires moisture retaining humus and a limited amount of decayed manure.

Sowing Sow the seed as for beetroot, in drills 18 inches apart and 1 inch deep and, when the seedlings are large enough, thin out to 12 inches in the rows. If sown in April, the leaves are ready for use in autumn and, if the weather is mild, they will continue to grow throughout winter. If another sowing is made in July, the plants will form their leaves in spring and early summer to provide an all the year supply. It is advisable to cover the rows of late sown plants at the beginning of winter for they will not have made much top growth by then and may be harmed by frost.

General cultivation The plants will benefit from a dressing with 1 ounce per square yard of common salt when actively growing but an excess will cause the top foliage to grow coarse. An occasional watering with dilute liquid manure will increase the quality of the sticks, making them tender and succulent. Ample supplies of moisture during dry weather are also necessary for the production of tender stems.

Swiss Chard is one of the most handsome of vegetables with its brightly coloured stems and leaves and may be planted in the herbaceous border. 'Ruby Chard,' makes a striking indoor decoration to use with autumnal flowers.

When required, always pull the stems as for rhubarb, for cutting them will cause the roots to bleed and will reduce the crop. If the outer leaves are gathered first, this will allow the centre leaves room to develop to maintain the supply.

Varieties
'FORDHOOK GIANT' The sticks are more than 2 inches thick and are pure white with fleshy dark green crumpled leaves. The stems may be prepared like asparagus; the leaves like spinach.

'RUBY CHARD' The sticks, which grow 15 inches tall, are of bright translucent crimson, the colour extending out through the veins of the leaves which are heavily crumpled and have a mild, sweet flavour.

Tomato
Lycopersicon esculentum

Tomatoes, or Love Apples, as they were once called, were introduced into Europe shortly after the journeys of Columbus to the new world, but did not reach England until a later date. To begin with they were grown merely for their ornamental and curiosity value, and were thought to be poisonous.

To grow them outdoors, a warm friable soil is essential and the ground should be trenched for best results. Soil to a depth of about 15 inches should be removed and into the trench should be placed as highly concentrated humus as it is possible to obtain. Farmyard manure is not as easily available as it used to be but if some can be acquired it should be incorporated into the trench or added to compost heap which is to be dug into the trench. The compost is made by composting a quantity of straw with an activator, to which is added some dry poultry manure to assist in fermentation. If the heap is stacked as high as possible to allow it to heat up quickly and turned at weekly intervals for three weeks, a very useful compost for tomatoes will result. This, is not the easiest way to grow tomatoes, but if one wishes to obtain the maximum crop, then one must be prepared to give the plants as much help as possible from the beginning.

Soil preparation It is an excellent plan to place in the trenches a straw compost that is only half composted, for fairly long straw will help greatly with the aeration of the trench soil, a free circulation of air being most necessary for a healthy rooting system. Some growers place completely uncomposted straw at the bottom of a trench and stand this on end as an extra aid to air circulation. This is a successful method, but it is preferable to use partly composted straw. Uncomposted straw will have a tendency to take up vital nitrogen from the soil whilst in the process of rotting down so, if used by itself, it must first be treated with sulphate of ammonia, which costs only a few pence per pound. Where it is required that the straw should be stood on end in the trench, the sulphate of ammonia can be sprinkled over the straw when in position, and it will then begin its decomposition before the top soil is added.

Horticultural peat and hop manure mixed together will also contribute to the humus content of the soil and should be used where possible. Chopped seaweed is also an excellent organic fertiliser and is used in large quantities by the tomato growers of the Channel Isles and West Country. Shoddy (cloth waste) is also valuable, especially when used in conjunction with partially composted straw. In all but the very lightest soils peat should be used in quantity, and again for mulching the plants when the fruits begin to form. Should it not be possible to compost a quantity of straw, then it would be advisable to place lawn mowings and garden refuse at the bottom of the trench.

The use of lawn mowings as a means of providing 'green' humus is not as universally popular as it should be. Experiments carried out at the Cheshunt Research Station have shown that where up to 40 tons to an acre was added, tomato yields increased considerably.

Another 'green' product that normally runs to waste is pea and bean haulm, which may easily be obtained for the asking in many parts of the country. This is a valuable source of nitrogen and will give excellent results in the ultimate crop yield. But, though bean haulm may not be available to the town gardener, lawn mowings usually are and, during the summer months should be stored for use in winter when the trenches are made. The allotment holder and country gardener should collect pea and bean haulm throughout the summer months, and have this available for incorporation into the compost heap in preference to using it in the uncomposted state. Where the soil is heavy, ashes which have been weathered and well mixed into the top soil will also help to encourage a strong rooting system.

It is suggested that a trench be taken out rather than a portion of the garden double-trenched and the humus placed in the trench so that the manures may be kept in as concentrated an area as possible. In the same way, one would not top dress the ground in between the plant rows.

Again a trench will help to keep the land free from tomato sickness where a yearly crop is being cultivated, for the exact position of the trench will have been marked and that for the following year's crop may be made some way from the old one. This is more satisfactory than using up a larger area of ground for the same crop year after year, with no exact knowledge of where last season's crop was set out.

Where 'new' land is being used to grow tomatoes, and this will be the case where one is taking up residence in a newly built house, the turf should be first removed and placed grass downwards at the bottom of the trench. The mass of tiny fibrous roots of the turf will be a source of additional humus and, for this reason, many growers use turf for lining the trenches in a glasshouse. Wherever it can be obtained turf will improve with stacking and will be even more valuable where mixed with farmyard or poultry manures.

When once the humus content of the trenches is established, and this will decompose either in a compost heap or in the trenches themselves during winter, the base fertilisers should be added. The humus forming materials should have been covered over with 2 inches of soil and trodden down. This treading will prevent air pockets forming but, where straw is present, treading will not cut off air circulation. Early in spring, the base fertilisers may then be mixed with the top soil before it is placed in the trenches.

For additional supplies of nitrogen, dried blood, meat and hoof meal are both concentrated and slow acting, thus the plants are enabled to take up food during the whole of their cropping. These prepared organic manures, when used with artificially composted straw or 'green' manures, have produced excellent crops and if horse manure cannot be obtained, the tomatoes will still yield well. Tomato plants starved of nitrogen show a tendency to become thin and lanky with a yellow blotching of the leaves, and also an uneven ripening of the fruit. Thus nitrogen is most important but, where ample supplies of horse, poultry and pig manures are being used, the addition of nitrogenous manures must be limited, otherwise a soft sappy plant and delayed ripening of the fruit will result.

A most important requirement of the tomato is potash. Poultry manure which has been stored dry before using in the compost heap contains almost ten times the potash concentration of farmyard manure, and where guano or poultry droppings have been used in this way almost no extra potash will be needed. Where farmyard manure only is being used and then only on a small scale, it will be necessary to give potash additions. Sufficient may be given in the form of wood ash which, like poultry manure, has been stored dry. Wood ash contains about the same quantity of potash as poultry manure; sulphate of potash may be used sparingly instead and this contains about eight times the concentration of pure potash. Where organic manures are not in concentrated form, a 3 ounce per square yard dressing of hoof meal (5 parts) and sulphate of potash (1 part) will provide the necessary requirements of the plant.

To counteract any tendency of the plants to suffer from lack of magnesium, which in recent years has become prevalent, a sprinkling of Epsom Salts (magnesium sulphate) should be forked in at planting time.

Raising the plants It is realised that not everyone possesses a heated greenhouse and will either have to purchase plants, well hardened off, for planting out early in May under cloches, or early in June when growing in the open; or seed may be sown over a hot-bed in a closed frame.

The hot-bed should be made to a depth of 8 inches early in April or two weeks earlier if situated in a favourable area. Over the hot-bed (which has been well trodden to conserve heat and moisture) is placed a 1 inch covering of sterilised soil made up to the formula of the John Innes sowing compost:

2 parts loam
1 part peat
1 part sand
1½ ounces superphosphate
¾ ounce ground limestone
} per bushel

Only the loam will need sterilising and if this cannot be obtained it should be taken from pasture-land from a depth of 8–9 inches. It should be friable and free from roots and stones.

The seed is individually sown spacing it 2 inches apart and just covering it with soil. It is watered and the light placed over the frame. Water sparingly and as soon as germination has taken place, the seedlings should be given ventilation on all suitable occasions.

When they have formed their first pair of leaves they should be moved to 3 inch pots containing the John Innes potting compost:

7 parts loam
3 parts peat
2 parts sand
¼ pound John Innes Base
¼ ounce ground limestone
} per bushel

John Innes Base consists of:

2 parts hoof and horn meal
2 parts superphosphate
1 part sulphate of potash
} per bushel

There should still be some heat in the hot-bed, and into the soil where the seedlings have been moved the pots are pressed, peat being packed around them to conserve heat and moisture. Carefully watered, by the end of May after being gradually hardened, the plants will be ready to be set out in the open in the south or under cloches in the colder districts. If no cloches are available the plants should remain in the frame until about mid-June. Do not plant out too soon, even where glass covering is available, for until mid-June the nights remain cold and there will be few insects about to pollinate the first trusses. If these lower trusses fail to set, the crop will not only be much lighter but later.

The plants should be set out 3 to 4 feet apart each way and in a position of full sun where there is some protection from prevailing winds. Plant firmly and water well, henceforth keeping the soil comfortably moist. Bud-drop will result if the soil is too dry. Plants which are growing on in large pots where they are to crop will require careful attention as to watering, for the soil will dry out more quickly.

Plants in the open ground must also be watered with care for otherwise the soil will be thrown up on to the foliage or flower trusses, with the possible result that fungus spores may cause damage. Such troublesome diseases as Botrytis and Buckeye Rot may be the outcome. The bush tomatoes are more liable to suffer in this respect owing to their dwarf habit, and many growers place a layer of clean straw under each plant about 3 weeks after they have been set out. This not only prevents splashing of the foliage and trusses which are formed only a few inches from the soil level, but the straw acts as a mulch, preventing the soil from drying out. A thick layer of horticultural peat may also be used in place of the straw but nothing should be placed around the plants until they are well established, for a mulch will prevent the warmth of the sun penetrating to the soil which will have a detrimental effect on early plant growth. If the plants are set out towards the end of May, mid-June will be sufficiently early for the straw to be placed in position.

Also, heavy splashing of the soil will cause it to 'pan' and form a crust through which oxygen is unable to penetrate to the roots of the plants, causing possible die-back of the plants which often suffer in this way. Should a crust form on the top of the soil (which it may do as the season advances however carefully the waterings have been done) this may be broken up by pushing a cane or a poker into the soil at regular intervals, taking care to keep clear of the stems.

Pollinating Pollinating the trusses by carefully brushing each flower with a small camel hair brush, or even with a few hen's feathers tied tightly together at the end of a small stick will assist in the formation of fruit. This procedure should take place around mid-day, when the flowers are open and when all moisture is off the flowers, so it is advisable to withhold overhead syringing until after hand pollinating has been done. A dozen plants can be pollinated in five minutes, and syringing can then follow.

Outdoor plants cannot be pollinated when they are wet from rain or mist and an appropriate time must be awaited. Plants grown under frames or cloches whilst forming their first trusses will be under a greater degree of control. As the season advances daily brushing of the plants will not be necessary, two or three times a week being ample, whilst plants in the open will receive all the pollinating they require from the work of bees and other insects. Where large numbers of plants are being grown and time is at a premium, the plants may be pollinated by merely shaking the supports to which they are fastened. This will produce a dusting effect on a small scale and is quite useful where plants are growing indoors. Plants growing entirely in the open are best pollinated by hand.

Bringing on the crop Those varieties of dwarf habit such as 'Atom', and 'Tiny Tim' will require neither 'stopping' nor the removal of any side shoots. They 'stop' themselves and will restrict themselves to only a certain number of shoots.

Those of taller habit should be 'stopped' at the fourth truss so that they will be able to ripen their fruit before the autumn. Most of the ornamental tomatoes will make tall bushy plants and so are better grown up pea sticks and allowed to grow at will. The ability of these plants to look after themselves makes them valuable to the gardener with only limited time at his disposal. Those orthodox yellow fruiting varieties should have the side growths removed with a sharp knife or even with the fingers, whenever they are observed growing from a leaf joint.

A light dressing of peat and strawy manure given early in July will help to preserve moisture in the soil and will keep down annual weeds, thus making hoeing and hand weeding with the danger of damaging the roots, unnecessary. Over the mulch a layer of clean straw should be placed to prevent soil splashing and on which the fruits may rest without damage though, if the trusses are supported by twigs this will be a help in ripening and keeping the fruit free from blemishes. As an aid to ripening a light dressing of sulphate of potash, 2 ounces per square yard could be given just before the mulch and, from the end of July until mid-September, a weekly application of dilute manure water will maintain the nourishment required by the later maturing fruit.

Defoliation also calls for attention as the crop is ripening. No leaves should be removed until they have completed their part in the health of the plant, for the function of foliage is just as important as root action, the two going hand-in-hand.

It is advisable to cut back the lower leaves when once the plant is thoroughly established. This will prevent an attack of Botrytis owing to the splashing of the bottom foliage with soil through careless watering, or due to heavy rain. It also allows for a free circulation of air, also a safeguard against botrytis or mildew. This is particularly advisable with bush varieties in a season of dull, damp weather where these particular varieties tend to form more foliage than is necessary. It is preferable to cut back the leaves just half-way, otherwise complete defoliation may be too drastic.

As the season advances and the plants appear to be making rather too much foliage due to a wet, sunless summer, it is permissible to thin out the leaves when the plant has formed its first trusses. Again, it is advisable to cut back only half of each leaf. Much will depend upon the season, and should the period of sunshine be above average, it is not only better to leave any defoliation entirely alone, but many growers even allow one or two side shoots to make more growth than usual before they are cut out. This will provide the plants with additional leafage for converting carbon dioxide and also to provide some protection for the plants for intense sunlight tends to dry up the foliage. So much depends upon the weather and the type of tomato being grown that no definite instructions on defoliation can be given. The removal of the leaves just for the sake of doing so is wrong; in fact, no gardening operation of any kind should be performed unless there appears a definite reason for doing so, and this applies particularly to defoliation. As the crop draws to its close, the sun's warmth becomes weaker and a certain amount of fruit remains to be ripened. Then considerably more defoliation may be done, for now the plant no longer needs the starches and sugars to produce its crop of fruit. The work is completed and all that remains is for the final ripening of the fruit, which should be given all the sunshine possible. Complete defoliation may then be done. The bending of the stem of the plant will also assist ripening, by restricting the flow of moisture.

Pests and Diseases

BLIGHT This is the same fungus that attacks the potato causing a grey mould to cover the underside of the leaves. With tomatoes, it causes dark brown spots on the leaves and grey patches on the green fruits. It is rare on plants in heated houses, troubling mostly those growing without heat or outdoors in a wet, sunless summer. Spraying the plants with Burgundy Mixture, once every 3 weeks from the time for the first fruit sets will prevent an outbreak. Or in wet weather, dust the foliage with the preparation.

BOTRYTIS This fungus disease is caused by careless watering splashing the soil onto the lower leaves:

it will spread rapidly under cold, damp conditions or those of excessive humidity. Too close planting should be avoided. The disease is diagnosed by the appearance of brown tissue which will spread to the calyces, causing the fruit to fall prematurely. Spraying with Shirlan AG at the first sign will usually give control and, as routine precaution, it may be advisable to water the lower part of the stem with Shirlan AG from the time the first truss has set.

BROWN ROOT ROT   This attacks indoor plants, causing the roots to turn brown and die back. Eventually the plant collapses. Soil condition plays a part in the appearance of the disease, a well aereated soil into which composted straw has been incorporated, rarely supporting the disease. A balanced diet is also important for a healthy rooting system.

BUCKEYE ROT   A disease of the fruit, usually of the lower trusses, it attacks at the point away from the calyx, the decay appearing as concentric rings making the fruit unfit to use. Careless watering of the lower trusses may be the cause and it is advisable to give them adequate support to lift the fruits from the soil.

CLADOSPORIUM   Also known as Leaf Mould or Leaf Spot and until the introduction of resistant varieties of hybrid vigour, it was one of the most troublesome of tomato diseases, especially in the low-roof forcing type house which it is difficult to ventilate efficiently. The disease takes several forms, hence the need for the varieties 'Antimold A' or 'B' raised at the John Innes Institute but several of the hybrids are resistant to all forms.

The disease appears as small yellow spots on the underside of the leaves. As it spreads, the whole leaf becomes a mass of brown mould whilst the fruits fall away without maturing. Spraying with a copper-oil compound will prevent it from destroying the plant tissues if caught in time but this should not be done until early July, until the plant is well established. It is advisable to plant resistant varieties, especially in forcing type houses.

EELWORM   This causes swellings to form on the roots and the plants may collapse. Where it has proved troublesome, and the plants are to be planted in permanent beds in the greenhouse, the soil must be treated with a liquid fumigant, that known as D.D being suitable, but the soil must be allowed 5 weeks to clear itself of the fumes before planting.

RED SPIDER   The red mites cluster beneath the foliage in a type of cocoon so that they they are difficult to reach except by pressure spraying which may damage the plants. The pest will be most prevalent in too-dry conditions. It may be exterminated by fumigating with an Azobenzene smoke or controlled by dusting the plants with Abol derris powder, which will also control aphis. Maintaining the correct humidity is also important.

TOMATO MOSAIC   The most dreaded of tomato diseases, causing the leaves to turn yellow and the plants to die back. The virus may also cause blemishes on the fruits. Smokers tending their plants with tobacco stained hands, may cause infection and 'Pagham Cross' an immune variety should be grown. Seedsmen now supply heat-treated seed for a small extra cost which will give immunity. Treated seed is more difficult to germinate, taking a week longer and allowance must be made for this.

WHITE FLY   Like a tiny white moth this is a dreaded pest amongst indoor tomatoes though it may be controlled by introducing to the greenhouse the white fly parasite supplied by several agricultural stations. Wettable DDT sprayed on to the plants once every 3 weeks from the time the first fruit has set will give control.

Varieties

(RED) 'ATOM'   Of almost prostrate habit and making little foliage, the plant needs neither staking nor stopping. When once the fruit has formed, it ripens very fast with the minimum amount of sunshine. Owing to its low habit it is the best of all tomatoes for an exposed garden, and may be brought into fruit by early July if planted under barn-type cloches or in frames.

Owing to the rapid maturing of the plant, seed should not be sown until towards the end of April for the plants must be kept growing without check, as it will not be possible to set them out before the second week of June except where glass is being used, and they can then be planted out early in May. These tomatoes need a well manured soil and when the trusses form, they should be kept above the soil by stout twigs, wood wool or moss being placed around the plants to prevent splashing. Cloches should be removed when the first ripe fruit is ready, and they may then be placed on their ends around the plants to give protection from wind.

Atom is not a large fruit, about the size of a golf ball. It ripens without any trace of 'greenback' and, apart from feeding with liquid manure each week, it requires no other attention.

'HISTON CROPPER'   Of dwarf habit and making little foliage, it carries a heavy crop of medium sized fruit with a unique 'tart' flavour. The crop ripens quickly in the minimum of sunshine. The plant is highly resistant to blight.

'HISTON EARLY'   Raised by Unwins of Histon, this is the earliest and heaviest cropping of the taller growing outdoor varieties. The plant is short-jointed with large potato-like leaves, the fruit being bright red, even in size and of excellent flavour.

'SLEAFORD ABUNDANCE'   An F_1 hybrid and one of the best of the outdoor varieties growing only 12 inches tall with little foliage. It bears enormous trusses and well shaped fruit which ripen quickly and possess delicious flavour.

'SUGARPLUM'   Excellent for growing in pots on a terrace or verandah or in the garden room, this is a tall growing variety bearing long, heavily packed trusses of small dark red fruits which are excellent in salads whilst, being sweet and juicy, are loved by the children.

'THE AMATEUR' This variety rapidly established itself with both amateur and market growers alike, not only for it matures quickly, but because of the high quality of its fruit, equal to that of most indoor varieties. It requires no stopping and is a tremendous cropper. Growing to a height of only 15 inches, well grown plants in a normal summer will yield up to 10 pounds of fruit. The first fruit matures a fortnight later than 'Atom' and has won praise for its excellent flavour and firmness. After bottling or in tins both 'Atom' and 'The Amateur' will retain their full flavour for two years. Processing should be done towards the end of August when there is often a surplus of ripe fruit, and before the autumn dampness causes any deterioration in its condition.

Yellow and white The yellow skinned varieties are not nearly so popular as they might be. Their fruit is never quite so prolific as the new red introductions, yet the flavour is rich and possesses a smooth sweetness, absent from the reds.

Those recommended for outdoor culture are:
'AMERICAN WHITE' This is included under yellow tomatoes for the fruit has a pale yellow shading. It is a novelty of exceedingly handsome appearance when mixed with red and yellow varieties in a salad. It is a heavy cropper producing large well shaped fruits, and does well both outdoors and in a cold house. The flavour is quite outstanding.
'GOLDEN JUBILEE' Bearing a large fruit of brightest yellow with the flesh almost the colour of an orange, this is a new and splendid variety. The habit of the plant is stiff and short jointed.
'MID-DAY SUN' A Stonor introduction, being a heavy cropper, especially in the south. The deep canary-yellow fruits are of medium size and particularly well shaped.
'YELLOW PERFECTION' An Unwin introduction having deeply cut fern-like foliage, like that of a potato plant. The plant is a vigorous grower and comes into bearing quickly. The fruit is the same size as that of 'The Amateur' and is an attractive golden yellow colour.

There are also other interesting tomatoes of ornamental value in salads and which make delicious eating, more like ripe, red gooseberries than tomatoes, being sweet and juicy.
'CHERRY TOMATO' The vivid scarlet fruits are about the size of a large cherry, having a rich flavour, and are borne in long clusters right through summer and autumn. They are used whole in salads and, eaten in this way, their full flavour is retained.
'GRAPE TOMATO' A new and unusual introduction, the fruit being borne in long sprays like grapes, which they resemble in size. They are very sweet and juicy, delicious in salads and are more like a fruit than a tomato in this respect.
'PEAR TOMATO' Tall growing but requiring the same treatment as that given to the more orthodox varieties. The fruit is crimson and in shape exactly like small pears. The flavour is outstanding and the plants are prolific: a splendid tomato for bottling.
'TINY TIM' This is a 'Currant Tomato', which makes a small bushy plant about 20 inches high, being a dwarf counterpart to the ordinary Currant Tomato which attains a height of 4 feet or more. Like 'Atom' it is suitable for growing in pots on the verandah or terrace of a town flat where its fruit will be particularly welcome through summer, the plants requiring the minimum of attention. With the Currant Tomato, the side shoots should not be removed for they will later bear fruit and here size does not matter. The tall variety is best grown up stout pea sticks.

Growing indoors The introduction of a number of varieties of hybrid vigour which, combined with a resistance to many of the destructive tomato diseases of the past, has revolutionised indoor tomato culture during recent years. A key roll in the hybridising programme has been played by the variety 'Potentate' which, of all ordinary varieties, produces more fruit on its lower (first) trusses and ripens it sooner than any other tomato, though its later trusses are liable to become smaller. It was therefore crossed with the variety 'E.S.1', which takes time to become established, and bears most heavily later in the season. The result of their crossing was a variety which combined the cropping qualities of both parents and set in motion a programme of crossing for hybrid vigour.

The two parents are grown in separate greenhouses, one acting as the seed bearer, the other as the pollinator. It is important that no stamens of the female or seed-bearing parent be allowed to ripen, otherwise the flowers will set pollen without having been crossed and would produce seed of the same variety. Every bloom must therefore be emasculated i.e. have its stamens removed so that it cannot pollinate the stigma, and this must be done before the stamens begin to shed their pollen, before the flowers open.

Pollen is removed from the other parent with an electric 'bee'. This is an ordinary torch case and battery, but in place of a bulb is a small glass bowl or cup with an opening large enough to take the stigma of a tomato flower. Inside the cup is a wire hook into which the stigma is placed, the pollen being removed by vibration of the hook and, as each flower opens, it is visited by the 'bee'.

The pollen is transferred to the stigmas of the emasculated or seed-bearing plants from the cup by means of a small camel-hair brush. This is done as soon as the stigma is exposed for if left too long the flower will die without being pollinated and will set no seed. After the seed has been grown, it must not be saved again from the fruits.

When to plant Light intensity will play an important part in planting for an early crop. Those living near to the south coast, where there is a higher rate of winter sunshine than elsewhere in Britain, may plant in a heated house towards the end of February, seed having been sown about mid-December. In the home counties, planting may be done early in March and on the east coast of Yorkshire where there are large commercial plantings, mid-March is the accepted time. It is incorrect to think that growers in the less favourable districts can obtain equally early crops merely by increasing the house temperature, for this would result only in 'drawn' plants. To grow early tomatoes, there must also be sufficient warmth to keep the plants growing whatever the weather. This will mean a minimum temperature of 50°F. during day time and 45°F. at night. Until these temperatures can be ensured, planting must be delayed.

In a cool house, planting should not be done before the first week of April in the south; mid-April in the Midlands; and the month end in the north. Again, the plants must be kept growing without check but if warmth can be provided at night by a paraffin oil heater or by electric heating, then planting may be done a fortnight earlier.

To obtain early crops in a cold house, plant an early maturing variety and stop some of the plants after they have formed four trusses. Others may be allowed to grow on to continue the cropping through autumn. Those plants at the back of a tomato house may be allowed to grow on to the top of the roof whilst plants of an early variety may be grown in large pots beneath them and these are stopped after forming four trusses.

Tomatoes may be grown on the greenhouse bench, planting either in boxes or in wooden troughs made at the back. The plants may be trained up the roof, being supported on long canes fastened to wires stretched across the roof; or in a Dutch-light house they may be planted directly into ground beds of prepared compost or in large earthenware pots placed on the floor. In a Dutch-light house the glass will reach down to the base, so that the plants will receive the maximum amount of light. Tomatoes may also be grown in deep boxes placed in rows on the greenhouse floor. The hybrids should be planted 18–20 inches apart, allowing them more room than ordinary varieties for they make plenty of leaf and form large trusses of fruit.

Experiments carried out by the Cheshunt Research Station on the relationship between crop yields and planting distances showed that, allowing 16 to 18 inches between ordinary varieties resulted in heaviest yields, 7–8 pounds of fruit per plant being obtained when stopped at the 8th truss. But the hybrids, which are shorter jointed plants and form their first trusses earlier, may be allowed to grow on to 12–14 trusses and will yield double the weight of fruit. They will also remain healthy to the end.

Sowing Where raising seedlings, the first sowings are made early in January and, where electricity is available, a simple propagating frame will be a necessity to maintain a temperature of 65°F. in the south (where there is a greater intensity of light). Germination will take 7–8 days. In less favourable areas, the temperature should not exceed 60°F., when germination will take 10–12 days.

Seed is sown in boxes or pans containing John Innes compost and the propagating unit will provide the correct humidity. Sow thinly, spacing out the seed so that the seedlings will not be crowded. When they have formed their first two pairs of leaves, transplant to small pots or to Root-o-Pots made of compressed peat and filled with the John Innes potting compost. There will be no further root disturbance for the plants may be set out in their fruiting quarters in the 'pots'.

Where sowing in boxes, it is a good idea to line them with moss or moist peat before adding the compost, then the seedlings will send down their roots into the moist lower layer and grow with additional vigour.

The seedlings and young plants should be kept growing on in a temperature of 58°F., falling to 50°F. at night. The atmosphere should be moist but buoyant; tomatoes will not tolerate 'stuffy' conditions. The plants must be kept comfortably moist and, for their watering, always use water heated to the temperature of the greenhouse. Water used from the tap will cause chilling which will bring about a check in plant growth. Well grown seedlings will set heavy first trusses and early tomatoes are always most in demand. Should the plants take on a 'blue' appearance, this may be due to cold conditions and may be corrected by increasing the temperature by several degrees; alternatively it may be due to lack of phosphates in the soil. This can be overcome by watering with $\frac{1}{2}$ ounce of superphosphate of lime dissolved in a gallon of water. Do not keep the plants in the pots too long before moving to their fruiting quarters or they may show signs of lacking in nutriment.

If planting in ground beds, double digging to a depth of 2 feet should be done, incorporating peat, decayed manure and garden compost. Tomatoes love peat for they like a soil with a pH value of about 6 which is slightly acid. A too alkaline soil will produce a light crop. To guard against wireworm, dust the soil with Lindex as it is prepared.

As an alternative to farmyard manure, 'Bio Humus' may be used. It combines bacterised peat and seaweed and is rich in nitrogen and potash, the phosphates being provided by a dressing of superphosphate of lime. Hop manure may also be used, augmented with sulphate of potash; or wool shoddy or hoof and horn meal which release their nitrogen over a long period, which is what the tomato requires.

To aerate the soil, which is so important for tomatoes, the method of planting between straw 'walls' has given heavier and healthier crops. Upright 'walls' of straw are made at intervals of about 2 feet along the beds after the soil has been prepared and between the 'walls' the plants are set out, one to every space of about 20 inches. The straw is taken from a bale and is inserted into the soil to a depth of about 18 inches and so that it reaches up to the surface of the bed. The 'walls' are made 6 inches thick and it is usual to water the beds through the straw 'walls'. This will ensure that the water reaches down to the roots of the plants and will prevent the soil from 'panning' at the surface.

Where growing in pots, a compost should be made up containing fibrous turf loam, preferably of a heavy nature but containing plenty of root fibres. Into this some decayed manure should be mixed ('Vitamure' or 'Bio-Humus' may be used instead), together with some peat or bark fibre to aerate the compost. To each barrowful of compost, mix in 1 pound of steamed bone flour and some sulphate of potash, at the rate of $\frac{1}{2}$ ounce for each pot. A 10 inch pot should be used and before filling with compost, it must be well crocked. Allow 2 inches from the top of the compost to the pot rim so that a mulch can be given when the first four trusses have formed. Plant firmly and water in. Ample room should be allowed between the pots for the plants to have a free circulation of air. Maintain a buoyant atmosphere by ventilating on all suitable days and, when the weather is warm, syringe the foliage frequently and water the floor of the greenhouse. Up to mid-May, the ventilators should be closed at night but from then onwards may be left open day and night except when unduly cold.

The lower (first) trusses will be opening their flowers when there are few insects about and should be assisted in their pollination by dusting them with a camel-hair brush. This is done about mid-day and the fertilisation will be more successful if a misty atmosphere is created in the house afterwards. Spraying the plants should continue throughout summer, not only to assist with pollination but to prevent excessive moisture evaporation from the foliage.

Water the soil only when necessary until the first truss has formed then, as the fruits appear and begin to swell, give ever increasing supplies, keeping the soil always damp. If the soil is allowed to dry out, and this is followed by heavy watering, it will cause the fruits to burst their skin.

When 12 inches tall, the plants should be supported by 8 feet canes to which they are loosely tied with raffia and, from this time onwards, all side growths which appear from the leaf axils should be removed by pinching out. Or use a sharp knife, taking care not to damage the main stems.

Bringing on the crop The plants will be ready for a mulch in June, a month later where growing in a cold greenhouse. A mixture of turf loam, peat and decayed manure will prove suitable. It should be given to a depth of about 2 inches around the base of the plants and the surface roots will at once begin to grow into it with the plant growing away with renewed vigour. These new roots will take up additional moisture and nutriment needed by the

plant in forming its top trusses. A $\frac{1}{2}$ ounce per square yard dressing of sulphate of potash given each plant in July will help the fruit to ripen well and prevent 'greenback'; or give a dressing of 5 parts nitro-chalk and 1 part potash which will keep the plants growing on and will help the fruit to ripen. Feeding once a week with dilute liquid manure will help to maintain the vigour of the plants and increase the yield. Shortage of magnesium will also reduce the weight of crop. This may be corrected by watering once every 3 weeks with magnesium sulphate (1 ounce to a gallon of water). As the fruit swells, the trusses should be supported by loosely tying them to the cane with raffia.

The correct time to stop the plants also calls for judgment, depending upon variety and the season. In a cold, dull summer it may be necessary to stop after 6 or 7 trusses for the top fruit to ripen, whereas in a year of prolonged sunshine plants of the hybrids may be grown on to 12 or 14 trusses before stopping. If the plants are stopped too soon they will not bear their maximum crop; if stopped too late, they will not bring their top trusses to maturity.

After stopping, the defoliation of the plant can begin. First, the lower leaves are removed and, as a rule, only the foliage below a truss is cut away when the fruit has matured. Then as the next truss ripens, the foliage below that truss can be removed and so on. Thus, the whole plant is defoliated to coincide with the ripening of the last truss. Too early removal of the foliage must be guarded against as this will upset the balance of the plant.

Tomatoes should always be removed with the calyx attached: this helps to retain the freshness and enhances the appearance of the fruit.

Varieties
'AMBERLEY CROSS' Raised at the Glasshouse Research Institute at Littlehampton and resistant to 'greenback', it is the earliest to ripen in a warm greenhouse and crops heavily. It makes a tall leafy plant and though setting heavy first trusses, it continues to grow with vigour and bears high class fruit until the end of autumn.
'ARASTA' A strong growing hybrid, forming its trusses on one side of the stem only. An easily grown variety, the fruits are of medium size and good shape, thick-skinned and fleshy.
'BIG BOY' An F_1 hybrid, this is the largest of all tomatoes, a normal sized fruit weighing more than 1 pound whilst, under good culture, fruits will weigh up to 2 pounds. There is nothing coarse about them, being round and of brilliant scarlet with a firm, smooth skin. Making plenty of leaf and continuing to bear over a long period, it must be grown well.
'EUROCROSS' A hybrid of the 'Moneymaker' type producing non-greenback fruits of excellent quality. Immune to Cladosporium and a heavy cropper, its fruits are of excellent quality, shape and size.

'INFINITY CROSS' The introduction of this cultivar heralds something of major importance in hybrid tomatoes for it has yielded up to 20 pounds of fruit per plant in an amateur's greenhouse and a single truss of 8 pounds has been recorded. As the trusses are so large that only 6 should be allowed from plants grown in a warm house and only 4 from cold house plants. It is necessary to feed heavily. The fruits are round and of medium size and ripen without trace of greenback.

'KELVEDON CROSS' This does well in a cold or a heated house, its trusses being closely spaced, the evensized globular fruits ripening evenly and early with no trace of greenback.

'LAVANT CROSS' This is derived from the excellent 'Amberley Cross' and shows all its desirable characteristics whilst it has the additional quality of being immune to *Verticillium Wilt*.

'PAGHAM CROSS' Smokers should grow this variety for it yields heavily and is immune to *Tomato Mosaic*. This is also a disease of tobacco and has been known to wipe out an entire house before the plants have yielded their full crop. It makes a tall leafy plant, is resistant to Cladosporium and crops over six months or more.

'PINK GOURMET' Raised by Dr. Lambert at the University of Missouri, this is classed as a 'beefsteak' tomato, being rough and uneven in shape with the flesh solid and meaty. The skin is of a lurid purple-pink colour with a flavour unlike that of any other tomato. It should be grown in large pots and confined to 4 trusses which will require adequate support.

'RED ENSIGN' A quick growing variety that ripens its first fruits early and is resistant to Cladosporium. It yields a heavy crop of well-shaped fruit of even-size with firm flesh and skin.

Turnip
Brassica rapa

A favourite vegetable of the Italians, the turnip may have been introduced into Britain by the Romans, whilst improved forms certainly came over with the Huguenots during the 16th century. It is the round flattish root that is most in demand rather than the leaves which are rarely used as a vegetable. By planting for succession, it is possible to have turnips throughout the year.

Sowing For an early crop, seed of 'Early White Milan' or 'Tokyo Cross' should be sown in a frame over a gentle hot bed at the end of February. Sow thinly and space the seedlings 6 inches apart, removing any which might cause overcrowding. Admit plenty of air when the seed has germinated, for turnips do not like coddling, and keep the soil comfortably moist. By early May, the roots will have attained the size of small tennis balls and will be ready to use.

This is a valuable 'catch' crop for the market grower, for there are few fresh vegetables in the shops in May. They are tied in bunches of 8 or 9 turnips.

Outdoors, a sowing is made early in April, between dwarf peas, to mature early July. Here, again, the roots are lifted when reaching tennis ball size, before they become coarse and woody.

Turnips require a rich, deeply worked soil which has been well limed and a firm seed bed containing plenty of wood ash. Sow broadcast and thin to 6 inches apart. Like radishes, turnips need to grow quickly so that they must never be allowed to lack moisture.

To mature early outdoors, 'Early Snowball' is recommended and this should be followed by a sowing made early July of 'Utility' or 'Golden Ball' to provide roots for winter use. Sown in July, the roots will have reached about 4 inches across by winter time and this is the size when they are at their best for culinary use. They are completely hardy and may be lifted as required.

If sowing in drills, make them 12 inches apart and space the seedlings to 6 inches apart in the rows. If the turnips are wanted for winter storing, they should be lifted early in December, the leaves being cut off but not the roots.

Exhibiting Lift as near to the show day as possible, wash away the soil and leave to dry for an hour or so before looking over the roots for any blemishes. They should then be sorted for uniformity and, on the morning of the show, cut the leaves back to 2 inches of the root.

Pests and Diseases
CLUB ROOT This attacks all the brassicas, the turnip being no exception. Well limed land will rarely support the disease and dusting the soil with Calomel before the seed is sown will afford protection.

MILDEW This occasionally attacks young plants, covering the leaves with a greyish mould. Spraying with Bordeaux Mixture as soon as noticed will give control.

TURNIP FLY This is a beetle which attacks the plants in the seedling stage, laying its eggs on the leaves in May. The grubs eat into the leaf tissues whilst the last of the three cycles which are produced each season winter in the soil as pupae. Before sowing, seed should be treated with a combined dressing whilst the young plants should be dusted with derris on a dry, sunny day towards the end of May and again a month later.

Varieties
'EARLY MILAN' A distinct variety with strap-like leaves, this is the first to mature. The roots are flattened and are white with a purple top.

'EARLY SNOWBALL' A white globe-shaped turnip with sweet and tender flesh and fine for exhibition.

'GOLDEN BALL' This stands through winter and is the finest for late summer sowing. The roots are ball-shaped and bright orange with the distinctive flavour of a swede.

'TOKYO CROSS' An F_1 hybrid maturing early and showing high resistance to disease. The pure white globe-shaped roots reach a diameter of 3 inches in five weeks and will grow to double the size without becoming woody.

'UTILITY' An outstanding all-round variety, being white with a purple top and with white close-grained flesh of excellent flavour.

Vegetable spaghetti
Cucurbita pepo

A variety of vegetable marrow, it is grown in the same way, planting on mounds of decayed manure in a frame or in the open, 5 feet apart when danger of frost is over. The seeds are sown in peat pots early in April for the plants resent root disturbance.

Keep them growing with ample supplies of water in dry weather and this will help the marrows to swell. An occasional watering with liquid manure will prove beneficial.

When the plants have made 18 inches of growth, pinch out the leader shoots to encourage the formation of side shoots and pollinate as for marrows to assist the flowers in setting their fruits. These are removed when only 9 inches long, whilst still tender and sweet. The marrows are bright yellow. They should be boiled for 30 minutes, then cut into halves, when it will be found that the inside flesh comes away in shreds like spaghetti. It can be served hot with meats or may be chilled and used in salads.

Water cress
Nasturtium spp.

A native plant of the British Isles water cress has been consumed for its pleasant taste and health-giving properties since the time of primitive man.

It is a creeping aquatic plant with hollow stems growing 12 inches tall. The dark green pinnate leaves have a high iron content and are rich in vitamins.

General cultivation The plants are set out 3 inches apart in a specially prepared bed with 3–4 inches of running water over them. The beds are made about 6 feet wide with a base composed of soil and decayed manure into which the young plants or rooted cuttings are set. Early summer is the best time to make up the beds for the plants will then become established before winter. In the warmer parts, they continue to grow and may be cut throughout the year so that many of the commercial growers are found in Hampshire and Dorset. Further north, the beds may be covered in winter with sheets of polythene raised several feet above the plants and this will provide sufficient warmth for them to continue growing in cold weather.

It is possible to grow water cress without running water. A trench is prepared 3 feet wide and 12 inches deep and into the bottom is placed 4 inches of decayed manure. This is covered with 2 inches of soil over which is placed 2 inches of sand. The plants are set out 4 inches apart and kept saturated with water.

Types There are no named cultivated varieties, though some growers have selected strains which are either more branched or else which bear larger leaves. There are, however, two distinct types of water cress, the green and the brown.

'GREEN WATERCRESS' So-called because it remains green through the autumn, though it is susceptible to damage by frost in winter and spring. This is the commoner of the native European species, *Nasturtium officinale*.

'BROWN WATERCRESS' or 'WINTER WATERCRESS' This is a hybrid between the above species and another wild species, *Nasturtium microphyllum*. The leaves turn purplish-brown in autumn, but it is less affected by frost than the green watercress.

Pea 'Histon Maincrop'. A pea that combines fine flavour
with exceptionally heavy cropping powers. The slightly
curved, medium-sized pods are almost invariably borne
in twos, producing a heavier crop than almost any other.
Heavy croppers like this need adequate support.
Courtesy of W. J. Unwin Ltd.

Turnip 'Extra Early Milan'. An unusual, mild-flavoured turnip with strap-shaped leaves and flattened globes with purple tops. It is by far the earliest turnip to mature, and is more successful on heavier soils than most.
Courtesy of W. J. Unwin Ltd.

Part 3

HERBS AND THEIR CULTURE

Angelica
Angelica archangelica

This is a stately and beautiful plant, native of Europe and growing as far north as the Arctic Circle. It may live for years in the garden but is usually treated as a biennial, seed being sown in August where it is to mature. As it grows 6 feet tall, it should be planted at the back of a border where it can be left to seed itself year after year. Alternatively it may be planted in the vegetable garden in an open, sunny position where it can be left un-disturbed to reproduce itself.

The stems are cut from early June onwards, preferably when young, when they are candied and used in confectionery or to flavour tomato chutney. The stems may also be used to stew with rhubarb or apples to which they impart a pleasant musky flavour. Rhubarb jam is improved by its inclusion which should be in the ratio of 1 part of angelica to every 5 of rhubarb. From the stems and leaves, a pleasant cordial water can be made which acts as an aid to digestion.

The garden angelica is distinguished from the wild form, *A. sylvestris* by its smooth, hollow stems, the latter having purple stems covered in small hairs. It flowers late in May or early June and, if the stems are cut before it does so, the plants will be long living whilst the stems will be sweet and succulent.

To candy the stems, cut them into pieces 3 inches long, peel and boil in a little water, until all moisture has evaporated. Then cover with sugar (1 pound to 1 pound of stems) and allow to stand for 2 days. Boil until clear, then drain and coat each piece with sugar, and place on a tray in a warm oven until they set firm.

Taken hot, the leaves infused in boiling water to which lemon juice and honey are added, is an excellent drink for a cold or to ease a sore throat.

Aniseed
Pimpinella anisum

This is properly Anise, as spelt in St. Matthew's Gospel and it is the seed that is used. It is a native of S. Europe, Egypt and the Near East and it may have been introduced into Britain by the Romans for, like caraway, the seed was used in Classical Rome to flavour cakes and bread.

It will flourish in a sunny corner but requires a better than average summer to ripen its seed in Britain. It is an annual, growing 18 inches tall, and has pretty white flowers and feathery leaflets of brilliant green which add to its charm.

The seed is sown in early April, in a light friable loam. Thin out the seedlings to 12 inches apart. Or sow in pans in a frame and plant out in May when large enough to handle.

Besides its use in confectionery, the seed, when dry, is included in cough mixtures and is used to flavour drinks. The seed when crushed and sprinkled on meat will bring out its flavour and help its digestion.

Balm
Melissa officinalis

This is a native of southern Europe but has been naturalised in Britain since earliest times. In Tudor days, no garden was ever without it for, with its powerful lemony scent was the most delicious smelling of all plants. The juice from the leaves and stems was used to rub on the furniture of manor house and cottage to which it imparts its pleasing aroma. In the Merry Wives of Windsor there is the famous Garter speech of Anne Page, dressed as the Fairy Queen and attended by her brother and others dressed as elves and fairies where she says:

The several chairs of order look you scour
With juice of balm, and every precious flower . . .

In cottage gardens, it was grown alongside a path or to surround a border for, though growing up to 2 feet tall and in its appearance resembling the dead nettle, it may be kept to half that height by pinching back the stems. Left to itself, it may be grown in a sunny border where it will make a bushy plant. There is also an attractive golden leaved variety.

Balm requires a light soil but one containing plenty of humus to retain summer moisture, and a position in full sun. It is readily increased by seed sown in shallow drills in early summer, the young plants being set out into their permanent quarters when large enough to transplant. Plant 2 feet apart and though a perennial and hardy in all but the most exposed gardens, the plants may be cut back in a severe winter but will come into new growth again in spring. It is also readily propagated by root division in March.

The young leaves make a delicious addition to a salad and from them may be made a pleasant 'tea' which is particularly good for the 'flu'. The leaves may also be used in a pot-pourri and were the principal ingredient for making Carmelite Water which had a great reputation as a restorative before the advent of Eau de Cologne. Balm wine is delicious and a salve made from the leaves used to be made in demand for healing skin wounds. With those of borage, the leaves may be used to impart their cool, aromatic flavour to claret cup and cider drinks.

Basil
Ocimum spp.

There are two species, the Sweet Basil *Ocimum basilicum* and the Bush Basil *Ocimum minimum* both being annuals though in all but the warmest parts of Britain, they must be treated as half-hardy for they will rarely survive a normal spring. Of the Sweet Basil, Parkinson said that it was 'used to make sweet or washing waters, yet sometimes it is put into nosegays' and Tusser included both species in his list of herbs for strewing. They are small plants with oval leaves which, when pressed, release the warm, aromatic smell of cloves. In France they are used in salads and to flavour soups and broths.

Seed is sown under glass early in March, the plants being set out, after hardening, to 9 inches apart early in May. They require a rich well drained soil. The leaves may be used from the time the plants are established.

Bergamot
Monarda didyma

This native of the swamplands of Eastern United States is named in honour of Dr. Monardes who, in 1569, wrote the first herbal of America. The plant takes its name from the likeness of its fragrance to that of the Bergamot orange and all parts of the plant have the same refreshing perfume. Its leaves, infused in hot water make a pleasing drink known in America as Oswego tea whilst both the leaves and flowers may be eaten in salads to which they impart a piquant taste.

A hardy perennial, it may readily be raised from seed sown in a frame in April, the young plants being moved to their permanent quarters before the end of summer. It grows 3 feet tall and is a delightful border plant, requiring a soil retentive of moisture so work in plenty of humus and select a position in semi-shade. It is readily increased by root division in November. Plant 2–3 feet apart.

Bergamot bears its red, pink or purple flowers (depending upon variety) in whorls and blooms from late July until the end of September. The leaves are used fresh in salads or to make a refreshing summer drink. In autumn, the stems are cut back almost to soil level when new growth will begin again in spring.

Borage
Borago officinalis

An annual or biennial plant that will seed freely where established. It is one of the most attractive of herbs and since earliest times, has been widely grown for both its leaves and flowers are used in salads and to flavour wine. Today, with their cool, cucumber-like flavour the leaves are much in demand by hotels to add to claret-cup and cider and to Pimms No. 1. which is never quite the same without its borage leaves. Gerard wrote that, 'the leaves and flowers put into wine makes men and women glad and merry'. The leaves are rough and Mr. Alex. Mackenzie is of the opinion that the plant takes its name from the Latin, *burra*, meaning

'shaggy cloth'. The leaves may also be cooked like spinach whilst an infusion in hot water will bring relief when suffering from a sore throat.

The plant grows 15 inches tall, the oblong leaves and stem being covered in stiff hairs. It blooms throughout summer, its deep sky-blue flowers having a contrasting spot of jet black at the centre. Sow seed in July where the plants are to bloom and plant on a humus-laden soil.

Burnet
Poterium sanguisorba

The Salad Burnet grows freely on the chalk downlands of Wiltshire and has been grazed by sheep there from the earliest times. It was a favourite with Elizabethan gardeners, to be planted in walks with camomile and thyme for, when trodden upon it emits a pleasant refreshing perfume. The leaves may be used in a salad for they have a mild cucumber taste whilst they may be placed in wine and summer drinks to impart a particular cool quality, like that of borage.

Burnet is a perennial plant, readily raised from seed sown under glass in spring or in shallow drills outdoors. The plants may either be thinned to 6 inches apart or transplanted to the same distance. It grows 12 inches tall and the toothed leaves, which are borne opposite each other, should be used when young and mild of flavour.

Camomile
Anthemis nobilis

This was used in Tudor times to make a fragrant lawn. It was Falstaff who said that 'the more it is trodden the faster it grows . . .' and once established, only occasional weeds will need removing. Its name is derived from the Greek meaning 'earth-apple' for when trodden upon, the plant emits the smell of ripe apples. Parkinson likened the pungency of its grey-green leaves to that of feverfew and, during Elizabethan times, before the introduction of tobacco, the leaves were dried and used for smoking, the rich aroma being regarded as a cure for sleeplessness. From an ounce of the flowers, infused in a pint of boiling water, a wine-glassful taken twice a day acts as a tonic for tired nerves. The same preparation may also be used as a hair tonic.

Sow in drills early in April, a half ounce of seed producing more than a thousand plants. If sown thinly, transplanting will not be necessary until the 'lawn' is made in autumn. A light, well drained soil is essential. Plant 8 inches apart and roll in the plants. Though evergreen, the 'lawn' will have a sparse appearance for a year or so until established and, until then, it should not be walked upon.

When established, the plants should be clipped back late in July and from then on they may be walked upon freely, when they will release a refreshing fruity smell. The plants will spread covering the ground and the 'lawn' will be green rapidly all the year round.

Only when young is there any tendency for the plants to die back and for this reason a few plants should be held in reserve to fill in any gaps, or pieces may be removed from established plants. Young plants should be kept moist during their first summer; afterwards, they will tolerate the driest conditions, remaining green during a drought.

Caraway
Carum carvi

A biennial, native of most parts of the northern hemisphere and grown for its aromatic seeds which are used to flavour bread and cakes and to serve with fresh or roasted apples. The custom of serving caraway seeds with dessert apples is still maintained by several of the London livery companies, at their dinners. On the Continent, the seed is used in the manufacture of the liqueur, Kummel, and to flavour cheese but its powerful taste does not appeal to all. At one time, the roots were boiled to accompany carrots and served with white sauce. They are sweet and tender if carefully cooked.

The plant grows 15 inches tall and has hollow stems. The white flowers are borne in umbels but to ripen the fruit a dry, sunny summer is necessary. Sow the seed in September where the plants are to mature and thin to 6 inches apart. The plants require a well drained soil and an open, sunny situation.

Chervil
Anthriscus cerefolium

This is a most attractive plant with its neat fern-like foliage and, as it grows only 9 inches tall, it makes a pretty edging to a path, the leaves turning to deep pink in autumn. Before lettuce came to be grown, the leaves were used in salads to which they imparted 'a perfumed relish' whilst the roots, which Parkinson described as being 'sweet, pleasant, with a spicy hot taste', were boiled and eaten with oil or vinegar in salads.

Seed is sown in autumn and the plant requires a light, well drained soil. Sow in shallow drills, thinning out to 4 inches apart. A second sowing is made in spring to maintain a constant supply of the leaves which may be used in salads and in soups, whilst they are a pleasing alternative to parsley for garnishing. If removed close to the ground, fresh leaves will soon take their place.

Water the plants in dry weather and to maintain a winter supply, protect the plants from frost by covering with polythene during periods of intense

Chives
Allium schoenoprasum

No garden should be without a few clumps of chives they remain green all the year to provide a mild onion flavour to salads and soups. Or the thin rush-like leaves may be shredded and used with cream cheese in sandwiches or in omelettes. It is the mildest of all onions.

Chives are readily raised from seed sown in a frame in spring, or they may be increased by division of the roots, splitting them into quite small pieces. Chives require a rich, humus-laden soil retentive of summer moisture when they will last indefinitely. They may be planted in partial shade and make a charming edging for a path or surrounding small flower beds.

Clary
Salvia sclarea

This is the most handsome of the sages, growing 2–4 feet tall with large basal leaves covered in hair and bearing pinkish-mauve flowers backed by deep pink bracts which persist well into autumn. It is suitable for the border and associates well with delphiniums and grey-leaved plants, whilst it requires a similar well drained soil so that winter moisture does not remain about the roots.

Its name is an abbreviation of 'clear eyes' for an infusion of its leaves was used to bathe tired eyes. The leaves, which have the refreshing smell of grapefruit, are also used in scent bags and pot pourris and from them an oil used as a fixative in perfumery is to be obtained. The plant is much visited by bees.

Plants may be raised from seed sown in a frame or in open ground drills in April transplanting to 3 feet apart; or propagate from cuttings taken and rooted in a frame or under cloches in summer. Plant out the following spring for like most 'blue' flowered plants, they should be removed only at this time, when root activity recommences. The leaves, fried in batter and served with lemon juice are an appetising accompaniment to meats and omelettes.

Comfrey
Symphytum officinale

This is a most attractive plant with dark green leaves and bearing pendulant clusters of bugle-like flowers of creamy white which appear in May. It grows about 2 feet tall and does well in semi-shade but requires a rich, moist soil. The old leaves may be used as a poultice to relieve sprains and swelling whilst the young leaves make an enjoyable salad with tomatoes, radishes and chives. The plant is perennial and is readily increased by division of the roots in autumn.

Coriander
Coriandrum sativum

A native of the near east, coriander may have reached England with the returning Crusaders for it was naturalised in Essex at an early date. In that part, where seed ripens better than elsewhere, the plant was grown to supply confectioners with the small ball-like seeds which they coated with sugar and which were much enjoyed by children.

Coriander is an annual, growing about 9 inches tall with solid stems and pinnate leaves of darkest green which are used to flavour soups and broths. The pinky-mauve flowers appear in July and are followed by seeds which are pleasantly scented and become more so as they dry. The seeds are used in curries and stews.

Sow in shallow drills in April, the plants being thinned to 6 inches apart. Ordinary soil will suit them but they require an open, sunny situation. To harvest, remove the seed heads on point of ripening and dry in an airy room. After removing from the capsules, place on trays in a warm room to dry further, when the fragrance will be pronounced.

Curry plant
Helichrysum angustifolium

A native of South Africa this is a perennial which will prove to be hardy in a sandy soil and in all but the severest of winters. It requires a sunny position where its attractive silvery foliage will scent the evening air with a strong smell of curry.

Late in summer, it bears clusters of bright yellow 'everlasting' flowers on 12 inch stems: the plants will bloom their first year from a sowing made under glass early in the year. Or propagate by cuttings, taken in July and rooted in a sandy compost under glass.

The leaves may be used either fresh or dry to impart their hot curry-like flavour to soups and stews. To dry the leaves for winter use, remove several from each stem and string up in an airy room when they may be rubbed down and stored in jars.

Dill
Anethum graveolens

It takes its common name from the Saxon verb *dilla*, to lull, for the seeds are soporific and were given to children to make them sleep, whilst women would rub dill-water on their breasts so that sucking babes would quickly fall asleep after their feed. For much the same reason, the plant came to be associated with black magic.

It grows 3 feet tall and has attractive fennel-like leaves which are used in sauces to serve with fish. They have a strong, 'quick' taste and may be boiled with new potatoes and garden peas, but should be used sparingly. The leaves are also used to pickle with gherkins, and impart their spicy taste to the vinegar. An annual, seed is sown in March, the plants being thinned to 12 inches apart. It requires a well drained soil and an open, sunny situation.

Feverfew
Chrysanthemum parthenium

This is a perennial herb, retaining its pale green leaves through winter whilst its small white button-like flowers are borne from July until September. The pungent scent of its foliage is known to all and in earlier times it was used for strewing the floors of cottage and manor. It takes its name from the Latin *febrifuge*, 'to drive away illness', from its tonic properties, whilst its bitter-tasting leaves are fried with bacon and eggs to counteract the grease.

Feverfew is an erect plant growing 15 inches high and is often used for summer bedding, the variety 'aureum' having golden leaves. It is readily raised from seed sown in gentle heat early in the year, or in March in a frame. Plant out 12 inches apart in May and do not let the plants lack moisture.

Fennel
Foeniculum vulgare

The Romans gave this herb the name *Foeniculum* because of its hay-like smell. It is one of the most handsome of plants, growing 5 feet tall and bushy, with bright green fern-like foliage which late in summer takes on bronzy tints. All parts of the plant emit a pleasant aniseed smell, the leaves being used with fish, either boiled with the fish or to make an appetising sauce. In Shakespeare's time it was always served with eels in city taverns whilst the roots were braised, like celery, and served with meats. The stems may be used in the same way, slicing them and stewing in butter until tender. But it was the seeds that were most in demand for it is said they allayed the pangs of hunger on fast days whilst the water, in which the seed has been steeped, is excellent to ease an upset stomach, like gripe water. The hollow seeds are used in commerce and are distinguished as 'shorts' and 'longs'.

The plant grows best in soil of a chalky nature. It is an annual or biennial, seed being sown in August or September where it is to grow or in boxes under glass, the young plants being set out in April. A sowing may also be made in the open early in spring, thinning the plants to 3 feet apart. It requires a sunny situation to ripen its seed, but if only the leaves and stems are required, the flower heads should be removed so that the plants may concentrate on making leaf. The leaves are used for garnishing in place of parsley.

Horehound
Marrubium vulgare

This is the White Horehound, with aromatic thyme-scented leaves and is grown to make a delicious beer or a syrup capable of easing the most persistent cough. It grows 18 inches tall and is clothed in white hairs which give the plant an appearance of being covered in hoar froast. The flowers are also white and are much visited by bees. They are borne in dense whorls all along the leafy stem.

The juice is extracted from the leaves and stems and from it is made a beer of wholesome flavour whilst an ounce of the fresh leaves infused in a pint of boiling water will make horehound tea, good for colds. Horehound is one of the most bitter of herbs, taking its name from the Hebrew, *marob* meaning 'bitter juice'. To place a leaf in the mouth will make one screw up one's face and, though the plant has an aromatic smell when fresh, when dry it is scentless.

A perennial, it is raised from seed sown in April and thinned to 12 inches apart. In the wild, it is found on chalk downs and in bare, dry places everywhere.

Horseradish
Armoracia rusticana

A perennial, this is grown for its roots which provide the pungent horseradish sauce served with beef. This is made by grating the roots and mixing with thick cream to give it a smooth hot flavour.

The plant should be confined to an out-of-the-way corner of the vegetable garden for once established it is difficult to eradicate, the parsnip-like roots penetrating to a considerable depth. Where grown commercially, they are marketed in bundles of a dozen or so, trimmed to the same length. To make sauce, it should be used as fresh as possible. It is as good for the kidneys and bladder as asparagus and barley.

Plant the thongs (roots) 18 inches apart in autumn and provide a well drained soil which has been liberally manured. Or sow seed early in spring and thin to the same distance apart.

Hyssop
Hyssopus officinalis

Since earliest times this herb has been held to be so sacred that it was used at the Consecration of Westimster Abbey. It is native of the cooler regions of Central Europe and possibly reached England during the Norman invasion for it is to be found growing on the walls of abbeys and castles of Norman origin. The poet Spenser writes of 'sharp isope' which was its name until recent times. It was planted with winter savory and thyme for these three herbs remained green throughout winter and could be used all the year round. It takes its name from the Hebrew *azob*, 'a holy plant' and is mentioned so often in the Bible that it is sometimes known as the Holy Herb.

Hyssop had all manner of uses in the old days, being strung up in rooms throughout the home to give off its pleasant smell whilst the leaves lend their spicy flavour to broths and soups. The leaves and flowers may be used in salads and from an infusion in hot water, a 'tea' may be made which brings relief for a tight chest.

The plant requires a light, well drained soil and an open, sunny situation. It may be planted alongside a path for it withstands clipping. This is done in April when fear of hard frost is over. Left untouched, the plants grow 2 feet tall and bear bluish-mauve flower spikes much frequented by bees. Both the leaves and dried flowers may be used in pot pourris.

Hyssop is propagated from slips taken during summer and rooted in beds of sandy soil in the open or in frames. It may also be raised from seed sown in shallow drills in spring, whilst a stock may be increased by dividing the roots in spring when new growth commences. There are also white and rose coloured forms which come true from seed.

Lavender
Lavendula spica

Though it has few, if any, culinary uses, lavender should be in every garden for the scent of the dried flowers has no equal. Langham in 'The Garden of Health' (1579) wrote, 'boil it in water, wet thy shirt in it, dry it again and wear it'. Until recently no cottage garden was ever without it, to supply dried flowers to make up into small muslin bags to place between linen and clothes, whilst the dried stems were burnt in sick rooms like incense, to cleanse the air.

Lavender prefers a light, sandy soil and is always more fragrant growing in the drier eastern side of Britain and in a chalky soil. It also requires an open, sunny situation. Dig in neither humus nor manure but give a light dressing of wood ash or of sulphate of potash raked into the surface at planting time: this will help to build up a 'hard' plant, able to withstand frosts.

Plant a lavender hedge to surround the herb garden, planting the more vigorous varieties 3 feet apart with the more compact varieties at half that distance apart. The plants will grow as wide as they grow tall. Propagate from cuttings or slips, taken off the half ripened wood in July and inserted into sandy soil. The use of a frame or cloches will provide protection from frost during their first winter and, in April, the young plants will be ready to move to their permanent quarters.

Lavender spikes should be cut when all the flowers are showing colour and will then be at their most fragrant. Cut the spikes about mid-day and spread out on trays in an airy room to complete the drying. When quite dry, the flowers are rubbed from the stalks and placed in muslin bags to put between clothes and bedding or beneath cushions and pillows.

Lovage
Levisticum officinale

Native of the Mediterranean countries, this herb has been grown in Britain since earliest times. It is a perennial plant growing 4 feet tall with parsley-scented leaves which look as if they have been polished. The leaves may be chopped and used in broths and stews or in a salad. They are extremely aromatic whilst the stems and seeds are also highly scented.

The plant is propagated by seed sown in spring in shallow drills, the plants being transplanted to 3 feet apart. It requires a soil well drained in winter but retentive of summer moisture. It may also be increased by root division in autumn.

English mace
Achillea decolorans

This is *Achillea decolorans* and should not be confused with the tropical mace, it has the same beautifully serrated leaves as all members of its genus. A perennial, it grows less than 2 feet tall, its pungent leaves being used to flavour soups and stews whilst they may be used sparingly in a salad.

The plant requires a well drained soil and an open, sunny situation. It is propagated by divisions of the roots in spring or from cuttings taken in summer and rooted in a sandy compost in a frame.

Marigold
Calendula spp.

Its botanical name is *Calendula* for it is perpetually in bloom and its flowers are to be seen on the calends (first day) of every month. Tusser includes it with those herbs of kitchen value and Fuller, in his 'Antheologia' (1655) says 'we all know the many and sovereign virtues . . . in your leaves, the Herb generally in all pottage', hence its name of Pot Marigold.

Being evergreen in mild winters and bearing at least a few flowers on each day of the year, the plant used to be found in every garden, the leaves and flowers placed in broths and stews to impart their pungent flavour, whilst they were also used in salads and to place, with cheese, between bread.

Gerard tells that so great was the demand for the flowers, that grocers kept them in barrels.

The marigold is a most accommodating plant, demanding no special treatment in its culture. It will grow well in ordinary soil and, though it prefers a sunny situation, it will do well anywhere, as long as it receives the early morning sunshine.

Seed is sown in a cold frame or beneath cloches in autumn, treating the plant as a biennial and moving to the open ground in April; or sow in the open ground in March, thinning the seedling to 10 inches apart. The variety 'Radio' with its blooms of brilliant orange and their long quilled petals is outstanding and a bed of a dozen or more plants will provide a splash of colour in the herb garden for fully 12 months. This is an annual and will seed itself each year. If not used in stews, the flowers make a charming display in the home, especially when arranged in green glass jars. Essence of marigold is used in hand creams whilst an infusion in hot water and allowed to cool, is a valuable lotion in which table cloths may be soaked to remove stains.

Majoram
Origanum spp.

The Greeks called this herb *Origanum*, 'joy of the mountain' and Parkinson mentions that it was used to make 'sweet washing waters' whilst from its dry leaves, a refreshing 'tea' was made. *O. vulgare* is a tufted perennial, to be found on chalky downlands, all parts of the plant being pleasantly aromatic. It grows 18 inches tall, and with its reddish stems and purple flowers, it is a handsome plant which makes a colourful edging to a border. In Tudor times, it was used with hyssop and thyme, for making 'knots' to surround pansies and primroses and from the flowering tops, home-made beer was brewed.

Sweet Marjoram, native of southern Europe is a more compact plant. This is *O. marjorana* which Gerard described as having a 'marvellous sweet scent'. It was used to make nosegays and garlands and was placed in windows, planted in small pots to release its scent about a room when a gentle breeze blew in from an open window. As Shakespeare said in 'All's Well that Ends Well', the leaves were used in salads. Though perennial, it is tender in all but the most favourable parts and should be treated as an annual, the seed being sown under glass in February, the seedlings planted out in early May. Plant 9 inches apart, in a well drained, sandy soil and in a sunny position.

Pot Marjoram, *O. onites*, is of more vigorous habit than the others, and its leaves were used to flavour stews and soups. They have a more pungent smell. All parts of the plant are tinted crimson but there is also a handsome golden-leaf variety. The species is perennial and is slow to increase from seed so is best propagated by division of the roots in April. Plant 12 inches apart in a rich soil. It is beloved of bees which visit its scented white flowers throughout summer.

Winter Marjoram, *O. heraclioticum*, should be confined to a warm garden where it will stay green through winter, its leaves being used in soups and broths. It is propagated by root division in autumn or in spring, and requires a well drained soil and an open sunny situation.

Mint
Mentha spp.

Natives of Europe including the British Isles, the mints may be divided into three main groups, (a) culinary, (b) medicinal and (c) fragrant. They are amongst the most rewarding of plants for the herb garden. There are between 20–30 species, each of them distinctive in their perfume. The most widely grown for culinary use is *Mentha viridis*, the Lamb or Pea Mint; *M. sylvestris*, the Hairy or Woolly mint, found in damp deciduous woodlands; and *M. rotundifolia*, the Round-leaf mint of which the best form is 'Bowles Variety'. They were grown in mediaeval times as a help to digest meat for which purpose the woolly mint makes an excellent sauce, as does the 'Apple' variety, a round-leaf mint of mild and pleasant flavour which is used in the confectionery trade for flavouring cakes. *M. cordifolia* with its large leaves possesses a distinctive spearmint flavour for sauce but the connoisseur will make up a sauce by blending several mints to suit the palate.

Of the medicinal mints, *M. piperita* with its black stems and high peppermint content is grown for the extraction of its peppermint to make sweets, whilst from the leaves and stems a 'tea' is made as a relief for indigestion. In Tudor times, peppermint was used to sweeten water whilst a sprig, placed in a jug of milk will prevent the milk from curdling. The dried leaves, placed amongst clothes will keep them 'sweet' and keep away moths whilst pressed against the temples it is supposed to bring relief to the most stubborn headache. To warm the stomach on a cold day, a 'tea' may be made by pouring boiling water on the dried leaves of *M. gentilis*, the Ginger mint.

The fragrant mints are used in pot pourris. *M. citrata*, with its green and yellow variegated leaves has a sharp and lasting lemon fragrance whilst *M. aquatica*, the Water mint, has the orange scent of Bergamot.

All the mints grow best in partial shade where cool, moist conditions can be provided and where few other herbs will grow. A soil containing plenty of humus should be provided, hop manure or old mushroom bed compost being ideal. Or dig in a quantity of old cow manure, together with some peat or leaf mould. With their creeping rootstock, mints are gross feeders and heavy drinkers.

The ground may be prepared in trenches made 6 inches deep, planting the roots 12 inches apart, spreading them well out; or it may be prepared as flat beds made 6 feet wide with a path on each side so that the sprigs may be removed without treading on the beds. A single root of a dozen different species or varieties will provide interest. Plant the roots 2 inches deep and riddle some fine soil over them. October is the best time to make up a bed for the plants will become settled in before the frosts and will then bear plenty of shoots in spring to use with lamb and the first garden peas. The first year should see only a few sprigs cut, to allow the plants time to become established. At the end of each season, cut down any stems to ground level and cover the bed with an inch of riddled soil and decayed manure.

To force mint, fresh beds should be made up each autumn, the roots being lifted the following November and planted in deep boxes in a greenhouse, or in prepared soil in a cold frame. In a temperature of 55°F. the shoots will reach a height of 6 inches within a month. If no heated greenhouse is available, make a mild hot-bed in a frame and cover with 6 inches of soil to retain the heat and into which the mint roots are planted closely together, covering them with 3 inches of loam. Water in and keep the frames closed. The mint will be ready for cutting early in the year, to place amongst peas and new potatoes.

An early supply may be obtained by covering open ground beds with cloches early in March when the sprigs will be ready to cut six weeks before those from uncovered plants. To propagate mint, either lift and divide the roots in autumn or take cuttings in July and root them in trenches filled with sand, keeping them moist during dry weather.

Nasturtium
Tropaeolum majus

An annual more often grown for its colourful flowers, this is one of the most useful plants for the herb garden for the large succulent fruits or seeds may be used as a substitute for capers to consume with fish, whilst the bitter leaves make an appetising sandwich used with cream cheese or with lettuce in a salad. The petals of the flowers may also be eaten in the same way whilst the seeds, pickled in vinegar may be used with meats.

The plant will flourish in ordinary soil but requires an open, sunny situation and plenty of sunlight. Sow the seed in boxes under glass early in March, planting out the seedlings early May. Plant the 'Gleam Hybrids' 12 inches apart, or sow the seeds directly into the open ground in April at the same distance apart. The plants will continue to grow and seed until well into autumn but need not be removed until the first hard frosts. If some seed is allowed to remain they will fall to the ground and produce plants the following year.

ne: an
o the
and a
r lust

n obscure herb rich in
help reduce coronary
nmunity to infections

Winter purslane

the fact that in Malawi purslane has a name which means: "buttocks of the wife of the chief", although this may simply be a reference to the succulent leaves and stems of the plant.

Because of these qualities the plant makes a crunchy salad. I managed to get some of the last of the summer crop and enjoyed its slightly sharp, clean flavour which as Gerard says: "is good for the teeth that are fet on edge".

In season, purslane can be obtained by mail from Rosemary Titterington, Iden Croft Herb Farm, Frittenden Road, Staplehurst, Kent, TN12 ODH. (From 35p a pack. Postage extra).

It can also be cooked and served as a vegetable. Irma and Marion Rombauer suggest in *Joy of Cooking* (Dent) that it should be blanched briefly in boiling salted water, drained and reheated in butter. But I would suggest using olive oil because animal fat is not kind on the heart. The Rambauers also suggest a soup, rather like watercress soup, which uses a large quantity of cream — again not the best food for the heart. If readers can write to me with suggestions for a healthier purslane soup or other ways of preparing it I will pass them on.

The following information on growing puslane has been gleaned from *Salads the Year Round* by Joy Larkcom (Hamlyn paperback) and other sources.

Purslane is a low growing, half-hardy annual, so it should be sown after frosts in a drill, like lettuce. It likes a sunny spot, needs plenty of moisture and a well drained soil. Mulching advisable. Keep well watered. Does well in greenhouses, under frames and cloches. Perhaps it can be during winter in heated green have success let me know useful tips. First months

A low-growing, half-hardy plant which likes sun and plenty of moisture

stems. Always leave two leaves at base of stem for regrowth. Do not allow plants to flower or leaves become coarse.

Keen gardeners should be sure to order *Portulaca oleracea* because there are other plants called purslane and I cannot vouch for their edibility.

The following stock puslane: John Chambers, 15 Westleigh Road, Barton Seagrave, Kettering, Northants, NN15 5AJ. Green and yellow varieties. (45p per packet plus sae). Down to Earth Seeds, Streetfield Farm, Cade Street, Heathfield, East Sussex, TN21 9BS. (35p per packet plus sae). Hollington Nurseries, Woolton Hill, Newbury, Berks. (35p plus sae). Rosemary Titterington, address as above. (40-45p per packet plus sae). Purslane can be served by itself with oil and vinegar, or in a mixed salad. In the Middle East it is served in elaborate salads. This recipe is adapted from *Queer Gear — How to Buy and Cook Exotic Fruits and Vegetables* by Carolyn Heal and Michael Allsop (Century Hutchinson).

To serve 6:
1 large bunch of purslane leaves
1 cucumber, diced, salted and drained
1 small lettuce, or lettuce heart shredded
4 tomatoes, diced
1 green pepper, diced
3 tablespoons parsley, finely chopped
2 tablespoons mint, chopped
1 onion, finely chopped
Dressing:
2 cloves of garlic, crushed
3 half tablespoons lemon juice
3 half tablespoons olive oil
salt and pepper to taste.

Put the vegetables and herbs into a bowl. Mix the garlic, lemon juice, oil and seasoning thoroughly and add to the salad. Toss well and chill for 30 minutes before serving with warm pitta bread, wholemeal if possible. It can be given as a starter or as part of light meal.

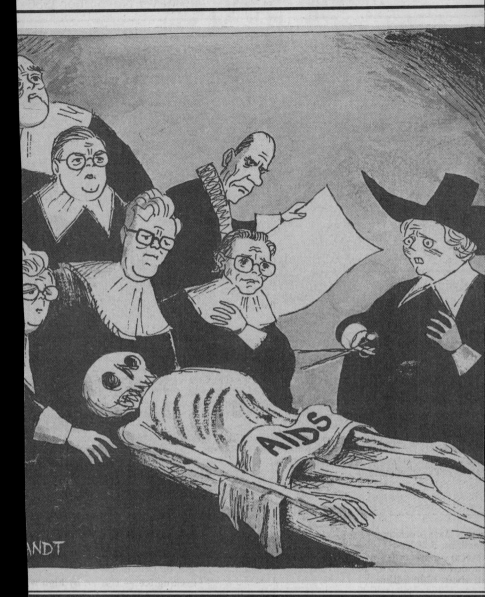

y the BBC ca

ead high over

William Rees-Mogg criticises Mr Tebbit's attack on the Cor

use of British bases. Tonight she shows her critics the proof of Libyan terrorism."

    Let us put them together. Both lead with international condemnation of the raid: ITN focuses on Mr Gorbachev, the BBC is more general, but the thrust of the lead item is the same. Both follow with the kiⁱⁱ ing of children, ITN agaiⁿ specific, but again tʰ area of attention. IT

of this kind is to count negative and positive statements from the complainant's view. The nearer ᵗ and positive equality tʰ The

any ca
Centra
le fo
ibil
b

Purslane aid heart cure

Oliver Gillie looks at the fatty acids which c...
disease and increa...

Green purslane

ACCORDING to a cookery book dating from the reign of Richard II, purslane "does extynct the ardor of lassyvousness [ascviviousness] and doth mytygate great heat in all the inward parts of man". Purslane was recognised, in the fourteenth century, as a powerful vegetable and today, after years of obscurity, it has again been recognised as a plant with unique virtues.

Purslane contains more omega-3 fatty acids than any other vegetable yet analysed. Omega-3 fatty acids are believed to be important in preventing heart attacks and in reinforcing the body's immunity to infections.

Over the last few years scientific interest in omega-3 fatty acids has increased greatly. This substance is found in relatively large quantities in fish which obtain it from plankton — minute green plants — on which they feed. Eskimos who eat a lot of fish are said to suffer rarely from heart disease because of the omega-3 fatty acids in their diet. Dutchmen, who eat fish several times a week, have fewer heart attacks than those who eat none at all. A diet with plenty of fish makes the blood clot less easily because of the fatty acids they contain. These fatty acids also reduce cholesterol and triglycerides (a type of fat) in the blood — another indication that risks of heart disease are reduced when fatty acids are increased in the diet.

The Department of Agriculture in the United States has analysed as many different vegetables as it can in order to find the best source of omega-3 fatty acids, but it did not analyse purslane because it is so seldom eaten in the United States.

However purslane, sometimes called continental parsley, is popular in salads and soups in Greece, the Lebanon and some other parts of the Mediterranean, where heart disease is relatively uncommon compared with Northern Europe and North America. It fell to a Greek Ameri-

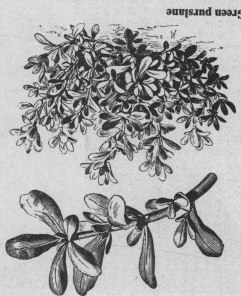

can, Dr Artemis Simopoulos and Dr... man Salem of the National Institut... Science in Bethesda, Maryland, to a... purslane (*portulaca oleracea*).

They found that it contains four ti... much omega-3 fatty acids as spinach, ... etable traditionally known for its str... ening qualities, and 12 times as much ... ga-3 fatty acid as lettuce.

Drs Simopoulos and Salem say in a ... to the *New England Journal of Me...* (September 25 1986) that purslane is ... richest source of omega-3 fatty acids ...

Popular in parts of the Mediterranean where heart disease is less common

vegetable yet exam... and suggest that "p... might benefit from... ing purslane". A ... which many peopl... find more accep... than to follow an ... mo diet. But the a... is not so easy to f... because purslane ... tremely difficult to ... tain — not least bec... winter is approac... During the sum... months purslane ca... found in some G... Cypriot and Middle Eastern shops. It ... not, at present, be bought at Safew... Sainsbury's or Waitrose, although thes... permarkets stock a lot of other exotic v... tables. Purslane can also be obtaine... mail and it does not seem to be diffic... grow (see details below).

But does this powerful vegetable ... side-effects which some might find un... come?

Gerard's *Herbal*, a great authority in ... sixteenth century, tells us that: "The l... of Purflane either rawe, or boiled, and ... en as falladed, are goode for thofe ... haue great heate in their ftomackes ... inwarde parts, and doe coole and ten... the inflamed bloud.

"The fame taken in like manner is g... for the bladder and kidnies, and alla... the outragious luft of the body; the j... alfo hath the fame vertue."

A welcome vegetable then, in the ag... Aids. However Gerard could have b... mistaken; I am encouraged in this belie...

Learning to paint the inner city red

REPORTS that the pop million-aire Richard Branson wants paint companies to sponsor graffiti in inner-city areas have caused much comment in progressive circles. The idea is get graffiti accepted as an art-form in its own right and provide "public art areas" where the new art form can be practised without fear of prosecution.

Laura Wallpaper, who with her husband Ashley runs the Hackney Artwork Cooperative held an immediate press conference to denouce the move. "It's outrageous. We thought of the idea months ago, and there's lots more to our plans than just graffiti. Would you like to see my video?"

Funded by grants from various friendly governments, the The Wallpapers have set up a two-year course called *Creative Vandalism: New Directions in Urban Despair*. On the extensive playing fields surrounding their converted warehouse I saw eager groups practising bowling in the nets. Ms Wallpaper explained: "Our research shows that throughout the riots of the last five years, missiles thrown at the police had only a one-in-seventeen chance of reaching their object. Here, we teach the boys and girls to go for height *and* length, and we stress the importance of allowing for crosswinds, particularly in a CS gas situation." One of the big brick companies has already expressed interest in a sponsorship deal.

The school kitchens are a model of their kind, clean, spacious and well-equipped. "Here," explained Ms Wallpaper, "we make cocaine *from the leaf*. Normally, as you know, cocaine is imported in powder-form. This means a serious leakage of employment-potential. Under this scheme, all those production jobs are done in Britain. We expect that when this project is up and running it will make a major impact on youth unemployment. And the scheme is, of course, fully self-financing."

Learning to Loot is one of the most popular courses. A realistic mock-up of a complete shopping parade has been built in one corner of the Wallpapers' warehouse. "The trouble with most urban violence is that it's so mindless. Here, we aim to put

---

hold

Libya

tion

: Govern-
ice, which
dcasting.
longs not
Douglas
etary.

clear and
t one. He
ndence of
s, as I do,
form, but
strengthen
ine press

This document is therefore bad for the cause of reform inside the BBC. It is also bad for the Conservative Party. When press freedom is attacked, or when thought to be attacked, journalists rally to defend it. The bees defend their hive with their stings. In 1967, Mr Wilson, in the D notice affair, appeared to want to bully the press. It did not do him much good in the 1970 election.

I have known almost all of the Chairmen of the Conservative Party since 1945. Few of them had much reason to like the press; all of them tried to get as

Parsley
Petroselinum crispum

This is one of the most widely used of herbs and is grown in large quantities for garnishing fish and for making sauce to accompany fish. The plant first reached England early in her history but Parkinson tells of having first seen it in 1600, growing in the garden of the Venetian Ambassador in London so that it could not have been well known in his time. An infusion of the leaves in hot water is supposed to be excellent for indigestion and for kidney ailments.

Parsley requires a well nourished soil, containing plenty of humus and decayed manure for it is perennial and sends down its tap root for some distance. To maintain its quality, a sowing is made in July each year so that the plants will be at their best the following year. The seed is slow to germinate. There is an old north country saying that 'parsley goes nine times to the devil before it grows'. Fresh seed must be used, sowing it in shallow drills 9 inches apart and thinning to 6 inches apart in the rows. Keep the drills moist to hasten germination and during dry weather for the plants will run to seed if lacking moisture.

Two rows should be sown, one to use through summer, the other to use in winter and any flower stems should be removed as they form. Only in the severest weather will the thick curled leaves be harmed but covering a row with cloches from December until March will ensure a continuous supply.

The plants will benefit from an occasional watering with liquid manure whilst a mulch of finely sifted soil and decayed manure given in autumn close up to the plants along the rows will help to maintain a supply of thick, succulent leaves for several years.

Parsley should be pulled close to the base of the plant and, if the leaves are to be dried, they must be removed to an airy room which receives sunlight or has artificial warmth for otherwise, the leaves are difficult to dry. When crisp (and this will take several weeks) the leaves are rubbed down for storing in jars.

There are several excellent strains which are a big improvement on the older types, forming an abundance of thick dark green leaves and standing the winter well. Outstanding is 'Cluseed Dark Green Winter', whilst 'Bravour' bears an abundance of dark green leaves which are closely packed and heavily curled. 'Champion Moss Curled' bears fronds of emerald green and makes a plant of neat habit so that it may be sown alongside a path or as an edging to a bed.

The old wives' tale that parsley will only grow for a woman if she wears the trousers in the family is something that has not been substantiated by scientific observation. Nonetheless it still needlessly deters many women from trying to grow parsley.

Pennyroyal
Mentha pulegium

This is a plant of almost prostrate habit found naturally growing close to water or on damp ground. At one time it was sold in the streets of London, to sailors to put in drinking water to 'sweeten' it whilst at sea. Its country name was Pudding Grass, for it was used as an alternative to sage for stuffings, its 'quick', minty flavour being so greatly esteemed that women would collect it at Mile End and sell it in the London markets. The stems were wound round the head to cure giddiness and to relieve a headache.

A creeping plant, it should be set amongst paving stones or in a damp, partially shaded place and it is one of those plants which releases its scent when walked upon. In the old days it was cut and strewn over cottage floors for it sweetened the air and was believed to rid the place of fleas, hence its Latin name.

Purslane
Portulaca oleracea

This annual was at one time a popular salad herb, its propeller-like leaves being sweet and succulent whilst the crimson stems were boiled and eaten with meats. Being half-hardy, seed is sown in an open, sunny position and in a well drained soil, about May 1st. This to 6 inches apart and begin using the leaves when young. They will then form three crops during summer. The plants grow only 4 inches tall and may be sown as an edging to a path. They are tolerant of dry conditions.

Rosemary
Rosmarinus officinalis

A native of the Mediterranean countries, Rosemary is believed to have been introduced into England by Queen Philippa, wife of Edward III, the gracious lady who begged her husband to save the lives of the six burghers of Calais. Rosemary was the herb of remembrance: 'There's Rosemary, that's for remembrance' wrote Shakespeare and it was the favourite evergreen for all solemn occasions, in demand both at weddings and at funerals, for its ability to retain its green colour and its fragrance throughout the year. This is because the microscopic pores through which water evaporates are sunk deep into the leaves whilst they also have a protective covering with tiny hairs. From rosemary and its ability to retain its freshness and scent longer than any other plant, comes the saying 'Rosemary keeping the memory green'.

Langham in 'The Garden of Health' wrote 'carry powder about thee to make thee merry, glad and beloved of all men. Lay it on thy bed to keep thee from evil dreams, seep rosemary with rose water, and drink it. To preserve youth, make a box of the wood and smell it'.

The potent seeds, dried and placed in muslin bags and put under the pillow case or hung above the bed are supposed to encourage deep sleep whilst the flowers and seed infused in water and drunk morning and evening are supposed to keep the breath always sweet.

Rosemary grows well near the sea and, though usually grown as a bush in the open, it grows best when trained against a sunny wall and planted in a dry, sandy soil. Plant early in May, 3 feet apart and if planting in the open, for the first winter give protection from cold winds. The plants will enjoy some lime rubble about the roots and, like lavender, will appreciate an occasional mulch of mortar.

It is propagated from 'slips' (which are cuttings of the half-ripened wood pulled away from the main stems) inserted in sandy soil in a frame or under cloches. If taken in July, they will have rooted by autumn but should not be planted out until the following May.

The distilled oil of rosemary is one of the ingredients of Eau de Cologne and water simmered from the leaves and stems is supposed to act as a valuable hair stimulant. Rosemary water is also a refreshener and purifier of the skin and may be used to wash the face at bedtime.

Rue
Ruta graveolens

Because of its intense bitterness, rue was the herb of repentance, though it takes its name from the Anglo-Saxon word 'ruth' meaning pity. Milton mentions the plant as being used as an eye ointment, and Turner says that rue 'made hot on the nipple of a pomegranate (a fruit widely grown in England at the time) was good for the ear ache'. Culpeper tells us that the leaves were used to strew the floor of workhouse and prison against evil odours and to keep away fleas. 'It is a most wholesome herb', wrote Parkinson, 'although bitter and strong'. The leaves have a pleasing orange-like smell which they release when pressed.

Rue is a perennial and grows 2 feet tall, its attractive leaves being of deep blue-green whilst the flowers are palest yellow. It retains its foliage all the year. It grows well in a calcareous soil but likes a well drained loam and an open, sunny situation.

Plants are readily raised from seed sown in drills in early summer, the seedlings being planted 18 inches apart. Or propagate from cuttings taken in July and rooted in a sandy compost in a frame.

Rue is an excellent tonic for humans and for poultry. It is strong in mineral salts and tones the system. Countrymen chop the leaves and place between bread with cheese. In continental Europe, rue sandwiches are often served for afternoon tea, with cress or lettuce.

Sage
Salvia officinalis

This is one of the herbs most widely used in modern cooking having retained its popularity through the years, along with parsley and mint. To the ancients it had so many qualities that at an early date, its name had become established in the English language as meaning 'wise', 'learned'. It is reputed to give long life to all who use it.

Sage cordial (made from the Red-leaf variety) is excellent for a sore throat whilst an infusion of the leaves (an ounce of dried leaves to a pint of boiling water) taken when cold, is supposed to help the digestion and to cure those suffering from anaemia. The same preparation, according to the old books, should prevent the hair from falling, whilst it should also darken greying hair. Sage water should be massaged into the scalp each day, using brilliantine once a week to prevent the hair from becoming too dry.

Since early times sage has been used to stuff the richer meats such as pork and veal but to have sage at its best, with its pronounced flavour, obtain a broad-leaf strain and propagate it from cuttings. These may be taken in summer and rooted in sandy soil in a frame or in the open ground. When rooted, plant 2 feet apart and, as it is shallow-rooting, give a mulch each autumn, preferably of decayed strawy manure or old mushroom bed compost.

To keep the plants tidy and to prevent them forming an excess of old wood, remove the stems in June and again late in summer but do so only when quite dry. Spread out on trays in an airy room for several weeks to complete the drying, then remove the leaves from the stems and rub down for storing.

Sage is readily raised from seed sown in April in drills made 9 inches apart. Keep moist to assist with germination and, later in summer, transplant to 2 feet apart. Plants raised from seed are all too often of the narrow leaf strain, which is not wanted.

Leaves of the broad-leaf variety may be dipped in batter or cream and fried, then served with orange juice, whilst the young leaves may be used in a salad. Deliciously pineapple scented are the young leaves of *S. grahamii* which may be used in a salad when fresh or in a pot pourri when dry.

The purple flowers of the ordinary sage are much visited by bees.

Savory
Satureia spp.

There are two species which are grown in the herb garden, the Winter Savory, *Satureia montana* and Summer Savory, *S. hortensis*. The latter is an annual resembling thyme in its pungent scent and flavour. It was scattered over fish and served with peas and new potatoes, like parsley. When dried, it was used with sage and onions to make stuffings. Seed is sown in drills in spring, the young plants being thinned to 9 inches apart. Sow fresh seed otherwise germination will be slow. It requires a rich soil and a position of full sun. The plant grows 9 inches tall and at the end of summer when the flowers begin to form, the stems are removed together, tied into bunches and hung up to dry. It may be used with all dry herbs.

Winter Savory may be raised in the same way but only in the milder parts of Britain is it not winter hardy. It is perennial and with thyme and rue is one of the few herbs to remain green through winter. It makes a dense shrub 15 inches tall and the same in width and is readily increased from cuttings taken in June and inserted in a sandy compost beneath a frame.

Its sharply pointed leaves used to be much sought after for dressing trout, together with thyme and rosemary. A sauce made from its leaves improves most fish dishes.

To withstand the winter, it must be grown in a poor soil containing some humus but no manure, as lush growth is not required. Provide it with an open, sunny position, protected from cold winds and plant 18 inches apart. To maintain a supply of young shoots, cut back the plants in April.

It is said that a sprig of Winter Savory rubbed on the skin after a wasp sting will give instant relief.

Southernwood
Artemesia abrotanum

This is better known by its country name, Lad's Love. It is a woody plant and, though native of southern Europe, it will withstand a hard winter in the British Isles. The pinnate leaves are grey-green with a refreshing lemon-like perfume.

It used to be placed amongst clothes to sweeten them and to keep away the clothes moth: hence its French name of 'garde-robe'. It was also used as an aid towards sound sleep, pounding the fresh leaves with sugar in a mortar until paste-like. A small quantity taken before bedtime, 'disposes persons to deep sleep'.

Sprigs of Lad's Love were burnt to sweeten the air of damp, musty cottages and it was used in salads, the pungent leaves bringing a piquancy to an ordinary lettuce salad.

The plant requires an open, sunny situation and a well drained sandy soil. To keep plants bushy, cut down to 18 inches from the ground in April each year.

To propagate, remove the woody shoots in spring and root in a trench containing sandy compost. Set the shoots well into the ground and keep them moist. They will root in 5–6 weeks. They are then moved to their permanent quarters and planted 3 feet apart.
Old plants are sometimes found to be suitable for division. This operation should be carried out in the spring.

Sweet Cicely
Myrrhis odorata

This herb is named because of its myrrh-like smell whilst the leaves taste as if they have been steeped in sugar, though they are also hot and spicy. The leaves and green seeds were popular in salads as John Evelyn recommended, whilst the nourishing roots were boiled and eaten with oil or vinegar or were braised and consumed with meats.

In northern Europe, since earliest times, the seeds were crushed and used to polish floors and furniture to which they imparted their myrrh-like fragrance and a glossy 'finish'.

It is a slow growing perennial, eventually attaining a height of 5 feet or more and, though it will die back in winter, it arises again from the old rootstock. Cottagers know it as the Sweet Fern for its bright green tri-pinnate leaves resemble those of the oak fern.

Seed is sown in spring where the plants are to remain, thinning them to 2 feet apart. A rich soil containing plenty of humus should be provided and, if the ground is undisturbed in autumn, the seeds will sow themselves.

The leaves when used in a salad are amongst the most delicious of all herbs with their slight aniseed taste but do not use too many until their 'taste' has been acquired.

Tansy
Tanacetum vulgare

This herb had many uses in earlier times. The bitter leaves added piquancy to a salad, whilst tansy-cakes were eaten at Easter. The leaves may be shredded and used in an omelette or they may be enjoyed with cream cheese in sandwiches. When there was no cold storage to preserve meats, tansy leaves rubbed on meat would keep away flies and at the same time would lend to it its unique flavour. For its supposed ability to keep away flies, it was used to strew over the floor of cottage and manor, whilst bunches hung up in a room would have a similar effect.

A handsome plant, growing 4 feet tall it bears in July and August flat golden flowers in large heads. It should, however, be confined to an out of the way corner of the garden for it has a creeping rootstock and increases rapidly, often at the expense of nearby plants. It is propagated by lifting and dividing the roots, all parts of which will grow if replanted. Allow 2 feet between the plants and provide a soil containing some humus.

Tarragon
Artemisia dracunculus

This is a perennial plant, native of southern Europe which grows 2 feet high. Its lance-shaped leaves with their aromatic scent are valued for seasoning when dried, whilst the fresh leaves may be used in a salad. When steeped in vinegar for several days, they provide a pleasing condiment to use with fried fish. Though able to survive an average winter in Britain, the plant will lose its leaves, like southernwood but will come again early in spring. It bears small white flowers in summer.

Seed is difficult to obtain and to germinate so the plant is usually propagated from cuttings, taken early in summer and rooted in sandy soil outdoors. Or increase by root division in spring.

Plant 2 feet apart, in an open, sunny situation and in a poor, sandy soil. It enjoys dry conditions at all times.

Thyme
Thymus spp.

Amongst the most pleasantly scented of all plants, the thymes may be divided into two main groups (a) the prostrate or creeping thymes; and (b) those of upright bushy habit, resembling small shrubs. The former are of the *T. serpyllum* group (serpent-like), the latter being represented by varieties of *T. nitidus* which are grown for their culinary qualities. All are native of the islands of the Mediterranean and of southern Europe, with the Wild Thyme, *T. drucei* common in the British Isles on chalk downs everywhere; and *T. serpyllum* found only on the Brecklands of East Anglia.

The flowers are much frequented by bees and thyme honey is the finest of all. Relying upon honey for sweetening, bees and the plants they visited were highly looked upon in olden times. Thomas Hyll in 'The Gardener's Labyrinth' wrote: 'The owners of hives have a perfect foresight and knowledge what the yields of honey will be each year by the plentiful or small numbers of flowers appearing on the thyme about the summer solstice'.

Varieties of *T. serpyllum* may be planted between paving stones and on the rockery whilst they make a pleasing 'walk', planted 8 inches apart in a well drained sandy soil. Outstanding is 'Bressingham Pink' which comes early into bloom, whilst 'Russetings' bears rosy-red flowers and has dark foliage.

The upright shrubby thymes are used in stuffings and to flavour meats with sage. The thymes are the most popular of all herbs when dried. Mixtures of the fragrant thymes are most appetising though *T. herba barona*, used in olden days to rub on Baron of Beef should be used by itself for its distinctive carraway smell.

T. nitidus, the Grey-leaf thyme with its rich pungency is widely grown for stuffings, also *T. vulgaris* the Black Thyme of which there is a golden leaf form. But it is the Lemon-scented thyme, *T. citriodorus* with its balm-like smell which is the most pleasing, the variety 'Silver Queen' having leaves of bright silver-grey.

The thymes grow well in a soil with a high lime content and this will usually be well drained. Plant the shrubby thymes 12 inches apart and, whilst the grey-leaved thyme is readily raised from seed sown in drills in April, most are best propagated from cuttings. These are removed with a 'heel' during summer and are inserted into sandy compost in a frame or under cloches when they will root in about 6 weeks. Or plants may be increased by division, the outer portions being the most vigorous. Plant in an open sunny position and to prevent them becoming untidy, cut the shoots down to the base in June and again at the end of summer. In this way, the plants will form plenty of young shoots which bear the most powerfully scented leaves.

To dry thyme, make up the sprigs into small bunches and hang up in a dry, airy room. When the leaves 'crackle' to the touch, spread them on trays and rub down the stems to remove the leaves which are placed in jars to be used when required.

Valerian
Valeriana officinalis

This is not the garden variety but *Valeriana officinalis*, the Great Valerian, that is grown for the extraction of its juices from the roots. These juices were used for nervous diseases and to some extent still are, the herb being included in the British Pharmacopaeia to this day. The leaves, pounded in a mortar, were mixed with fat and applied as an ointment for healing wounds. They were also used in broths and stews and to serve with meats.

The plant enjoys a dry soil and is raised from seed sown in shallow drills in spring. A perennial, it grows 3 feet tall and bears flesh pink flowers in July and August.

Part 4

THE HISTORY OF VEGETABLES

Early man, like his ape-like forebears, lived literally off the fruits of the land. He gathered whatever he could, according to the season. Winter would have been his hardest time, for in this season there is little in the way of tender greenery about. He would have had to rely for food largely upon the tender inner bark of trees, on nuts (which he probably stored in much the same way as squirrels do to this day) and on the underground reserve organs of various bulbous, rhizomatous and tuberous plants, among which were the wild onions, the rhizomes of Solomon's Seal and those of bracken, *Pteridium aquilinum*. In addition there is archaeological evidence to show that the storage organs of water-plants were particularly favoured, especially those of the arrowhead *Saggitaria* and the bullrush *Schoenoplectus*. In early spring he would have had to tap the rising sap of trees, while in full spring there would have been a glut of tender green leaves and shoots for him to eat. Full summer would have been a leaner period for him, for the greenery would by then have become tough and mucilaginous, but by late summer the first of the fruits and berries would have been beginning to ripen. Autumn would have been his 'glut' season, when wild plants produce a veritable cornucopia of fruits, nuts and seeds.

To live like this, from hand-to-mouth, early man must have led a nomadic existence. Precisely how he came to domesticate wild food plants and to adopt a settled way of life is a question which is still being debated. However it happened, it is certainly the most important event in the whole history of mankind.

Certainly the great majority of the foodstuffs eaten by man to-day were being eaten by his ancestors many thousands of years ago. Excavations of human remains from the Iron Age in Denmark show that a number of grass-seeds (ancestors of our modern cereal crops) were already being used as food in those days. The archaeological evidence of early vegetables is less certain, the vegetable remains rotting away too quickly to have been preserved.

The change to a settled agriculture must have been a gradual one. Early man would have found that seeds of many of his foods germinated readily on his refuse tips, for refuse tips are rich in nitrogen, essential to most vegetables. Thus the discovery of settled agriculture and of manure must have gone pretty much hand in hand. This discovery would have led to early man changing his nomadic habits: instead of wandering at random he would have returned to the sites of previous camps to collect the foods growing on the refuse tips the following year, when the seeds had time to germinate and grow.

The forward step from this type of agriculture, which is still basically of the hand-to-mouth type, to a settled, deliberately cultivated agriculture is an obvious one—in retrospect. What is surprising is that in fact the step was taken only in the relatively recent past—as little as between 8,000 and 10,000 years ago. And what is even more surprising is the fact that those crops which were first brought into cultivation are still the major food crops of the world to-day.

Settled agriculture does not appear to have been a single discovery made once and once only, and in only one part of the world. To begin with, the discovery was made independently in the Old World and in the New World. Moreover, even in the Old World, the discovery seems to have been made independently to the west of the Himalayas and to the east of the Himalayas: the Himalayas would have proved a virtually impassable barrier to early man.

So far as the western world is concerned the domestication of food plants began in that area of the world known as the Fertile Crescent. The Fertile Crescent is a great arc of land that runs for about 1,500 miles from southern Palestine, north through Lebanon and Syria, across the south of Turkey and down through northern Iraq to the Persian Gulf. It lay cradled between two great rivers, the Tigris and the Euphrates, rich and fertile, nurtured by rains. There, some 10,000 years ago, some forebear of ours munched the kernels of some heavy-headed grass and liked them. Even to-day, wild wheat and barley can be found growing in the hills 2,000 or 3,000 feet above the now arid plains that were once the Fertile Crescent.

Few parts of the world are more arid to-day than the Fertile Crescent, but there is ample evidence that some 7,500 years ago the first plots of cultivated wheat were harvested all the way from Natuf in Palestine to Tepe Sarab in Iraq. Climatologists believe that in those days the annual average temperature in that part of the world was much lower than it is to-day. The last fingers of the glaciers of the retreating Ice-age still lingered in the high mountains of Asia minor, and those lands were then much more heavily forested than they are now, and a heavy covering of forest gives a land a moister and a cooler climate than it would have without forest. Besides, the east wind of those days was a wet wind, sweeping up off the Mediterranean, not a dry wind as it is to-day.

From the Fertile Crescent the Agricultural Revolution spread southwards into Egypt, and
westwards through Europe, reaching Britain probably no more than 3,000 years ago. As the
Agricultural Revolution progressed it took with it food plants already in cultivation, adding a
few new species as it went. For this reason it is interesting to trace the origins of certain vegetables
in their movement both through history and through geography.

Foods of ancient Egypt   Ten thousand years ago, the population of Egypt may well have been as
high as ten million for in 57 B.C. the Greek historian Didorus Siculus who wrote 'A History of the
World from the Creation', then put the population as more than seven million and by then,
Egypt was past her splendour. Using only the most primitive methods of cultivation, it is remarkable that the land, much of it desert, was able to support so many. This was possible only
because the area was so rich in edible plant life. A list of the important food producing plants
which grew in ancient Egypt or were readily available from those lands which extended from
the Nile delta to the Black Sea and eastwards to the two mighty rivers, the Tigris and Euphrates,
is of interest:

Almond, Barley, Broad bean, Cabbage, Chicory, Dates, Endive, Figs, Garlic, Grapes, Leek,
Lettuce, Melon, Olive, Onion, Pea, Radish, Shallot, Water cress and Wheat.

From them it will be seen that many are bulbous plants, tolerant of winter cold and which are
able to store up moisture to ensure their successful cropping during times of drought and exposure
to hot sun. Like most bulbous flowering plants, many retained their quality when in storage and
as with dates and figs, will keep through winter to be used whenever required. Cereals and
legumes which do not need artificial drying in that part of the world, were also grown in large
quantities and formed the staple diet of the people. At the height of her glory, Rameses II built
large 'treasure cities' in Israelite territory to store the crops. The only other important food crop
known to man, the potato, is a product of the new world and was, of course, unknown to the
Egyptians whilst rice, the staple diet of the eastern peoples requires to have its roots submerged in
water and is Asiatic in its origin.
    Of the food producing plants known to the Egyptians, those held in most esteen were the garlic
and the onion. The Greek historian Herodotus has recorded that in the Great Pyramid of Cheops
at Giza which covers an area of 13 acres and at one time reached a height of 481 feet, there is an in-
scription which states that 1600 talents of silver (about a million pounds in today's money values)
had been paid to supply the workers with onions, garlic and radishes during its building. So
highly esteemed was the onion that the Egyptians worshipped it as a deity, believing that the
concentric layers of the bulb represented the various spheres of heaven, earth and hell. Rich in
vitamins and mineral salts, all members of the onion family are remarkably sustaining and the
builders of the Pyramids would consume their daily ration, sliced between bread made from the
flour of wheat and broad beans, in exactly the same way as England's ploughmen obtained their
daily sustenance until almost the present day. Egyptian onions are sweet and mild of flavour and
are baked or fried, or used for making soup. In the homes of the wealthy, baked onions are usually
served with meat.
    The Israelites, returning to the Promised Land after two hundred years in captivity, deplored
the absence of these vegetables as they made their way through desert lands of blistering heat.
In Numbers it is written: 'We remember the fish, which we did eat in Egypt freely; the cucumbers
and the melons, the leeks and the onions, and the garlic'. Never again were they to enjoy so rich
a diet.
    The water melon, native of tropical Africa was as highly prized in Egypt and the Near East
as it is to this day. From earliest recorded times, it was used both as food and drink, to give during
times of fever. The people considered the season of water melons the best of all and extending
from mid-May until almost the year end, they were easily grown and reached a weight of 20
pounds or more. The juice was pressed out and mixed with sugar and was a pleasant and sustaining drink. The plants were readily raised from seed sown directly into the sandy soil, surplus seed
being roasted and salted, to be consumed during wintertime, like salted almonds.
    Almost as widely cultivated as the onion was the Broad Bean, thought to be native of Persia.
Seeds have been found in early Egyptian tombs and, like wheat, the beans were made into flour

for making bread. In Ezekiel it says, 'Take thou also unto thee wheat and barley, beans and lentils, millet and fitches, put them into one vessel, and make thee bread thereof . . .' In Egypt, the beans are sown in October and the crop is ready to harvest in March. The seed is dried and stored until required.

Amongst the common weeds of Egypt are the lettuce and endive, the chicory and the sorrel, the leaves of which are used fresh in salads. Since the dawn of civilisation, these plants have appeared exactly to modern gardeners as they did to those who built the Pyramids and those who came before them. Water cress, the dandelion and the sorrel may have been the 'bitter herbs' eaten during the Passover in about 1500 B.C.

Vegetables of Greece and Rome   Gradually, the foods of the Egyptian people came to be used by more northerly civilisations for all those crops which could be harvested and stored, were readily transported either by land or sea. It is likely that many would be introduced into Greece by the armies of Alexander who, following his defeat of the Persians at Issus in Syria, marched south into Egypt and there founded the seaport bearing his name. Soldiers of Alexander's armies made use of the garlic and onion in their diet, for it endowed fighting men with great physical strength. Aristophanes made frequent mention of this quality.

The Greeks borrowed their love of wine drinking from the Egyptians and their custom of eating boiled cabbage before taking wine with their food. Athenaeus said that 'many people add cabbage seed to their potions as an antidote against drunkenness' and the cabbage became as popular in Greece as it was in Egypt. In Greece and later in Rome, cabbage was seasoned with cummin and coriander, with salt and pepper and served with salad oil or gravy.

Almost all those vegetables we now call 'greens' belong to the Cruciferae family. The kohlrabi and the turnip are bulbous rooted cabbages and broccoli and kale, cabbage and savoy, Brussels sprouts and the cauliflower are all derivatives of *Brassica oleracea*, native of Egypt and the Near East. Perhaps the cabbage in something like the form we know it today came first and this took on another form with the crinkled leaves of the savoy. From the savoy, the curling of the leaves is taken a stage further in the Cottager's Kale and from this was evolved the green sprouting calabrese. The short stem of the cabbage and the savoy lengthened and when the stem buds began to form miniature cabbages, the Brussels sprout made its appearance. Plants with stem buds are observed by Gerard though they were probably known to the Greeks and Romans.

The lettuce, a cultivated plant during the time of the Pharoahs, was well known to the Greeks, Theophrastus knew four kinds, possibly derivatives of the tall growing cos lettuce grown by the Egyptians. Its narcotic effect was well known to the ancients, and to Gerard some years later. But it was the Romans who gave most attention to the lettuce, considering it of greater importance than all other foods with the possible exception of the garlic upon a diet of which the Roman legions conquered the world. Pliny tells us that the lettuce came into prominence during the time of the Emperor Augustus whose life was saved by consuming large quantities prescribed by his doctor, possibly to correct a deficiency of Vitamin C. Martial, the most famous satirist of ancient Rome, mentions that from that time onwards lettuce and radishes began to be consumed at the beginning of every meal instead of at the end, a custom perpetuated by the serving of hors d'oeuvre:

Tell me why lettuce, which our grandsires last did eat,
Is now of late become to be the first of meat?

The reason for consuming lettuce at the end of a meal was that like cabbage 'it kept away drunkenness which commeth by wine' and in many wine drinking countries, the custom is practised to this day. The Anglo-Saxons knew the lettuce well for seed would have been introduced with the coming of the Romans. This would be the Roman or Cos variety which is still known in France as 'romaines'. The Saxons called it lactuce, from the Latin, lacta, milk, because of the milk-like juice which exudes when the stems are cut. Gerard distinguishes several forms, including a lettuce with curled leaves and one 'drawn together like a cabbage', in addition to the more familiar cos variety.

By the beginning of the 17th Century, varieties must have increased considerably for in the 'Paradisus', Parkinson writes, 'there are so many sorts that I shall scarce be believed of a great many' and he goes on to mention 'our winter Lettice (which is) wonderful hardy to endure our cold', this being the first intimation we have of a variety capable of standing through an English winter.

A plant well known to the ancient Greeks and Romans was the Globe Artichoke which grew wild along the northern coast of Africa and which was most plentiful around Carthage. It was not, however, held in very great regard by the Roman historian Pliny who writes of it disparagingly, calling it a 'thistle'. He tells of small plots of land around Carthage which produce from its culture, a yearly income of 6000 sesterces, 'such being the way in which we make the monstrous productions of the earth subservient to our gluttonous appetites'. Though there is no mention of the plant reaching England until Tudor times, it is more than likely that it was one of the vegetables introduced by the Romans, together with the leek and onion both of which were grown in Saxon times. The leek became the symbol of Wales and the Tudor dynasty took on its green and white colouring as a symbolic gesture, due to its being so widely cultivated in that part of our islands where Owen Tudor was born. Parkinson said that it was 'a great and general feeding in Wales with the vulgar gentlemen'. Possibly its ease in culture compared with the onion and the fact that it could remain in the ground all through winter, added to its popularity with the cottager. There has been some improvement in its size but it remains comparatively unchanged since Parkinson's time and indeed since cultivated by the Israelites during their time of captivity in Egypt.

Vegetables of early England   The leek was one of the vegetables mentioned by Alexander Neckam, Abbot of Cirencester in the year 1200, as growing in a typical monastery garden of the time. Other vegetables mentioned in his essay, 'Of the Natures of Things' were smallage (celery), lettuce and garden-cress, and he recommends that 'there should be beds planted with onions, leeks, garlic, pumpkins and shallots. The cucumber growing in its lap . . . nor are there wanting if occasion furnish thee, pottage herbs, beets, mercury, orach, sorrel and mallows'. Cabbage is not mentioned but in 'The Natural History of Selbourne', Gilbert White has this to say: 'Our Saxon ancestors certainly had some sort of cabbage, because they called the month of February, Sprout-kale; but long after their days, the cultivation of gardens was little attended to. The religious, being men of leisure and keeping up a constant correspondence with Italy, were the first among us that had gardens in any perfection, within the walls of their abbeys, priorys and monasteries' and it is fairly certain that those vegetables introduced by the Romans came to be perpetuated in the gardens of the religious houses which arose at the time of the Norman Invasion. The vegetables mentioned by Alexander Neckham were all those grown by the ancient Egyptians and which were familiar to the Israelites. They reached European soil following the conquests of Alexander and when Greece lost something of her splendour, they found accommodation in the gardens of ancient Rome, eventually reaching Britain with the Roman armies.

In addition to the delicacies brought here by Caesar were a number of the Umbelliferae, native plants like smallage (celery), carrot, chervil and parsley which must have been in cultivation long before the Roman Invasion. They are plants which are widely distributed throughout Northern Europe. Prolific in the production of their seeds which were used for flavouring (as they are to this day), they were also grown for their highly flavoured roots which bore little resemblance in size to those grown today to win acclaim on the Show bench.

Besides the Umbellifers, around the coast in the warmer parts grew asparagus and seakale, skirret and beet. Of the beets, that native to Britain is *Beta maritima* which was in earlier times grown for its foliage which was boiled and used as a substitute for spinach. In his essay, the Abbot of Cirencester mentions 'beets', in the plural, and also known to him would be *B. vulgaris*, the red beetroot, a native of southern Europe and which the Romans held in greatest esteem. They would surely have brought it to this country and with it, the greatly prized Silver Beet or Swiss Chard, *B. sicla*, native of Sicily and southern Italy which was widely grown in England during Tudor times. It is described in detail by both Gerard and Parkinson, the latter calling it the Italian Beet 'with great white ribs', the leaves being boiled and served hot with oil and vinegar, a delicacy which the modern gardener knows not. In Parkinson's time, those beets grown for their enlarged roots were candied, like eringoes and used as a sweetmeat; or they were boiled and used in salads.

The diet of the Englishman from the time of the Roman Invasion would be reasonably varied if only because of the edible plants which were native to these islands and with those introduced by the invaders. The leaves of water cress and dandelion were put in sandwiches whilst parsley and fennel were in daily use, to stay the pangs of hunger on fast days or whenever food was scarce. Highly flavoured foods were most in demand, to counteract the saltiness of badly cured meats and to provide more interest to the labourer's diet. Of the Sompnour in the 'Canterbury Tales' Chaucer says:

'Well loved he garlic, onions and the leek'. In 'Piers (the) Ploughman', written when Chaucer was working on his epic poem, William Langland has told of how the poor lived almost entirely on fruits and vegetables from the countryside with the occasional luxury of a rabbit poached from the manorial lands.

The earliest instruction for the sowing of vegetables is in the MS by John (the) Gardner written in 1440. In it he says that onions and leeks are to be sown on St. Valentine's Day and parsley 'in the month of March'. Cabbage and kale were amongst the crops to be sown then and a cookery book of about the same date, suggests serving cabbage dressed with saffron for which John Gardner also gives instructions for planting. Gradually small cottage gardens came to be stocked with all manner of vegetables and with fruits and herbs removed from the hedgerow, together with violet and primrose flowers to use in salads which were also cooked with other foods to impart their sweetness and flavour. Many herbs, too, were grown for their medicinal value. 'The juice of lettuce', wrote Parkinson 'mixed with oil of roses and applied to the head of those unable to sleep encourages rest'.

Broad beans and peas grew in every cottage garden, not to cook fresh but to dry and use through winter, to cook with lentils to make 'pottage' which was a most nourishing dish. The most famous pea was known as the Runcival which takes its name from the French village of Roncesvaulx, from which it originated. Thomas Tusser, in his rhyme of a 'Hundred Points of Good Husbandry' (1557) which he later extended to 'Five Hundred Points', suggests planting the Runcival pea in February:

'Strike plentie of bows among Runcival peas,
To clamber thereon and to branch at their ease'.

Parkinson gives it chief place amongst a dozen or so varieties and he also mentions the Sugar Pea which is illustrated in the 'Paradisus'. This pea, which is sliced and cooked like a runner bean is available to modern gardeners and has changed but little since Stuart times.

The garden pea received little attention through the ages except for making 'pottage' whilst dried, it was used at sea to provide sailors with a similar diet. It was the petit pois of the French Court which first gave the pea a popularity when boiled and eaten freshly picked which it has retained until today. So popular did it become during the reign of Louis XIV that Mme. de Maintenon, writing in May, 1696, said: 'The chapter of peas still goes on. The impatience to eat them, the pleasure of having eaten them, and the joy of eating them again are the three points of private gossip (at Versailles)'.

But the first break through in giving peas a more popular image in England did not occur until early in the 19th Century when Thomas Knight a Herefore squire, took up its hybridising and introduced the first wrinkled variety. This characteristic is due to the pea changing its starch content into sugar whilst in the pod. The round pea does not undergo this change and so it is never as sweet. With their sweet and tender flavour, the new peas of Thomas Knight became known as Marrow peas or Marrowfats and were the foundation upon which the later breeders took up the work. Dr. McLean of Colchester followed with both early and late varieties, thus extending the season and towards the end of the century, Laxton and Veitch brought about further improvement and gave their name to several varieties which are still in cultivation.

About the same time, Gregor Mendel was conducting his genetic experiments on breeding with peas in the monastery in Czechoslovakia, His paper, 'Experiments in plant Hybridisation', written in 1866 but only rediscovered in 1900, in the words of Sir Roland Biffen (of wheat-breeding fame) was to 'completely alter the outlook of all concerned with plant breeding'.

The catalogues issued by the seed houses at the beginning of the century, show the results in this great improvement in plant breeding. 'Thomas Laxton' was generally listed as being by far the finest of all early peas. Messrs. Fidlers of Reading described it as 'a wrinkled marrowfat raised by crossing Gradus with an early seedling'. They considered it to be the best early pea ever introduced. Other popular varieties of the year 1900 were 'Gradus', 'Duke of York', 'Harrison's Glory' and 'Alderman' all of them still in commerce, with the latter still unsurpassed as a maincrop pea. Of other vegetables, then being widely acclaimed and which have stood the test of time was the dwarf bean, 'Canadian Wonder'; broad bean, 'Bunyard's Exhibition'; asparagus, 'Conover's Colossal'; Veitch's self protecting broccoli; Brussels sprout, 'The Wroxton'; celery, 'Clayworth Prize Pink'; melon, 'Hero of Lockinge'; and those two enormous leeks, 'Musselburgh' and 'The Lyon'. This selection would stand comparison with the finest vegetable introductions of modern times though hybrid and vigour has, in more recent years ensured greater reliability and heavier crops. In the years following the First World War, it was the American and Japanese who first became interested in hybrid crossing. First Cross (F_1) hybrid seed is obtained by artificially crossing two distinct parent strains by controlled hand pollination, the result being to transmit the special qualities of both parents to the first generation progeny. These qualities may be earliness to bloom or freedom of flowering.

Whilst the Americans and Japanese have concentrated their experiments more on flowers, in Britain and in Holland, the horticultural stations have been working mostly on food crops, especially tomatoes, cucumbers and sweet corn and it has been found that certain varieties at the first generation crossing produced qualities which appear to have become lost (bred out) in later generations in trying to 'fix' the results of the original cross. Amongst these desirable qualities are earlier fruiting; a longer season of production and heavier crops, together with greater freedom from disease.

Being hybrids and thus not coming true from their own seed, it is necessary to carry out the crossing of two selected varieties each time seed is to be saved and not only have special varieties to be selected but special strains which show no deterioration in their original characteristics.

Plants of the New World Few, if any, new vegetables reached this country after the Roman Invasion (for those which came with them, together with those native to our islands constituted the diet of our people) until late in Tudor times. For at least 1500 years, there had been nothing new of any note. Not until the arrival of the tuberous potato into Europe. Holinshed, writing in Elizabethan times said that the rich and poor alike were eating 'melons, gourds, cucumbers, radishes, skirrets, parsnips, carrots, cabbages, turnips, and all kinds of salad herbs'. No mention is made of the potato but the first important food to have reached Europe from the New World was, in fact, the Sweet Potato, believed to have been amongst the treasures brought back by Columbus following his first voyage westwards. Later, it grew in Gerard's garden in Holborn and Shakespeare knew it well. When Falstaff shouted 'let the sky rain potatoes', these are what he was referring to.

It was from Spain also that the ordinary potato reached Britain, possibly by way of Holland or Belgium, or it may have been brought over by the Huguenots fleeing from the massacre of St. Bartholomew. Its introduction is shrouded in mystery for some believe that it may not have reached this country until about 1586 upon Raleigh's return from the New World. It certainly grew in Gerard's garden at the end of the century and in 1664 appeared the first ever treatise on the plant. It was called 'England's Happiness Increases'; or 'A Sure and Easy Remedy against all Succeeding Dear Years' and was written by one, John Foster. But few heeded his sound advice and another two centuries were to elapse before the potato received any attention.

With the potato, came the tomato, introduced into Europe from Peru by the Portuguese or Spaniards early in the 16th century. It also grew in Gerard's garden and in Elizabethan times was known as the Love Apple. The fruit, wrote Gerard 'is of a shining bright red colour, of about the bigness of a good egg or pippin', and he goes on to say that 'in Spain and other hot regions they eat the 'apples' prepared and boiled with pepper, salt and oil' or serve them as sauce to have with meat, the pulp being mixed with oil, vinegar, salt and pepper. Of the same family as the potato and tomato, is the Aubergine and Sweet Pepper, also native of South America. They may have reached England with the tomato but were not widely grown until Sir Joseph Paxton's glasshouse introductions at the middle of the 19th century enabled them to be grown in the warmth so necessary for their successful culture at that time.

The discovery of the New World saw the introduction of a number of other choice vegetables amongst which was the Runner bean, native of Mexico and which reached England during the early years of the 17th century. Closely related is the Haricot or Lima bean, the seeds being used by the Aztec Indian as a staple food and they have been found in their ancient tombs, preserved as if just harvested. From north America, Champlain, the French botanist, sent home some strangely looking roots which, in England were known as Potatoes of Canada. We know them now as Jerusalem Artichokes though they are in no way connected with the biblical city nor are they of the Globe Artichoke family. 'Being put into seething water,' wrote Parkinson, 'they are soon boiled until tender. They are sliced and stewed with butter, and with a little wine are a dish for a Queen'. Later, the Dutch settlers of New Amsterdam sent back a number of vegetables including the Pokeweed or Pocan, its young shoots being boiled and treated like asparagus. Treated in a similar way were the shoots of *Ornithogalum nutans* which grew in such profusion on the outskirts of Bath that its young shoots became known as Bath Asparagus and at one time were as popular as real asparagus in the fashionable city.

One of the last of vegetable plants to reach this country was New Zealand spinach which Sir Joseph Banks discovered when accompanying Captain Cook on his first voyage. They returned to Deal in 1771, having used the plant to supplement their diet the way back. Banks was to raise Kew Gardens to a position of pre-eminence and it was through his exertions that Australia and New Zealand were colonised. At about the same time, William Cobbett, after his sojourn in America, extolled the merits of the sweet corn and though it was grown under glass in the gardens of the wealthy, it was not until the arrival of the American forces during the Second World War that the British realised its delicious eating qualities and took advantage of new varieties which would ripen outdoors in a normal English climate.

Of the vegetables we grow, the greater proportion have been known to man since the dawn of history, but the knowledge of modern plant genetics is only now enabling man to enjoy the many derivatives to the full.

From this table of the more widely cultivated vegetables and their families, it will be seen that the greater part of the vegetable and food crops of the world are represented by only 8 or 9 plant families out of the 300 or more which comprise the earth's flora. Of these families, there are only about 40 genera represented by some 50 species and from this comparatively small number of the many thousands of plant species, the greater part of the population of the world is fed. To these may be added *Lens esculenta*, the Lentil, a legume with a distribution similar to that of the Pea; and the rice, *Oryza sativa*, native of India and S.E. Asia. Like sweet corn and other cereal crops, it is a grass, amongst which are numbered the most important of the world's food crops and as with several of the more important vegetables rice is a plant of the marshlands.

Table 1
Vegetables and their families

Family	Vegetable	Botanical name
Chenopodiaceae	Beetroot	*Beta vulgaris*
	Good King Henry	*Chenopodium*
	Orach (Mountain Spinach)	*Atriplex hortensis*
	Spinach	*Spinacia oleracea*
	Swiss Chard	*Beta sicla*
Compositae	Artichoke, Globe	*Cynara scolymus*
	Artichoke, Jerusalem	*Helianthus tuberosus*
	Cardoon	*Cynara cardunculus*
	Chicory	*Cichorium intybus*
	Dandelion	*Taraxacum officinale*
	Endive	*Cichorium endivia*
	Lettuce	*Lactuca sativa*
	Salsify	*Tragopogen porrifolius*
	Scolymus	*Scolymus hispanicus*
	Scorzonera	*Scorzonera hispanica*
	Seakale	*Crambe maritima*
	Skirret	*Sium sisarum*
Convolvulaceae	Sweet potato	*Convolvulus batatas*

Table 1
Vegetables and their families

Cruciferae	American Cress	*Barbarea praecose*
	Broccoli	
	Brussels sprouts	
	Cabbage	
	Calabrese	
	Cauliflower	*Brassica oleracea*
	Collards	and derivatives
	Kale	
	Kohl-rabi	
	Pe-tsai	
	Savoy	
	Radish	*Raphanus sativus*
	Turnip	*Brassica campestris*
	Water cress	*Nasturtium officinale*
Curcurbitaceae	Cucumber	*Cucumis sativus*
	Marrow	*Curcurbita pepo*
Gramineae	Sweet Corn	*Zea mays*
Labiateae	Artichoke, Chinese	*Stachys tuberifera*
Leguminosae	Asparagus pea	*Lotus tetragonolobus*
	Bean, broad	*Faba vulgaris*
	Bean, butter	*Phaseolus lunatus*
	Bean, dwarf	*Phaseolus vulgaris*
	Bean, runner	*Phaseolus coccineus*
	Pea	*Pisum sativum*
Liliaceae	Asparagus	*Asparagus officinalis*
	Garlic	*Allium sativum*
	Leek	*Allium porrum*
	Onion	*Allium cepa*
	Shallot	*Allium ascalonicum*
Malvacea	Okra	*Hibiscus esculentus*
Polygonaceae	Sorrel	*Rumex scutatus*
Umbelliferae	Carrot	*Daucus carota*
	Celeriac	*Apium graveolens*
	Celery	
	Chervil	*Caherophyllum bulbosum*
	Finocchio	*Foeniculum dulce*
	Hamburg Parsley	*Carum petroselinum*
	Parsnip	*Pastanaca sativum*

Table 2
Vegetables and their habitat

Vegetable	Botanical Name	Family	Habitat
American Cress	*Barbarea praecox (20)*	Cruciferae	N. Temp. regions
Artichoke, Chinese	*Stachys tuberifera (300)*	Labiateae	Sub. trop. Asia
Artichoke, Globe	*Cynara scolymus (14)*	Compositae	N. Africa
Artichoke, Jerusalem	*Helianthus tuberosus (110)*	Compositae	N. America
Asparagus	*Asparagus officinalis (300)*	Liliaceae	Old World
Asparagus Pea	*Lotus tetragonolobus (100)*	Leguminosae	Temp. Europe, Africa, Asia
Aubergine	*Solanum melongena (1700)*	Solanaceae	~~S. America~~ Tropical ASIA

129

Table 2
Vegetables and their habitat

Bean, Broad	*Faba vulgaris (1)*	Leguminosae	Near East
Bean, Butter	*Phaseolus lunatus (250)*	Leguimnosae	Sub-trop. America
Bean, Dwarf	*Phaseolus vulgaris (250)*	Leguinosae	Sub-trop. America
Bean, Runner	*Phaseolus coccineus (250)*	Leguminosae	Sub-trop. America
Beetroot	*Beta vulgaris (6)*	Chenopodiaceae	S. Europe
Broccoli			
Brussels sprouts			
Cabbage			
Cauliflower	*Brassica oleracea*		Temp. regions of Old
Collards	*(and derivatives)*	Cruciferae	World
Kale			
Pe-tsai			
Savoy			
Cardoon	*Cynara cardunculus (14)*	Compositae	Near East
Carrot	*Daucus carota (60)*	Umbelliferae	Cosmopolitan
Celeriac	*Apium graveolens rapaceum*		
Celery	*Apiun graveolens*	Umbelliferae	Europe, W. Asia
Cherry, Ground	*Physalis ixocarpa (100)*	Solanaceae	Trop. America
Chervil	*Chaerophyllum*		
	bulbosum (40)	Umbelliferae	N. temp. regions
Chicory	*Cichorium intybus (9)*	Compositae	Europe
Cucumber	*Cucumis sativus (25)*	Cucurbitaceae	Africa, Asia
Dandelion	*Taraxacum officinale (60)*	Compositae	Cosmopolitan
Endive	*Cichorium endivia (9)*	Compositae	Mediterranean
Finocchio	*Foeniculum dulce (5)*	Umbelliferae	Europe
Garlic	*Allium sativum (450)*	Liliaceae	Near East
Good King Henry			
(Mercury)	*Cheopodium (100)*	Chenopodiaceae	Europe
Hamburg Parsley	*Corum petroselinum (30)*	Umbelliferae	Europe and sub-trops. of Old World
Leek	*Allium porrum (450)*	Liliaceae	Near East
Lettuce	*Lactuca sativa (100)*	Compositae	Temp. Europe, Asia
Marrow	*Cucurbita pepo (15)*	Curcurbitaceae	Near East
Okra	*Hibiscus esculentus (300)*	Malvaceae	Trop. America
Onion	*Allium cepa (450)*	Liliaceae	Near East
Orach	*Atriflex hortensis (200)*	Chenopodiaceae	Temp. and sub tropics
Parsnip	*Pastinaca sativum (15)*	Umbelliferae	Europe
Pea	*Pisum sativum (6)*	Leguminosae	Mediterranean, W. Asia
Potato	*Solanum tuberosum*	Solanaceae	S. America
Radish	*Raphanus sativus (8)*	Cruciferae	Near East
Salsify	*Tragopogon porrifolius (50)*	Compositae	Europel Asia
Scolymus	*Scolymus hispanicus (3)*	Compositae	Mediterranean
Scorzonera	*Scorzonera hispanica (150)*	Compositae	Europe, Asia
Seakale	*Crambe maritima (25)*	Compositae	Europe
Shallot	*Allium ascalonicum (450)*	Liliaceae	Near East
Skirret	*Sium sisarum (12)*	Compositae	Cosmopolitan; not S. America or Australia
Sorrel	*Rumex scutatus (200)*	Polygonaceae	Temp. regions of world.
Spinach	*Spinacia oleracea (3)*	Chenopodiaceae	Near East
Sweet Corn	*Zea mays (1)*	Gramineae	S. America
Sweet Pepper (Capsicum)	*Capsicum anuum (50)*	Solanaceae	Trop. America
Sweet Potato	*Convolvulus batatas (250)*	Convolvulaceae	S. America
Swiss Chard	*Beta sicla (6)*	Chenopodiaceae	S. Europe
Tomato	*Lycopersicum*		
	esculentum (7)	Solanaceae	S. America
Turnip	*Brassica campestris ( )*	Cruciferae	Europe
Water cress	*Nasturtium officinale (6)*	Cruciferae	Europe, N. America

The numbers in brackets indicate the number of species of that particular genus.

INDEX